THE HOUSE OF
LANCASTER

NEIL SQUIRES

THE HOUSE OF LANCASTER

How England Rugby Was Reinvented

YELLOW JERSEY PRESS

LONDON

1 3 5 7 9 10 8 6 4 2

Yellow Jersey Press, an imprint of Vintage,
20 Vauxhall Bridge Road,
London SW1V 2SA

Yellow Jersey Press is part of the Penguin Random House group of companies
whose addresses can be found at global.penguinrandomhouse.com

Penguin
Random House
UK

First published by Yellow Jersey Press in 2015

www.vintage-books.co.uk

A CIP catalogue record for this book is
available from the British Library

ISBN 9780224100007

Printed and bound by Clays Ltd, St Ives Plc

This book is not authorised or endorsed by Stuart Lancaster

MIX
Paper from
responsible sources
FSC   FSC® C018179
www.fsc.org

Penguin Random House is committed to a sustainable future for
our business, our readers and our planet. This book is made from
Forest Stewardship Council® certified paper

For Sam – who began this journey

Contents

Foreword by Sir Ian McGeechan OBE 1

Introduction 5

1. The Mess That Came Before 13
2. Caretaker Duty 29
3. Playing For Keeps 51
4. Who Is This Lancaster Bloke Anyway? 64
5. The Coaching Road 79
6. The Impossible Job 93
7. National Service 106
8. California Dreaming 120
9. The Jersey 135
10. The England Plan 154
11. Know Your Enemies 172
12. Know Yourself 188
13. Holding Your Nerve 209
14. The Miracle Shot 224
15. Leadership 245

Conclusion 271
Postscript 279
England Tests Under Lancaster 281
Test Nations' Results During Lancaster's Tenure 283
Bibliography 284
Acknowledgements 288
List of Illustrations 290

Foreword

by Sir Ian McGeechan OBE

It is a great pleasure to have been asked to write the foreword to this book. The paths of Stuart Lancaster and I have crossed in many different ways, of course all associated with rugby.

These crossings have been at each of the different stages of Stuart's rugby journey, and particularly in coaching. We have shared notes as club coaches – him with Leeds, me with Wasps – as well as at Academy meetings with his role with the Rugby Football Union, and most recently in the process of his becoming England head coach.

He and I also share an association with one club, Leeds (or in my day Headingley). I have returned to the club, now known as Yorkshire Carnegie, to carry on with Stuart's legacy of player development, which he left in fine shape. We have many similarities in approach and as a reader you will find his journey both fascinating and uplifting.

Having taken on the England role, a major challenge, Stuart

had clarity of purpose and belief in how he wanted his England side to look and why the players wanted to wear the rose on their chests.

The journey on which he has taken his England group is also the journey of someone developing his coaching personality. Why we do something is the most important question to ask continually, both of yourself and collectively. What we get is in this book, very clearly, is the 'why' of Stuart Lancaster.

People make the difference; they set the environment, the group atmosphere. Stuart has been exceptionally good at building connections and making them feel like partnerships. He has made it personal: meeting every Premiership club coach, discussing players and planning, speaking to the media as individuals, and being very open about his approach and intentions. He has created an environment both inside and outside the England team that is stronger than any of his predecessors managed.

Those connections he has forged go all the way to the grass-roots of the English game. Holding training at West Park in Leeds highlights awareness of the privilege and responsibility he recognises are so important for him and his players.

There is no doubt we both believe the international arena is a very special place to be. Access to it cannot be bought, but comes from an extraordinary commitment and attitude. To perform at this level requires the ultimate in honesty, trust and respect, and building those things is a significant part of the journey in representing your country.

After the 2011 World Cup, England were in a poor place because these key elements were not part of the players' mindsets. That is why England needed a coach with this core understanding and belief in what make the strongest team environment.

He now has an England team who are a solid unit, who will be challenged on and off the field, but will not be split. This is a unity built on the experiences shared with many people outside as well as inside the sport. Stories of challenges and bravery from our armed forces personnel, rugby league and American football all form part of Stuart's bank of knowledge and inspiration, these things tell us about the man, these things matter to him. What Stuart has given to everyone directly involved with England is a reason to believe, a reason to support, a reason to play.

This book shows the development of a modern coach with the appreciations of age-old values: some things never change. He is a presenter, a teacher, an educator – for me, the essential requirements of a good coach. What he has learnt, like me, is that as you become more experienced and work at the highest level, simplicity and clarity are the keys to repeatable world-class excellence.

Stuart Lancaster has got England in good shape because he has taken nothing for granted. He has a team playing for all the right reasons, who are giving England supporters a reason to believe as we go into the 2015 Rugby World Cup.

I am sure you will be captivated by his journey.

Sir Ian McGeechan OBE
April 2015

Introduction

Once more unto the breach, dear friends, once more,

Or close the wall up with our English dead.

In peace there's nothing so becomes a man

As modest stillness and humility,

But when the blast of war blows in our ears,

Then imitate the action of the tiger.

Stiffen the sinews, summon up the blood,

Disguise fair nature with hard-favoured rage.

Then lend the eye a terrible aspect

Henry V, Act 3, Scene 1

England vs France, Twickenham – Saturday, 21 March 2015
It is England's final competitive match before their home World Cup, the last match of the 2015 Six Nations' Championship. Stuart Lancaster's squad disembark from the gleaming black team bus with the red rose proudly displayed in the window to a rapturous welcome.

As is Lancaster's habit, the set-down point in Twickenham's buzzing West Car Park 50 yards away from the Lion Gate is meticulously planned. It means the players have to walk through their army of support before entering the stadium. The crowd get to see the players; the players get to see the crowd. Those who are first off the bus pause to wait for the rest of their team-mates. Again, this is carefully choreographed by the head coach. If they are to play as a unified team they must look like a unified team.

Headphones, the ever-present companion of the modern professional sportsman, are banned. Lancaster wants the players to hear the applause and the cheering.

In their purple tracksuits, they set off behind their captain, Chris Robshaw, through the funnel of England fans who spill out 20 deep on either side of them. Cameras flash, children on parents' shoulders crane for a glimpse of their heroes. As the players pass through the gate, the outer shell of a stadium which will soon be filled to its 82,000 capacity rises imposingly in front of them. A giant rose decorates the third tier. Every vantage point is taken by supporters in white shirts, applauding from steps and balconies. Lancaster, at the back, looks up, smiles warmly and waves.

A band strikes up with the strains of 'Swing Low, Sweet Chariot' as a smiling Robshaw leads his team forward before stopping to receive a single red rose from eighty-six-year-old Twickenham debenture holder Mary Tootell. It is a gift she has given to every England captain for the past 30 years. He thanks her politely before entering the stadium with his team-mates. The door closes behind them and the tumult subsides.

Entering a corridor, England's players are immediately con-fronted by a giant image of themselves singing the national anthem which fills the wall at the end. It is a powerful picture.

In a parallel corridor a few yards away the French team will be greeted by an equally powerful picture – a life-size image of Manu Tuilagi in full flight, bandage around his head, rampaging through their defence on their last visit. Welcome to Twickenham, *mes amis*. Enjoy your stay.

As they walk along the corridor, the home team pass a pictorial timeline, starting with the invention of the game at Rugby School in 1845. Rugby, England. Our game.

There are images of towering figures throughout English rugby history. Ronnie Poulton Palmer, killed by sniper fire during the First War World after captaining England to their second Grand Slam, 1920s poster boy Wavell Wakefield and Eric Evans, who led England to their 1957 Grand Slam. A few steps more and into the modern era with England's Grand Slams under Bill Beaumont and Will Carling before the crowning glory – Martin Johnson lifting the 2003 Rugby World Cup. Great men of English rugby; great acts to follow – visual reminders of the team whose history they carry forward today.

The players make their way down another corridor towards Changing Room No. 1 where they are greeted by a huge English rose on the wall in front of them. On their left they pass a dark grey wall decorated with the names and milestones of more England legends – Jason Leonard 114 caps, Lawrence Dallaglio 85 caps, Jonny Wilkinson 1,179 points...

Five trophies are engraved into the history wall, too. The World Cup stands centre stage, flanked by the Calcutta Cup, the Triple Crown, the Cook Cup and the Sir Edmund Hillary Shield – a reminder that even New Zealand can be beaten.

Turning right at the end they are into the inner sanctum – the England dressing room itself. It is a big space yet it feels intimate. The colours strike you immediately – it is decorated entirely in the colours of the flag of St George.

Suspended from the ceiling is a giant oval disc spelling out five illuminated words: teamwork, respect, enjoyment, discipline, sportsmanship. Rugby's core values as defined by the Rugby Football Union.

Brass plates adorn each changing place, inscribed with the player's name and their number in England's chronological list of internationals. Hanging from each peg is a white England shirt.

This is the first England shirt presented to the player when he joined the squad. On it is written, in his own words, what that shirt means to him. At the bottom is his signature. It is intensely personal and yet available for all his team-mates to share. If he, and they, need a reminder of why they are here, there it is writ large.

Billy Vunipola's shirt has just three words on it. Family. Honour. Sacrifice. Family is everything within the Pacific Island culture in which he was raised. As well as his brother Mako, another England international, he has two sisters, Tiffany and Ana. His mum, Singa, is a Methodist minister, whom the Vunipola boys go to hear preach on their free Sundays at the Avenue Methodist Church in London.

The honour he feels playing for England mirrors that which his father Fe'ao felt in captaining Tonga. His grandfather and six uncles have also played for the island nation. The sacrifice refers to everything his family has given up to enable him to become part of the England brotherhood.

Behind the shirt, there is a plaque on a cross of St George bearing the names of ten great players who have represented England in that same position. A link to his forebears, a pointer to the standards expected.

The players change, stretch, strap themselves up and kill time. Some read the match programme, some chat nervously, others just stare into the distance, thinking, visualising.

INTRODUCTION

With 40 minutes before kick-off, they make their way out on to the pitch in dribs and drabs. They turn left to warm up in front of Twickenham's sparsely filled South Stand, a bank of green seats greeting them. The movements are low key, the acclimatisation gentle. Chris Robshaw and James Haskell pass a ball to one another, George Ford knocks over a shot or two at goal and then a few drop kicks; the scrum-halves hoist box kicks to each other. After ten minutes they head back down the tunnel and briefly back to the changing room. The bars start to empty and the stands begin to fill.

With 30 minutes until kick-off the England team emerge again – this time as one. The mood is suddenly much more urgent. A switch has been flicked. The forwards and backs split to be put through their paces by the fitness coaches, Dave Silvester and Tom Tombleson. Press-ups for the forwards, stretches for the backs. Quickly, they are into three-on-two passing drills with the skills coach Mike Catt urging them on. Across the field the pack run through a line-out drill with forwards' coach Graham Rowntree.

The murmur around the stadium is growing. More and more fans are filing in and the seats are being taken. The greensward is being replaced by a white backdrop.

Under the crossbar, arms folded, Stuart Lancaster is watching impassively. The backs and forwards come together in open field to run through attacking moves. They are slick and sharp. All the time the intensity is increasing.

Fifteen minutes. Backs' coach Andy Farrell gathers the team together in a huddle in the centre of the field and barks out his orders. Then it is into their pattern for a last test of the defensive shape before a few smashes into the tackle shields – a precursor of the enormous impacts to come.

Eleven minutes. England run off to return to the gleaming dressing room, leaving the swelling noise behind. The door closes. This is their space. Their territory. The players sit in their places, gathering themselves. There is no management now, no replacements even, just the 15. The chosen few. It is calm and quiet but there is an intangible energy pulsing through the room.

The team leaders go through the detail with each other one last time. Ben Youngs reminds Geoff Parling what sort of possession he wants from the first line-out, Dylan Hartley talks to his props about the first scrum. Then the captain brings the team together into a final huddle in the centre of the room. Robshaw is measured but determined. His brown eyes wide, he reminds the side of what they have talked about all week – smashing France hard in defence, taking out Thierry Dusautoir at the breakdown and trusting their fitness to run the French around Twickenham. The messages are simple, the conviction total. This is no place for doubt.

With six minutes until kick-off, the referee, Nigel Owens, knocks. Off they go.

Ten paces along the corridor and then they turn left and emerge into a tunnel illuminated from the low ceiling by thin strips of red and white light. Beside them on the wall is a flag of St George with hundreds of messages and images from well-wishers up and down the country. Screaming out from it is one simple, powerful slogan – 'Hundreds before you. Thousands around you. Millions behind you.'

One last reminder to the players of what is at stake here. They are not just playing for themselves. Or their team-mates. Or even the shirt. They are playing for the cause.

Ten more paces, then it is out of the tunnel and into the

concrete coliseum where a wall of noise hits them and a white cloak embraces them. It is time.

Almost two hours later they return to the sanctuary of the dressing room having just beaten France 55–35 in one of the most remarkable games Twickenham has ever seen. The ovation is still ringing in their ears.

They have posted a record score against the French, running in seven tries. The last time an England side did that was in 1911. At times the stadium was shaking, such was the response to the points avalanche which concluded the dramatic final day of the tournament.

This is an England team to be proud of.

1

The Mess That Came Before

There lives not three good men unhanged in England,
and one of them is fat and grows old
Henry IV Part I, Act 2, Scene 5

Since England's first game in 1871, fewer than 1,400 players have felt the unique surge of pride that comes with pulling on the England jersey. These are disparate brothers linked across the generations by a common cause: of playing for their team-mates, their families and their country. And of upholding the honour of the England shirt. It is taken out on loan, to be worn in the prime of their physical life, and then passed on.

When Stuart Lancaster took charge of England that message had been corrupted. The England he inherited after the calamitous 2011 World Cup campaign was a dysfunctional landscape where team trust had broken down. There were splits between players and coaches, between senior players and junior players, and divisions within the coaching group. Worst of all, a schism had developed between the England team and the shirt itself.

In team sport sides need a point to rally around. For England's rugby team, the pure white shirt with the beautiful red rose should have been it. But for players whose childhood dream had been to wear that jersey, it had lost its true meaning. The jersey had become less about honour than the privilege, fame and money owning it brought. The 2011 World Cup in New Zealand had exposed an empty void where the heart of English rugby should have been beating strongest.

The TSD. That was how England's World Cup campaign was referred to, disparagingly, by the New Zealand press. Three letters which spelled out the depth of ridicule to which it was being exposed. TSD stood for Tindall Stag Do. The team had become an international joke.

The dreary on-field performances were bad enough; what made England's image immeasurably worse were the off-field escapades which accompanied them. In rugby union's long amateur era excesses came as part of the package – boys on tour, that sort of thing – but these were supposed to be professional athletes representing their country on the greatest stage of all.

Tindall, a hero of the 2003 triumph and the captain of the side in their opening game against Argentina, was captured on CCTV stumbling around a Queenstown bar days later hopelessly drunk, balancing only with the help of a supportive blonde's cleavage. As Tindall's future wife was the Queen's granddaughter Zara Phillips, the scenes soon found their way to a wider audience. Jonathan Dixon, a bouncer at the Altitude bar, released the CCTV footage on YouTube having failed to find a buyer among the red-top tabloids.

Pictures also emerged from the same bar, on what was billed the 'Mad Midget Weekender', of Chris Ashton and Dylan Hartley indulging in horseplay with dwarves. Other desperate images showing a dishevelled Hartley and Tindall sprawled on top of Ashton made England look more like Old Knobendians' Vets on tour rather than an elite sports team.

Subsequently it emerged that even before the opening game England players were making trouble for themselves. A Dunedin hotel maid complained about a group of them making suggestive comments to her in the confines of one of their rooms. James Haskell and Chris Ashton were handed suspended fines for using 'inappropriate language'. It was just the sort of situation the team had been primed to avoid. To cap it all, after they had been eliminated, Manu Tuilagi jumped off a ferry in Auckland Harbour, was warned by police and then fined by the RFU.

On the field England were also in trouble. Kicking coach Dave Alred and conditioner Paul Stridgeon were suspended for a match by the RFU after changing the balls to ensure Jonny Wilkinson received the best ones for his goalkicking against Romania. The batch of balls may have been inconsistent but the RFU decided the actions were against 'both the laws and the spirit of the game'.

England's 67-3 victory against Romania, one of rugby's backwater countries, was the high point of their tournament. Although England won all their group matches, the stodgy nature of most of their rugby was chronically uninspiring.

An unconvincing 16-12 victory over Scotland in the final group game hinted at what was to come in the knockout stages and, sure enough, the roof fell in against France in the quarter-final. The game was as good as over by half time as England fell 16-0 behind, and although they fought back to lose 19-12 they were out. They were missed like rotting fish in a heatwave.

England's appointment of Johnson as manager three years

earlier had been intended to rekindle the embers of 2003 when, as captain, he lifted the World Cup. England had not scaled the same heights since.

As the distance from the 2003 campaign grew, it became increasingly clear that there had been little succession planning. As Johnson, Jason Leonard, Will Greenwood, Neil Back and Richard Hill reached the end of their careers with England, the ready-made replacements were simply not there.

Sir Clive Woodward left in a huff in September 2004, taking a swipe at the RFU for failing to deliver the central control over players he thought essential and it was left to his deputy Andy Robinson to pick up the pieces. He was never able to finish the jigsaw.

A respected hands-on coach, Robinson never convinced when it came to swapping the track suit for the pin-stripe. He endured some bad luck – the icon he chose to lead the side into the new era, Wilkinson, saw his body fail on him – but as a selector he was found wanting and after two years of struggle and a 40 per cent win record, he was replaced after the 2006 autumn internationals by Brian Ashton.

The drudgery of the Robinson years gave way to a sense of optimism under the maverick Ashton which wins in his first two games in the 2007 Six Nations helped to stoke. A record defeat by Ireland at Croke Park in the next game brought England back down to earth.

They were billed as the worst holders in history when they went down 36-0 to South Africa in the World Cup group stages but after a player rebellion came up with a new approach, they somehow scrapped their way past Australia and France to the final where they lost much more narrowly to the Springboks. No. 8 Martin Corry compared the campaign to *Cool Runnings* – the film of the Jamaican bobsleigh team's unlikely passage to the Winter Olympics.

It was, in the end, a spirited defence of the trophy as, in reaching the final, they had overshot expectations. Their motto 'Shock The World' had given away the fact that they were in reality a modest side who was big on heart but some way short of world class.

Ashton was rewarded with a new contract but defeats by Wales and Scotland in the 2008 Six Nations saw reality dawn. England still weren't very good and Ashton was gone.

The RFU decided star power was the solution and turned to Johnson, at that point a visibly frustrated TV pundit, in April 2008 to try to restore their lustre. He was a figure of authority, revered and respected by the English game as a whole, who could shape the side in his own indomitable image and conquer the world again. Couldn't he?

That was the theory. There was a problem, though. Johnson was a towering rugby player, a colossus as a captain, but he had never managed a rugby team before. Not at international level, not at club level, not even at mini-rugby level. Here was a man who knew everything there was to know about rugby but nothing whatsoever about rugby management. He was being asked to sit an entirely different exam paper.

The flame flickered during his reign – his win record was respectable and England claimed the 2011 Six Nations' Championship title – but when it came to the ultimate test, a World Cup in New Zealand, it all fell apart for Johnson.

The players were always going to be under intense scrutiny in a country where rugby union is front-page news at any time. When a World Cup came to town they were on a petri dish under a microscope.

There had been a clear warning of what to expect on England's tour to New Zealand in 2008 which the recently appointed Johnson missed to attend the birth of his second child. Mike Brown and Topsy Ojo were fined and reprimanded after an all-night drinking session in Auckland.

A report by RFU disciplinary officer Judge Jeff Blackett, which cleared the pair of the much more serious allegation of sexual misconduct with a young woman the same night, clearly spelled out the standards expected of England players in the professional era.

'No doubt in the past England players on tour have stayed out too late, drunk excessive quantities of alcohol, invited guests back to the team hotel and missed physiotherapist appointments or training the next morning,' wrote Blackett. 'But such activity is now inconsistent with the life of an elite professional rugby player in the modern era and with membership of a team seeking to be the best in the world.'

The class of 2011 should have worn that message across their foreheads. Instead, they left a trail of embarrassment across New Zealand.

In a succession of team meetings Johnson and other members of his sizeable management team delivered the message that they needed to be mindful of allowing themselves to be seen in compromising situations, but they were ignored.

The fall-out followed quickly. Twickenham ordered a series of three reports into the failure – one from the players' union, one from the Premiership clubs and one from the England players and management by the RFU.

Questionnaires were issued to the players by their trade union, the Rugby Players' Association. They were assured their contributions would be treated in confidence. They were leaked.

The revelations shone a torch into the darkness of a rancid squad culture in which the honour of playing for England had seemingly been lost.

The RPA report noted: 'Senior players behaving like they were owed something and leading drinking games. There was also, alarmingly, a culture where it was not cool to train hard.' There was more. 'Some of the younger players trained their hearts out in pre-season and were mocked by some players. What happened to the culture where everyone was training to be the best in the world?'

This was a team preparing for the third-biggest sporting event in the world and 'senior' elements inside it did not think it appropriate to give their all.

In some cases it was no longer about playing for the rose any more, it appeared, but the pound. The RPA report noted: 'The off-field culture was, allegedly, quite money-focused for senior players.'

That was backed up by the following damning observation from one player. 'To hear one senior player in the changing room say straight after the quarter-final defeat: "There's £35k just gone down the toilet" made me feel sick. Money shouldn't even come into a player's mind.'

There had been arguments about money right up until departure. The squad, the highest paid in world rugby, had threatened to boycott the World Cup send-off dinner at Twickenham unless their financial demands were met. 'It suggested that some of the senior players were more focused on money than getting the rugby right,' complained one RFU official afterwards.

The squad had gone into the tournament with a motto to live and play by. Together. Relentless. Trusted. The words were rendered utterly meaningless in the context of what emerged from England's World Cup.

Dave Alred, who had been used to working with dedicated professionals such as Wilkinson, was left exasperated by the indiscipline. 'The culture of "together, relentless, trusted" was only lived by a few,' he wrote in the RFU's debrief. 'The critical mass of the group was not mature or responsible enough to live the culture without continual checking and chasing as, in part, was illustrated by the off-field foolishness.'

The prevailing culture appeared instead to be: Expectation. Earnings. Entitlement.

Always, always it was the 'senior' player group which was in the firing line. Those who should have set the standards had manifestly failed to do so. When the standards of the influential senior England players in New Zealand sank, it dragged the rest of the squad down with them. When Tuilagi, a freewheeling twenty-year-old kid, jumped off the ferry in Auckland Harbour he was merely following the indirect example of his peers. In such an environment no one can prosper.

'We should have been harder on key senior individuals. From early on in the camp some of them should have been told to put up or leave. I felt we listened to these senior players' needs too much. They affected the group,' reported one member of the England coaching staff.

Another added damningly: 'The squad contains a very limited number of individuals whose attitude is, in my view, on occasions unacceptably selfish, arrogant and ill-disciplined. These individuals were not (in hindsight) adequately dealt with at the time. Again with the benefit of hindsight I would not have put as much trust in senior players as we did concerning off-field standards. In some cases they let Martin Johnson down in this regard.'

Senior players were accused of operating to their own agenda and with a total lack of respect to support staff and sponsors who were helping to pay their substantial wages.

In her World Cup report, the RFU's sponsorship account director Jenny Simms reported 'significant abuse' for the RFU's commercial partnerships team at a shirt-signing event and players greeting sponsors at squad appearances with the question: 'When can we leave?'

One of the principal backers, Land Rover, subsequently delivered a formal complaint to the RFU over the players' attitude. They claimed players had used inappropriate language and had driven dangerously at a driving day in New Zealand. The players involved claimed to have been misled into attending a corporate event which they believed would be a day of R and R. There was fault on both sides but the resentful response mirrored that which the coaches claimed to be experiencing on a daily basis.

'A small minority lacked respect and continually lacked humility and understanding of the situation around them, the challenges management faced and if something wasn't quite right or didn't work instantly they moaned and blamed and expected instant resolutions,' reported one. 'Some influential players within the group lack self-awareness and how, whether they recognise it, they influence others around them.'

The World Cup was a high-pressure environment and emotions were bound to be running high. Honest exchanges on the training ground were natural but each fresh off-field incident ate away at the coaches' faith in their players.

'By the end of the Rugby World Cup campaign the players had, in my opinion, lost the trust of the management (on and off the field). Trust is born of competence and character,' said one coach.

'A minority of players needed a greater sense of responsibility as to what and who they were representing, higher self-awareness...world class is not just about what happens on the pitch, it is a 24/7 attitude to all elements,' said a colleague.

Another recommended that in future: 'Everyone, particularly players, to take more responsibility and not expect everything to be done for them. Players to understand that they are in a privileged position and they should recognise their role as someone representing their country.'

How had it come to the situation where they had to be reminded of this? Where had the honour of playing for England gone? There seemed to be plenty of take but not much give in return.

The knock-on effect from the failure of some players to live up to their responsibilities was to open up fault lines within the squad. Some of the younger players were appalled by the extravagances and lost respect for their seniors.

'The players were trusted by Johnno to behave in a way which allowed them to socialise and enjoy their down time but unfortunately a few overstepped the mark, which in turn, I believe, affected how together the players were with each other,' one member of the management reported.

In his own post-tournament debrief to the RFU, Johnson maintained his loyalty to the players. Never a fan of the media, he fell back on blaming the messenger. 'The reporting of the team's off-field behaviour became a huge issue in the English media and this was then picked up by the local press who published a number of these articles. The incident that happened early in the tournament involving Mike Tindall became a catalyst and the story became far greater because of his status,' reported Johnson.

'We held a meeting during the first two days in Auckland to highlight the risks associated with being an English player in New Zealand during the Rugby World Cup and the escalation that can occur from any incident.

'Richard Smith QC [the team's lawyer] spoke and we thought left no one in any doubt as to how closely they would be scrutinised. Unfortunately in some cases even after the incidents and subsequent media coverage some players still do not understand that the facts and size of the story do not correlate.'

Underneath, though, even Johnson tacitly acknowledged the existence of a discipline problem in the England squad. Only cover-ups by their clubs and representatives had prevented previous excesses reaching the public domain.

'The fact is, for a few, these messages do need to be repeated on an almost daily basis. A minority of players are at risk through lack of self-awareness and in some cases the past experience of being protected by teams/agents from exposure of being involved in an incident whenever they are out socially,' he admitted. 'The impact of off-field coverage is difficult to judge. We certainly felt it affected Mike's [Tindall] performance although he claims that wasn't the case and he had simply played poorly.

'For the squad as a whole, I think it did become tiresome but how much it affected performance is questionable. It was certainly time-consuming for the players involved and parts of the management. We had to tread the line of being supportive, keeping the squad together and letting people know that it was not acceptable and was putting us under needless pressure.'

Johnson's coaches were in considerably less doubt that the distractions had impacted on the squad's performance. In fact they could not have been more clear on the subject afterwards. 'Off-field dramas killed us. They took over. Management/players affected by a few immature individuals. Lads should have come home early that night in Queenstown,' wrote one in the England team debrief.

Another pointed to the link between England's high penalty count in their early matches and their inability to control their behaviour away from the games. 'Indiscipline was a massive issue both on and off the pitch. The two are very much related and both had a massive impact on the team's performance. Whilst on-field discipline did improve significantly the damage had been done off the pitch with the media and public's perception of the group – and Mike in particular. Going forward significant education to the group is required.'

Perhaps if England had been world-beaters some of the excesses could have been overlooked. But the reality was the excesses contributed to the fact that they weren't world-beaters. England's players were nowhere near as good as they seemed to think they were. The basics – which was frankly all England were about by that point – broke down under pressure and their decision-making was simply not up to it at the highest level.

One coach went so far as to contribute the following telling paragraph to the RFU debrief: 'Sore point this one but no point burying our heads in the sand. We do not have a single world-class player in our squad. In fact we might struggle to get a representative in a Home Nations' XV never mind a Six Nations' XV.'

If management had their doubts over the players, it was a two-way street. The contempt in which the players held most of the coaching staff was startling. The RPA report was highly critical. 'The feedback on the majority of the on-field coaching is brutal. There was a culture of self-interest and the players noticed the coaches did not share the same philosophy on how the team should play,' it read.

John Wells was described as 'archaic', defence coach Mike Ford's analysis 'a white wall of jargon' and attack coach Brian Smith 'way out of his depth'. Smith drew particularly heavy criticism and was ridiculed by several players for borrowing an attack move from minnows Romania. 'Attack analysis so poor it's unreal – he is clueless,' reported one player.

In a survey of the squad 27 per cent rated the attack coaching very poor and 64 per cent poor. One labelled the attack strategy a 'disgrace'.

'Attack is a huge problem. We don't have any structure, we don't have a game plan, everyone is not sure of what they are meant to be doing. There is no plan against the opposition and it's not good enough in all areas. The training drills are not at all beneficial to any of us,' wrote one player.

'To go into World Cup games not having a game plan, any structure or any clear idea of what we were going to do in attack was astonishing,' complained another.

'They'd had four years to develop a plan for the World Cup and it felt like they were doing it off-the-cuff in New Zealand,' added a team-mate.

In frustration the players took it upon themselves to try to sort out the muddle. 'In the end it was more player-led with little coach input,' revealed one.

Tactical deficiencies were highlighted in the same survey. Of the players who responded, 27 per cent thought England's negative approach very poor and 55 per cent poor.

England, under Johnson, had played some lively rugby at times but a 24-8 defeat by Ireland in Dublin during the 2011 Six Nations had narrowed their horizons considerably. England had fallen back on risk-free rugby which was as unfulfilling to play as to watch. The grey brand of rugby was 'terrible', complained one.

'We had no identity. We weren't the best at anything and we weren't encouraged to be,' added another.

A quarter-final exit matched England's worst performance at a World Cup but felt like over-achievement to some in the grim circumstances. 'I really can't believe we lasted as long as we did in the tournament. We played like crap,' was one player's succinct summation.

England's preparation also came under fire. The pre-World Cup camp at the lavish Pennyhill Park Hotel in Surrey, which had been the squad's base since the Woodward era, was criticised for being a slog. Rabbit holes in the practice pitch there were also highlighted.

When it came to the tournament itself there was disgruntlement over the quality of the physical work they were asked to do. 'Physically, weights programmes provided are not good enough – felt weaker and slower than I ever have before,' confided one player.

Of course players will always be internally critical when the team loses – particularly when they are not being picked – but all this went way beyond the normal boundaries of disgruntlement.

Even Johnson, who retained the widespread admiration of a group who had grown up with him as a hero, was taken to task over his selection. The job description was to select the best players – rather than the players he knew best – and to blend their contrasting skill sets into the most potent unit possible. But Johnson leaned heavily towards former team-mates – those he knew and thought he could trust – rather than those in form. Of the squad, 27 per cent thought his selection very poor and 45 per cent poor.

'Clearly, to me, five players should not have been involved in the Rugby World Cup. Loyalties made favouritism,' complained one player.

That was in the original squad selection; once in New Zealand the sense of a closed shop grew. The most glaring example was Johnson's resistance to picking Flood ahead of the struggling Wilkinson as playmaker. He was an English sporting icon, the consummate professional and the perfect ambassador but Wilkinson was in a personal rut and, according to one team-mate, not 'an attacking threat any more'. Even his fabled goalkicking was on the blink but Johnson seemed to be permanently drawn back to past glories. When he eventually did call up Flood for the quarter-final it was – despite the fact he had barely trained there all tournament – as a centre outside Wilkinson.

The sense of banging hard against a locked door created resentment within the squad. 'Too many old players in it for the wrong reason – young players performing better but overlooked and the squad knew this,' wrote one.

The bitterness came to the surface in one scathing comment by a player in the report on his England colleagues. 'Most of them think they have a divine right to walk on the pitch and win. No desire, no ethic, no one willing to be accountable.'

The management feedback had also picked up on a work ethic shortfall which some players within the squad acknowlededged. 'Boys just don't get it,' said one. 'That comes from a culture that Johnno needs to create and would have done if he wasn't stopped by certain players who think they are above the law!' Another spelled it out straight, citing the 'complete lack of respect for Johnno, their team-mates and the England shirt' within elements of the team.

For a country to have a chance of winning a World Cup they need very good players but they also need very good players who will put the team first. Not enough of them were willing to do so in Johnson's squad. 'Some players were there for themselves and not the team,' reported one England player.

It seemed that as the England shirt had become ever more valuable financially, it had become virtually worthless in spiritual terms. 'The team identity is in ruins,' concluded the RPA report.

Johnson, the greatest enforcer of his generation – a player who could curdle milk with a single glance – had proved powerless to do anything about the decline into anarchy. He resigned.

Twickenham took the unprecedented step of saying sorry for the England team. 'The most important thing I can say on behalf of the RFU is to make an apology to the fans, to the clubs and everyone involved in rugby – everyone who loves rugby – for the performance in the World Cup and surrounding events. Fundamentally, we have let ourselves down as a sport and as a team. We've let the sport of rugby down,' said the RFU's acting chief executive Stephen Brown.

'The standards of our performance and our behaviour were below what we would expect, as was our preparation. We had a lot of off-pitch disciplinary problems which have attracted a lot of negative coverage. We need to fix this going into 2015.'

England were beaten, bedraggled and rudderless. They had hit rock bottom.

2

Caretaker Duty

It was always yet the trick of our English nation,
If they have a good thing, to make it too common
                                                Henry IV Part 2, Act 1, Scene 2

Watching all this unfold with increasing unease and agitation
was Stuart Lancaster, the coach of the second-string England
Saxons.

He knew Martin Johnson well from his Saxons role and
believed he had been let down by his players at the World Cup.
He had huge respect for him as a rugby legend and as a man of
integrity and honour. But he also felt there had been a failure
of management in allowing such a decrepit culture to develop.

He was so frustrated that the day after England's quarter-final
exit in Auckland he headed off to a library in Leeds and wrote
down a list of what he felt had gone wrong. Several hours later
he re-emerged. The list stretched to 159 separate points.

Lancaster had a good insight into what had gone awry with
the England squad. He had spent a fortnight in New Zealand,
taking in the final group game against Scotland and the

quarter-final against France, as part of his RFU brief. It had offered him the chance to see the decay from within and the disdain in which England were widely held at the tournament. Nineteen nations seemed to be welcome in New Zealand as ambassadors for their countries and the sport; one wasn't. They wore white.

Lancaster also had a keener sense than most in the professional game of the growing distance between the English grass-roots rugby supporter and the national team.

Despite being based at Twickenham, Lancaster lived in Yorkshire where his son Daniel played for West Park Leeds under-11s. He was the assistant coach. Lancaster had watched England's opening game in the bar at West Park and what he had heard from those around him disconcerted him.

Despite the growth of the professional club scene, England had always been the crown on the head of a unified English game but a disconnect seemed to be emerging.

This was before all the off-field antics. What Lancaster heard on the touchline on Sunday mornings after he returned from New Zealand indicated something even more alarming for English rugby. Mini-rugby man and woman were appalled at what they had seen and heard at the World Cup. Appalled and angry.

They not only had a failing national side but one who had lost the faith of the common rugby man. They could take defeat with honour if they had to but there had been only dishonour in New Zealand. This England team had betrayed them.

English rugby union had always given its players a certain licence. In the amateur days bonhomie and boorishness had been comfortable bedfellows. A drink or several remained central to the culture of a game which retained its thirstiness at most levels.

This was England, though, and England in the professional era. The players were ambassadors as well as athletes. What were they thinking? Lancaster shared their sentiments. What differed was that he was in a position to do something about it.

As well as being Saxons coach, Lancaster was also the RFU's head of elite-player development, overseeing all of the national age-group sides. He had in-depth knowledge of the next generation of English talent coming through and believed there was something to work with – if the correct parameters were put in place to guide them. He had his own ideas on what they should be.

The players were not, in his view, a lost cause, just lost sheep who needed a shepherd's crook. And, having been raised on a farm in Cumbria, he knew all about that.

Lancaster was convinced that if they were put on the right path and made to understand what playing for England should really be about again then the connection to their army of disgruntled supporters could be restored. The link was broken but it was fixable.

Johnson's resignation created a vacancy for someone able to enact the turnaround, but with the Six Nations' Championship only a couple of months away, time was short for the RFU to find the right man.

The RFU itself was in a state of chaos at the top with an inquiry underway into who had leaked the World Cup reports. Chairman Martyn Thomas was on his way out with Stephen Brown holding the fort until a permanent successor could be found. In the middle of the mess was Rob Andrew, the former England stand-off who, as the RFU's Professional Rugby Director, was charged with finding a replacement for Johnson.

'We were in a state of flux,' said Andrew, with some under-statement. 'We'd gone out of the World Cup in the quarter-final, there were political issues at the RFU – we didn't have a full-time chief exec – and Johnno announced he was stepping down. There was a whole heap of stuff going on. We were pretty much all at sea to be honest.

'We decided we weren't going to make a rushed appointment of a permanent head coach – there was too much going on in the organisation – so it was agreed by the board that we would make an interim appointment and they asked me to put in place some plans.'

A caretaker would buy them time to find the right man to take England through to the 2015 World Cup. A home World Cup would be the biggest event English rugby had ever seen and it was critical to get the long-term coach right.

That could wait. In the short term, they needed someone to restore order, someone who knew the players and the English system.

The most logical call would have been to headhunt one of the Premiership coaches who had up-to-date knowledge of both. Northampton's Jim Mallinder, a calm head and respected director of rugby at the Saints, was flagged up as one possibility. But the RFU were loath to risk antagonising the clubs by poaching a contracted coach mid-season for what might well be only a three-month appointment. The most critical factor on the CVs of the potential candidates became availability.

As Andrew sifted through options such as the great All Black John Kirwan, recently departed from Japan, he kept coming back to the same problem. None of the established Test coaches who wanted the job and were free to take it knew much about England's players.

Andrew, a former director of rugby at Newcastle, did know them and had briefly filled the void in 2008 in New Zealand, before Johnson took hands-on control, but had no wish to do so again.

There was one other man who ticked the boxes of familiarity and availability and he was sitting in the Twickenham offices opposite Andrew. Stuart Lancaster.

'Stuart was very keen to do it and he was very clear on what he wanted to do,' said Andrew. 'He'd been in New Zealand so he had a handle on the problems but he also knew all the players who were coming through. There were people floating around who had put their hands up who I spoke to but Stuart was effectively the in-house candidate. We had various meetings and he very much impressed on me in typical, down-to-earth Stuart fashion that he really wanted to do the job and that he could do it. "This is how I'll do it. Don't worry about it. I'll sort it out."

'He'd done a fantastic job with the Saxons over the previous three seasons and there comes a point with coaches, like players, when they just need to be given a chance. If nobody ever gave a chance to someone who hadn't coached at international level before, then we'd never have any new international coaches. It became a reasonably straightforward decision for me to recommend to the board that we hand the reins to Stuart for the Six Nations.'

Andrew had some trepidation over whether his colleagues at the RFU would be reluctant to put such an unfamiliar face in charge of their most valuable commodity, but they bought his pitch. 'I didn't have to do a great deal of persuading. The board accepted that we needed to steady the ship,' he said. 'You could argue that we were buying ourselves a bit of time in terms of the longer-term appointment but it just felt right for everybody.'

To outsiders, it looked like the RFU grandees had been on the super-strength skunk. Not only had Lancaster no experience of playing or coaching Test rugby, but he had spent very little time in Premiership rugby either. He had never played in the top division of the English game and in his one full season coaching in it, Leeds were relegated after winning only two matches.

While he had guided the Saxons to nine wins in ten matches, he remained a virtual unknown outside Twickenham. Where Johnson was a global icon, Lancaster was the invisible man.

It may have looked like a kid being handed the keys to the sweetshop but this was not quite the blind punt it appeared. Lancaster had already turned the heads of the RFU Council with a flawless presentation for a job of performance director, a position which never saw the light of day. In it, he outlined how, with a side based on the talented young players who had reached four of the last five junior world championship finals, England could win the 2015 World Cup.

He showed a chart which revealed that the average number of caps for a World Cup-winning side was 663. If England backed the gifted young players currently making waves at junior level, he argued, they would reach that target figure just in time for the start of the 2015 tournament. The prospective team he showed the council members had George Ford, the 2011 world junior player of the year, at No. 10 and another highly promising uncapped Lancastrian called Owen Farrell at No. 12.

In the end he was not appointed to the job of performance director – the post was scrapped – but he had made a strong impression with his plan and his delivery.

Insiders at the RFU knew all about his drive and energy too. This was a man who would set off at 3.15 a.m. from home in Yorkshire to make sure he was first in the office for 8 a.m. meetings at Twickenham. 'Everyone who had worked with him knew he had this remarkable work ethic,' said Andrew.

Even so, when it came to the role of England head coach – even an interim version – there were many within the inner circle who harboured serious doubts. The RFU needed a strong character who could bring England's players back into line. Was the outwardly calm and measured Lancaster really that man? Did a man who had spent half his working life as a PE teacher ordering children around have the necessary clout?

He would have to win over a group of established international players and persuade them that his opinions on a game he had never himself played at Test level were worth listening to. The consequences if he failed would be grave. If Lancaster proved as much use as a chocolate teapot, the Six Nations could end up being one of the biggest embarrassments in English rugby history.

The RFU took a deep collective breath and went for it. The announcement was made on 8 December 2011 that forty-two-year-old Stuart Lancaster was taking charge as England caretaker coach.

'We were at Twickenham in the office when I told him. He was delighted but he was also desperate to get on with it,' said Andrew.

Misgivings behind the scenes remained. Even those who had known him for a long time like England second row Tom Palmer, a former team-mate in the Leeds pack, raised their eyebrows at the appointment. 'When I first heard, I was quite surprised. I thought they would have gone for a bigger name,' admitted Palmer. Lancaster was, in global rugby terms, a nobody. He had a lot to prove, a lot on his plate and just 58 days before the start of his first tournament in charge, the 2012 Six Nations' Championship.

And so the whirlwind blew. If this was to be a three-month role, Lancaster wanted to make every second count. The first job was to sort out the management team. The RFU still had Johnson's four main World Cup back-up coaches on their payroll but the poisonous tone of the tournament debrief made it impossible for the quartet to survive. Lancaster kept the one member of Johnson's unit who came out of the leaked report intact, Graham Rowntree, and promoted him from scrum coach to forwards' coach. The other three – John Wells, Brian Smith and Mike Ford – had to go. In their place he wanted just one other coach – Saracens' Andy Farrell.

'He was very clear on the coaching team he wanted,' said Andrew. 'He was absolutely adamant he wanted to keep Graham and he wanted to get Andy Farrell in. We went to Saracens and asked them if they could help us out. They were fantastic in that Six Nations – although they weren't best pleased when we went back afterwards and asked if we could have him full-time.' The pair had worked together at Saxons level and, as straightforward northerners, spoke the same direct, honest language.

Rowntree, too, as a former member of the Leicester front row, did not do bullshit. He still had the respect of the players – even after the World Cup experience – and, like Farrell, he had the experience of playing international rugby. They were shrewd appointments to flank Lancaster and men who gave him instant credibility. In an era of bloated management teams, a three-man operation looked thin but it was what the head coach wanted.

There was talk of an experienced manager being put in place above him. Lancaster said no. He did not want his message diluting. He also wanted to ensure the big-picture planning was all his own work. Despite the temporary nature of his appointment, Lancaster's vision for England stretched all the way to the next World Cup.

He embarked on a whistle-stop tour around all 12 Premiership clubs to visit each director of rugby in person. These were the relationships he would have to rely on however long he had the job but he was starting from an awkward position. Relations between the clubs and the RFU had been allowed to wither on the vine – the clubs' own World Cup report was the most damning of the three.

While the owners were relieved that none of their directors of rugby had been poached for the England interim position, the directors of rugby themselves may well not have felt the same way. A proportion of those club coaches would have viewed themselves eminently better qualified for the England job than Lancaster. He had to prove himself to them.

They were the men who knew their players best and for the high-wire act Lancaster was about to undertake he needed the best possible information. There would be no safety net. He believed there was no point picking players who were too old to stay the course, particularly the ones who hadn't exactly covered themselves in glory at the World Cup. While the safe option would have been to hang on to a few of Johnson's warhorses to help assist with the transition in his first squad, Lancaster knew the depth of young talent in England and was prepared to give these players their break. The new England was to be no country for old men.

At the time, it felt bold to the point of recklessness. Hindsight has not altered that impression. Three years into his reign Stuart Lancaster gave a talk to a group of businessmen in which he acknowledged the gamble he took. 'It was a big risk – we could easily have lost three or four of the Six Nations' games and if we had, I wouldn't be in the job now. Someone else would be doing it. Fortunately, we won four out of five,' he said.

'There was a strategy behind selecting young players, sticking with them and developing experience within them so that there would be 500 or 600 caps' worth by the time of the 2015 World Cup. Experience isn't the only thing that wins you games but going through tough times together and learning together and to fight and commit to each other certainly helps.

'People criticised me for my selections, saying I should always pick my best team for the here and now. But if we'd have done that we'd have picked players who would have retired before the World Cup and our young players would have been even less experienced because we'd have been pitching them in later. When you are building a team you can't just aim to win in the here and now. You have to build for the future as well.'

In December 2011 Lancaster had embarked on a culling tour, breaking the news in person to the old guard that their time was up. It was no fun touring around delivering bad news but he wanted to do it face to face. For all that the World Cup had been a disaster, these were players who had represented England in better times, too. In some cases the best of all. An honourable end was what they deserved.

Lancaster met with England's 30-somethings – men with more than 50 caps such as Mike Tindall, Mark Cueto and Simon Shaw – to pass on the message. He said farewell, too to Nick Easter although that turned out to be more of an au revoir. At the same time Lewis Moody, Steve Thompson and Jonny Wilkinson all announced their retirements. Lancaster flew to Toulon to see Wilkinson, partly to thank the great stand-off for his service to England but also to pick his brains. He talked to him about the ingredients which had made for the most productive England environment in his remarkable 13-year Test career, and also the least productive. It was an informative three hours.

On 11 January 2012 a new 32-man England elite squad was announced containing 13 changes from the World Cup squad.

The squad was stripped bare of hundreds of caps in one go. There was no Riki Flutey or Shontayne Hape while Matt Banahan and Delon Armitage were dropped to the Saxons squad as Lancaster prepared to turn to a fresh page.

It was a risk but, for an unknown coach trying to prove himself, sweeping away the veterans who had seen it all before had an advantageous side effect. The last thing a new coach with no profile needed was a cynical old lag undermining him. Lancaster chose big hearts ahead of big egos. Players like Chris Robshaw, who had been overlooked for the World Cup squad despite tearing up trees in training, would be central to the reconstructed, resolute England.

It looked more like an England Saxons squad such was the absence of recognisable names – nine of the players had never played Test rugby before – but the players had been sifted and selected carefully. The players he brought in were so hungry to play for England it hurt. Lancaster had inside knowledge of the majority of them from his time with the Saxons, from where he promoted reliable individuals such as Geoff Parling and Lee Dickson. He also picked stars of the future who had excelled in England's age-group sides like Owen Farrell and Joe Marler who he had overseen in his years at the RFU's National Academy. He knew they were inexperienced but also knew they were made of exactly the right stuff for Test rugby.

He had come up with a list of individuals who he believed had the character to give their all for England on the pitch and also represent the country with honour off the field.

If they failed to do so, they would be dropped – as Danny Care found out. He was set to return to the national squad after missing the World Cup through injury but, after he was arrested twice in three weeks for drink-related offences, Lancaster axed him for the Six Nations.

One of Lancaster's protégés from his five years with the Leeds Academy, Care could have been expected to be one of his key allies in winning over the squad but a line in the sand had to be drawn, and the Harlequins scrum-half found himself on the wrong side of it. 'I think it was awful for both of us,' said Care. 'Stuart said that the last thing he wanted to do as his first act with the squad was to throw me out of it but it was something he felt he had to do. I just got on with it, accepted it and realised I had to change a few things to earn a bit of trust and respect back. It took a lot of hard work but I did it.' Delon Armitage was also excluded from England Saxons after being arrested over an assault allegation.

These cases were difficult but they were also timely for Lancaster in that they offered him the chance to show he meant what he said about building a new England. It was not just hot air: if they wanted to play for England, players had to behave. Being an England player was a privilege but it came with responsibilities. It was a 365-day-a-year job. When behaviour failed to live up to expectations, the players had to know their actions would lead to consequences. Selection was Lancaster's nuclear option.

Not all of the bad boys from the World Cup were banished – Chris Ashton, Manu Tuilagi and Dylan Hartley were named in the 32 – but they were about to re-enter a very different set-up from the one they had left.

Lancaster ripped up Johnson's plan to fly the squad out to Portugal on a warm-weather training trip ahead of the Six

Nations in January and took them to Leeds for the week instead.

As conference-centre hotels on the ring roads of industrial cities go, Weetwood Hall is not unattractive. Built around a seventeenth-century manor house in nine acres of gardens with well-kept lawns and pleasant views of Leeds University playing fields, it has gone upmarket from its previous guise as a student hall of residence. To the players, though, the sandstone pile with its courtyard and cupola cannot have felt that welcoming. For most, it was a long way from home at the end of the M1 and it was inescapably northern – a sculpture of a Leeds owl on a metal tree surrounded by white Yorkshire roses greeted the players as they walked into the hotel where a complimentary copy of the *Yorkshire Post* awaited them in their rooms.

Then there was the uncertainty of what lay around the corner over the next few days. Lancaster had announced that the squad would be training at his Yorkshire Division Two club, West Park Leeds, for the week. The words 'boot' and 'camp' sprang to mind as the players booked in. The England rugby team had misbehaved and this must be their 'grim up north' punishment.

There was a reason for the location. 'It wasn't because it was near to where I lived,' said Lancaster. 'The main reason I did it was because I wanted to get the grass-roots rugby fan to understand that the England rugby team had their feet back on the ground. The grass roots is where I have come from. There was no point in going to a warm-weather camp anyway. Our first game was in Scotland!'

Training at West Park was certainly a throwback experience for stand-off Charlie Hodgson, a West Yorkshire lad himself exiled in Hertfordshire with Saracens, who had played under four previous regimes, beginning with that of Sir Clive Woodward, but never experienced anything quite like this with

England. 'I would question the pitch – it was pretty muddy and not something we would play on too often – but Stuart wanted us to go back to grass roots,' said Hodgson. 'He wanted us to reconnect with the England fans and for us all to feel part of the same thing.'

In fact, as Lancaster knew it would, West Park Leeds turned out to be a long way from the primitive hell some had imagined. Housed in the leafy-lane village of Bramhope, the modern facility they encountered would not have looked out of place at a Premiership training ground.

It might have belonged to a level-eight club in the English structure but it featured ten pitches spread over 42 acres including one all-weather surface. Inside the smart two-storey clubhouse, which cost £3.2million, was a gym, medical room and ten dressing rooms. True, the planes from nearby Leeds-Bradford Airport could be a little distracting and they did not have cows quite so close at Pennyhill Park, but if this was back to basics they could live with it.

While it was unfamiliar to most of the players, the quirky venue put Lancaster on the front foot. He knew the area like the back of his hand so he knew exactly what he would be exposing his players to. The only surprises would be for them.

When it came to the training itself, Lancaster was starting from a position of weakness as a non-international player and rookie Test coach. His lack of experience placed extra pressure on his authority. If the players did not believe in the messenger, they would not believe the message. This was a step up and, if he was bluffing, his players would have seen through him straight away, but Lancaster was confident in his ability to deliver.

He came prepared. He had kept a written copy of every single training session he had taken since he started out as a coach in a neatly stacked pile of A4 Collins diaries he stored in his loft. They contained everything from West Park minis to England. He was not short of material to draw on.

As de facto attack coach, Lancaster kept it simple. A solid set piece – Rowntree's area of expertise – and a watertight defence – Farrell's parish as a former rugby league man – were the priorities for a new team just getting to know each other. 'He brought in good people around him. They were excellent coaches,' said Palmer.

The clear-out meant a widescale lack of exposure at Test level within the squad. Having not been there and done it, there would naturally be questions in many heads as to whether they were up to it. So, on their first full night together Lancaster gathered the squad at their Weetwood Hall base to watch a DVD.

'He showed this video of all the talent that was in the room. There were clips of every single player. It was phenomenal,' said Hodgson. 'Regardless of experience and caps, that helped us to really believe in ourselves. I think it made a massive difference.'

For Palmer who, like Hodgson, went all the way back to 2001 as an England player, sitting there watching his new teammates doing great things for their clubs up on the screen felt like a page turning. At thirty-two, he might not have been in it for the long haul but many of those surrounding him intended to be as, by the sounds of it, was Lancaster.

'There were lots of players experiencing that environment for the first time but Stuart did a good job right from the start setting the tone – he's a very modern coach. He is really excellent at presenting, at getting his message across,' said Palmer. 'Even then it wasn't as if he was going to be around for a few months. The way he presented to the guys sounded like he was planning for four years. "This is where we are now," he said. "And this is where we're going to get to.'"

The players left that short but inspiring meeting with a spring in their step. 'The start point was to get the team looking ahead to the World Cup in 2015 and get people excited about that. I picked a team that I felt we could grow and develop so it would peak for 2015,' said Lancaster. 'Early on I made that decision, and started with a new group of players. I reminded them of the reason why playing for England is special and focused all my effort and energy on that to get them committed to the team, to the shirt and to each other.'

The comedown arrived after training the next evening when Lancaster took them through a damning debrief of the World Cup campaign in the company of the RFU management board. It was much longer and much more painful.

For Chris Robshaw, the message was as agonising as if he had been in New Zealand himself. 'Stuart outlined where we stood with the public in our first week together but I already knew. I saw the papers and spoke to people in the pub who'd happily tell me what they thought of England,' said Robshaw. 'We had to reconnect with the fans and with the community work we did, the public training and most importantly our attitude, humility and results.'

Each player was instructed to reread the terms of his RFU elite-player contract in which his disciplinary responsibilities were listed. If they needed a visual reminder of what would happen if they failed to meet them, the forlorn sight of Care's framed England shirt on the wall of the West Park clubhouse underlined it. Care might have played mini-rugby for the club, he might be the local hero, but there were to be no exceptions to the standards which would have to be met from this point onwards.

While Lancaster was not shy in emphasising that a line had been drawn in terms of behaviour, he tried to stress to the players why they should feel it necessary to toe the line in the first place. He had expressed it clearly when he was unveiled as England's interim coach to the national media, many of whom were meeting him for the first time, at Twickenham a month beforehand.

'If we give a strong enough reason to the players about why it's important to be responsible and be respectful of the rose and what the rose represents then everything falls into line behind that. It's about creating an environment that shapes behaviour,' he explained. 'Environment shapes behaviour. For the first twenty years of my life I lived on a small farm in Cumbria where you have to graft and work hard. I spent the second twenty years in Yorkshire, where you get "nowt for owt". There'll be no airs or graces in this camp.

'I'm from a teaching background and a group of pupils can go through five different lessons in a day and behave differently in every lesson because of the standards of the teachers and the values they set.

'Little things to me are important. Things like being on time and being courteous at all times. I'm confident in our ability to create the right environment and the right vision so that they'll come motivated and desperate to get back on the field to represent England and improve on the last World Cup.'

As England players, they were role models to some and heroes to others, carriers of a proud flame. They were the honoured few habiting a space thousands of others would give almost anything to experience. The question was not why should they behave but, in such a position, why shouldn't they? It was not a question of them and us either. The management, too, had a code of conduct drawn up to which they had to adhere.

Lancaster pledged to do away with the culture of expectancy within the England squad. With this is mind, he took a calculated risk. When the squad was reduced to 24 after ten players were released back to their clubs for Premiership duty, he asked for eight of them to give up their free time the next day. He wanted them to coach eight local under-13s sides. For nothing. This was giving back instead of taking.

When Dylan Hartley marched up to him and said: 'We've got a problem with coaching the kids', Lancaster feared the worst.

'What's that?' asked Lancaster.

'All twenty-four of us want to do it,' said Hartley.

It was the first sign to Lancaster that the change in outlook he was striving for was beginning to bite.

So it was that the following afternoon 96 disbelieving Yorkshire schoolchildren had a head coach and two assistants each from the England rugby squad putting them through their paces at West Park. It was more competitive among the internationals than the minis at times. 'In terms of the buzz it created among the England lads, I was running around like I was playing the game,' said Hartley.

There was a wholesome innocence to the scene completely at odds with what had gone before. It was freezing cold with a biting wind but the smiles were genuine and the laughter infectious. The England squad was beginning to look a much more positive place to be.

The team also held an open training session for fans in Leeds. It was not a city strongly associated with rugby union, the national side was at a low ebb results-wise and it was a workday. It could have been the proverbial one-man-and-a-dog event if the dog could have been bothered but, astonishingly, more than 3,000 turned up.

Maybe it was the Yorkshireman's love of a free event but it added to the sense that change was in the air. Hope, too. Optimism even. Broken bridges had begun to be rebuilt. Lancaster had made a flying start in his battle to win over the squad and the public.

To conclude their first week together, Lancaster took the squad out for dinner to Napa, a cosy restaurant he knew well in the affluent Leeds suburb of Roundhay. Squeezed into a dimly lit corner at the back against the purple, velvet-coated walls, the squad was joined by footballer Gary Neville and England rugby league star Jamie Peacock, two players from other sports who embodied the fighting spirit Lancaster wanted in his side.

The place might have had a nightclub-style ambience but the players were not there for a night of revelry. They were there to listen. They had been addressed earlier in the week by Hugh Morris, from England Cricket, who talked about his experience of building a winning side and England rugby league international Kevin Sinfield who struck a more personal note.

'He asked us: "What are you doing when no one is watching?"' recalled Chris Robshaw.

'It's easy to do the right things at your club where everyone is watching and you are being pushed hard but what are you actually doing away from that? If it's a wet, cold day at home and you've had a bad training session, are you still eating well? Are you still making sure you are recovering the right way? Are you making sure you are doing everything you can to make sure you are ready for Saturday? That stuck with me.'

Peacock, a hulking, relentless machine of a forward, went deeper. He spoke to the squad about how he had dragged every inch of ability out of himself over his career. Saracens' full-back Alex Goode came from a family of sporting high-achievers – his aunt Jo had won a badminton bronze at the Sydney Olympics, He absorbed Peacock's words intently.

'His message was that he wasn't the fastest, the strongest or the most skilful but that he believed that to help his team he had to run into the hardest guy the opposition had enough times to break his will. That really struck a chord in terms of what he was willing to do for his team,' said Goode.

Neville, whose own career had been built on a similar story of mental fortitude, spoke about how he wished the success of his Manchester United career could have been replicated for his country. 'He made an interesting point. For all the success he'd had with Manchester United, he said he played lots of games for England but never won anything with them. That's what us, as players, would remember from our careers,' said Tom Palmer.

The speakers had been carefully chosen. Lancaster wanted to instil in his players just what an opportunity they had been presented with and how they had to make the most of it. He also invited along another guest from outside sport's narrow confines, someone who knew what fighting for Queen and country really meant. British Army veteran Simon Brown had lost an eye saving six comrades in Iraq.

'He spoke about what had happened to him and what he'd had to overcome. His situation underlined the point about reacting to those negatives. It's how you come back from them and fight which counts. He put everything in perspective for us,' said Goode. 'To hear him say: "We're 100 per cent behind you and we want you to do well" meant a lot.'

The evening had hit just the note Lancaster intended but he had one more ace up his sleeve. He wanted the players to know just what it meant to those closest to them to see them wear the white shirt. When the players had eaten, Lancaster rose and announced that he had a gift for everyone. He had secretly written to the parents of every player and asked them to write down for him what it meant to them to see their son play for England. He had then asked them to track down up to five of the most influential figures on their son's rugby journey, whose comments would also be included on an individual plaque.

Brad Barritt, a South African-born centre who was about to represent his mother's country for the first time, recalled that special moment: 'It was a complete surprise to the players. We didn't know anything about it. 'Mine was written by my father, my brother and my high-school coach and it was something we kept with us for the whole season. I would read it the night before games. It uplifted me and gave me that extra little bit of motivation. I've still got it.

'Small things like that made the team feel a greater sense of responsibility to those people close to us and the jersey and really bonded the team. It grew exponentially from there. That night, for me, was truly the birth of the new England culture.'

Some of the players were in tears.

As the players stepped out on to the wide sweep of Street Lane to board the bus back to Weetwood Hall, outwardly everything was as normal. The estate agent's, the shoe shop, the bus shelter and betting shop – they all looked the same. Inside, though, England players felt different. The retreat into chaos had stopped; the first steps had been taken towards a brighter future.

Unbeknown to Lancaster, while he had been phoning every player's parents to set up the surprise, his wife had been ringing around his family and his foremost influences. When Lancaster left Napa that night, his secretary handed him a package which he eventually opened back in his room at 1 a.m. It contained a plaque of his own with messages from his school coach, from his mentors, from his friends – 40 people in all – telling him how proud they were that he was the England coach. Lancaster is not an overtly emotional man but that touch meant everything.

3

Playing for Keeps

Lean raw-boned rascals, who would e'er suppose
They had such courage and audacity?

Henry VI Part I, Act 1, Scene 3

The first game of the new England era was away to Scotland. Good England teams had lost at Murrayfield before, never mind totally untried ones. Andy Robinson, the Englishman in charge of Scotland and a former England coach himself, must have been licking his lips.

Robinson had taken something of a gamble in his first game as England coach, throwing four uncapped players into his first match-day squad against Canada in 2004. Every new coach likes to put his stamp on things. When Clive Woodward took the job in 1997, he threw in five debutants – Will Greenwood, David Rees, Matt Perry, Andy Long and Will Green – against Australia in his first Test in charge. Martin Johnson also had five new faces in his first match-day squad against the Pacific Islanders in 2008, while Brian Ashton included three against Scotland in 2007.

Lancaster named eight uncapped players in his squad for the 2012 Calcutta Cup match. England were so wet behind the ears they needed snorkels and flippers to move around the dressing room.

Would a seasoned coach have taken the risks Lancaster did with selection and discarded almost all of his experienced players? Probably not. But this was the direction in which he wanted to go and he was willing to be bold to the point of recklessness.

Chris Robshaw, whose one cap had been won against Argentina three years beforehand, was chosen to lead the team. Only four times in their history had England chosen a captain with less experience – Nigel Melville, in 1984, was the most recent of the quartet of uncapped captains. But Lancaster was in no mood for caution.

The only concession to pragmatism was the selection of an experienced stand-off in Charlie Hodgson who had endured ups and downs at Twickenham over the years. Lancaster wanted Hodgson, who had last started a Test three-and-a-half years previously, to direct the operation and hold the hand of his Saracens club mate Farrell as he took his first step in Test rugby as a centre.

'I obviously knew it would be a short-term thing – I knew there were guys coming through who were better than me – but it wasn't a hard decision to make to come back. I bought massively into what Stuart wanted because I knew he had the team at heart and wanted it to succeed,' said Hodgson. 'It felt different to other England squads I had been involved in because there were no egos to it. There were only two or three players who had played more than thirty Tests so there was a real fresh enthusiasm and a real excitement about the place.'

There were 233 caps in the starting XV and only 42 more on the bench; Scotland had 499.

England had no right to win but somehow they prevailed 13-6, their first victory at Murrayfield for eight years. Scotland dominated possession but blew their chances; England rode their luck and tackled like madmen. The quality was, frankly, poor but there was something there in the performance against the Scots. In rugby, defence usually tells the story of a team's togetherness and in this respect England were ferocious. They made 142 tackles compared to Scotland's 62.

After only a fortnight together, it was less about precision than throwing themselves with kamikaze abandon at anything in a blue shirt. They had prioritised defence in their short training time together, worked to a clearly defined, if restrictive, formula and it had paid off.

'Our defence was based on the Saracens system – it was very similar – and Andy Farrell had an unbelievable amount of enthusiasm for it. Everyone was super-excited about it and it just took off,' said Hodgson. 'We were probably underdogs going into that Six Nations but we wanted to succeed so much. We knew we had to get ourselves going in that first game against Scotland and we did so. Kevin Sinfield had said to us when he spoke to us in Leeds: "don't dip yourself into the water, throw yourself into it and enjoy every minute because it won't last forever" and that's what everyone did.'

The same spirit shone through in the snow in Rome a week later. It was needed as, after a poor first half, England were staring a first defeat against Italy in the face but, after going nine points down, they came back to win 19-15. It was a tightrope walk but they stayed upright as Hodgson's second charge-down try in successive games saved the day. With twenty-year-old

Farrell rewarding Lancaster's faith in youth with his goalkicking, England triumphed. Played two, won two.

The new collective was made up of individuals from clubs with vastly different approaches. While Harlequins used every blade of grass on the pitch to play open rugby, Northampton sent big forwards rumbling around the corner to batter opponents into submission. Saracens put an emphasis on a low-error kick-chase game while Leicester relied heavily on a strong set piece. Distilling all this into an England formula was going to take time so, while Lancaster might have dreamed of sweeping backline moves lighting up Twickenham, there were priorities to address.

There simply was no leeway to move far beyond the basics so England built from the back – a dry stone wall can rise only from a stable base, as any Cumbrian farmer will tell you. Stopping tries rather than scoring them was the main aim when Lancaster's England took their first stuttering steps together.

'Stuart wanted to change the attack shape but early on we spent longer on defence than attack,' recalled Tom Palmer, the team's line-out general. 'There was a lot of emphasis on line speed and getting up fast to get at the opposition.' With the team flying up to shut down opponents' space, there was an acceptance that some tackles would be missed but an expectation that the pressure it created would force mistakes.

It was manically committed, terrifically focused, but to call it a work of creative genius would be a grotesque exaggeration. When it came to attack, England relied on Hodgson's charge-downs and . . . er . . . that was it.

'Initially the game plan was pretty basic but attack is one of those things that takes time to develop,' said Hodgson, Lancaster's first playmaker. 'Defence is quicker. You put the systems in place, get people's attitudes right and off you go. Stuart laid out a framework, explained how it was going to work and then let us develop it. He didn't give me a play-book, he wanted me to write down the things I thought were important. Because I didn't want to leave anything out, I wrote down everything!'

One thing was obvious, however – England's players were all on the same page. 'From the start, Stuart's team showed a great unity and desire and that was probably down to the kind of players he picked,' said Palmer.

'He was very brave in his selections but he brought in lots of young guys who he obviously had faith in. I suspect there were some players who never had a look-in because Stuart thought they would be difficult to manage. He'd done a lot of work looking at other teams and at where they'd got winning cultures from because he obviously thought that was an issue with the previous group. It was very easy for him to mould what he wanted in such a new group because there were so few experienced guys left. Stuart put the framework in place and it evolved.'

For players like Phil Dowson and Brad Barritt, who had played under Lancaster for the Saxons and been promoted to make their full debuts in the championship, his ability to pull a side together quickly and have it ready for international competition was no bolt from the blue.

'I had worked under Stuart for two years with the Saxons and they had been unbelievable experiences,' said Barritt. 'He puts a lot of hard work into the detail of a team and what they want to achieve. He has the man-management skills to get the best out of players but also the organisational skills to steer the ship. Both were brilliant for the team.'

Lancaster might not have carried the kudos of a Nick Mallett or Eddie Jones but Dowson saw how his team-mates responded to a coach who radiated integrity. 'The first word which comes to mind about Stuart is "honest". He tells players how it is and that is what players want,' said Dowson. 'Beyond that what stands out about him is hard work and organisation. There is no stone left unturned in preparing for a game, which is exactly how it should be in international rugby.'

The opening fortnight of the championship had created a feel-good factor which had been missing from England. Lancaster had succeeded in shaping an upbeat environment in which players felt valued but knew exactly where the boundaries were. Two wins over the two weakest sides in the championship had not made England world-beaters but there was a resolve in the team again. They were not the greatest rugby team in the world but they were, already, a team.

When Lancaster had been appointed to the position of interim head coach no one had seriously thought of him as a candidate to do the job full-time. The Oxford University-educated Mallett, who was rugby royalty as a highly regarded ex-coach of the Springboks and Italy, was the favourite for the position. But the flying start and the clear change in the atmosphere around England meant Lancaster suddenly had a foothold in the contest for the permanent post. He thought he could do the job and, increasingly, others did, too. If this was what he could achieve with England in just over two months, what might he manage with a long-term contract?

Large swathes of a media who had never even considered him a runner in the race were being won over. Lancaster, in keeping with his open, uncomplicated personality, had taken a wholly different approach to them than his suspicious predecessor.

Johnson's policy had been to view the press as the opposition and give them nothing; Lancaster was much more willing to indulge his critics with increased access and extra briefings.

The players were also encouraged to reach out to their interrogators – literally. They made a point of shaking hands with journalists before interviews. If this had happened in Johnson's time there would have been an electric buzzer hidden in the palm of the hand but in one simple gesture it created a link and watered down the 'them and us' mentality. The PR stuff was window dressing in one sense but it helped to reinforce the message that this was a team on the straight and narrow again.

Communication was a big issue for Lancaster. Wales were up next – a huge challenge for England – but on the afternoon before the game Lancaster took time out to address the RFU Council and outline what he was doing with the England squad and how he saw them developing. It was an unusual step for a serving coach – even more so on the eve of an international match – but with the team's preparations complete he saw no harm in broadcasting his message to a wider audience. He spoke to Twickenham debenture holders the same day. At the same time he was also preparing for an interview for the role of permanent head coach.

As man-manager, hands-on head coach and salesman for the restored England, Lancaster was flying at the job at 100 miles per hour. It was impressive but it was also over the top. Playing so many parts was leaving him precious room to think. Lancaster is not an automaton. He feels stress like anyone else and exercise is his release. He will often go for a run through the streets at night after a match just to clear his head. As the Wales game approached the walls were closing in.

After their northern odyssey, England were back *in situ* at Pennyhill Park. A plush five-star hotel set in 123 acres of prime Surrey parkland, with its own beehives in the grounds and Prince Edward as a neighbour, it wasn't really Stuart Lancaster. With its nineteenth-century manor house, its formal gardens modelled on those of Château de Villandry near Tours, its Michelin-starred restaurant and its glorious spa, it was all too fancy. If he had been starting from scratch, Lancaster would probably have abandoned it and moved to somewhere less grand but the RFU had agreements in place and Pennyhill Park was within an hour of Twickenham.

Its roaring fireplaces and hunting tableaux were not what he needed at that moment. Lancaster, being a Cumbrian, rang his secretary and asked her to find him a hill to climb somewhere nearby. She came up with Virginia Water. It wasn't quite Helvellyn but it was open space and with a little room to breathe he was able to order his thoughts.

England went on to suffer their first defeat under Lancaster – 19-12 to Wales – but the performance, against top-class opponents, was the best so far in his time in charge. If David Strettle's touch-and-go try at the end had been allowed by the Television Match Official, England could have drawn the game.

And Twickenham? This was the really interesting part. Even in narrow defeat, the old cabbage patch shook with passionate support for the new side. It was as if all the pent-up frustration with the old regime had been released. The public were voting with their stamping feet. Theirs wasn't the casting vote, however.

The RFU had, in time-honoured fashion, appointed a committee to deliver a recommendation as to who should be England's next permanent head coach. It comprised two Twickenham figures – Rob Andrew, Kevin Bowring, the RFU's head of elite coach development, and two Premiership represent-atives – Harlequins director of rugby Conor O'Shea and Sir Ian McGeechan, who was then at Bath, with the recently installed RFU chief executive Ian Ritchie heading it up.

The position itself was, despite all the baggage which had surrounded England, still an attractive one. 'There were five very senior people in for the job, including Stuart,' revealed Andrew. 'It was a very robust and professional process which was undoubtedly the most extensive there has ever been to appoint an England rugby coach. It involved two rounds of interviews in front of a very experienced panel and lots of meet-ings. Not only was Stuart going through an audition on the pitch but one off it as well. He had one of his interviews during the tournament.'

McGeechan, a coaching legend with Scotland and the Lions, had been the RFU's top target for the England job that Woodward took in 1997. He explained that the panel were looking for a leader capable of restoring English pride through humility not bombast. 'We talked together and decided on the type of personality England needed and the things that needed to be looked at,' said McGeechan.

'The way Stuart was talking was excellent for that. The changes he was proposing and the parameters he was setting were spot on. At the same time you could see how he was pro-gressing the environment, which was a powerful argument for him getting the job. A lot of my thinking was like his so, for me, it was an easy decision in some ways.'

McGeechan also took a look behind the scenes at Pennyhill Park and liked what he saw. 'You know when a group is coming together and has the right priorities and that group had it. Stuart's priorities were right from the word go,' said McGeechan.

'He knew how important it was to get over what playing for England means. He did a lot in moving the players towards making England a very special group where people can see what it means to play for that jersey. The players wanted to be in that camp. If they got it wrong, if their behaviour was not up to scratch, they wouldn't be in. He was very strict on laying that down and they benefited from that.'

O'Shea, whom Lancaster had replaced at the RFU when the Irishman moved to the English Institute of Sport, was aware that many outside the room believed England needed an experienced big hitter. Woodward, treading water in a largely ornamental role at the British Olympic Association, had influential backers in the media supporting his return and would almost certainly have jumped at the chance to try to revisit past glories with England.

'There was a groundswell of opinion that we had to go for someone big who could shake things up. My thoughts were: "Why can't Stuart shake things up?"' said O'Shea. 'How do you play for someone for the first time? How do you become a captain for the first time? How do you become a chief executive? Someone has to trust you. You have to be given an opportunity. You don't have to have experience. Sometimes freshness and a new voice is important. For me it was a case of the best man for the job and he was the best man.'

A stunning 24-22 victory in Paris a fortnight later gave Lancaster all the momentum. It was the first time he had ever set foot in the Stade de France.

Again it was the defence that stood out – England made 111 tackles to France's 59 – but they also shredded the French three times to score tries through Manu Tuilagi, Ben Foden and the outstanding Tom Croft. 'Having come close against Wales, it would have been a kick in the teeth to go down to defeat again. It was a real marker for the side,' said Croft. 'Winning in Paris is never easy and for the side to do so, that early in their development, was incredibly satisfying. I think it was obvious how we had come on.'

England's third victory on the road for the first time in a Six Nations' Championship was further evidence both of the side's growth and the close bond Lancaster had fostered in them. Robshaw summed it up simply, after the triumph at the Stade de France. 'Stuart has given us the chance and we want to play for him and the shirt,' he said.

The bandwagon was in motion and Ireland could not halt it. They were demolished 30-9 after being scrummaged into the Twickenham turf as England rounded off their Six Nations in ruthless fashion.

It was a proud moment for forwards' coach Graham Rowntree for whom the championship had represented an exorcism after the pain of the World Cup. He put the transformation in quasi-religious terms after the final match of the championship. 'We've been born again as a new team under Stuart,' he said.

For the players, a runners-up finish from the rubble of what had gone before was something to be proud of, too. 'There was a real sense of pride and achievement from a young group which had come together in those few weeks,' said Palmer. 'We'd come out the other side playing some decent rugby and there was a real sense of excitement going forward.'

It was time to celebrate. The beer flowed – but this time behind closed doors. 'When Stuart came in he decided we still could have a night out at the end of a campaign but it had to be in the team hotel. So we let our hair down and enjoyed ourselves together as players at Pennyhill Park,' said Palmer. Lancaster, usually seen with a glass of tap water for company, allowed himself a quiet beer.

When Woodward first took charge of England in 1997 he did not register a win for his first five games, Johnson lost five of his first seven, Ashton six of his first ten and Robinson four of his first six. England had won four out of five games under Lancaster.

Not only was he ahead of the game, results-wise, but the reconnection he had sought with the English rugby public had been emphatically achieved. If the RFU wanted to give the England job to someone else, fine, but they would have to man the barricades to confront a rebellion. Even Mallett was saying Lancaster should be handed the job.

'The team got better and better through the Six Nations. He steadied the ship and got the team headed in the right direction again, but the single most important thing he had done was reconnecting the team back to the English rugby supporter,' said Andrew. 'The team had lost the respect of English rugby fans in 2011 – there's no doubt about that – but the atmosphere for the two home games in the 2012 Six Nations was very, very special. Everyone had banished the memory of the World Cup and the crowd was back behind a young England team.'

The following weekend Lancaster was back in his other role – assistant coach of West Park under-11s – swapping the elation of 82,000 at Twickenham for the more down-to-earth surroundings of Castleford and a crowd of 35 parents at a mini-rugby match.

It being Yorkshire – and the rugby league heartland of the county at that – Lancaster was not mobbed or chaired aloft as the saviour of English rugby union. Asked to pose for a picture with the Castleford under-11s by their coach Ian Brooksbank after a win for the West Park boys and two tries for his son, he smiled obligingly.

'Does anyone know who this chap is?' Brooksbank asked his players enthusiastically.

Silence.

'He's not from rugby league, he's from rugby union.'

Blank looks.

Eventually, a small voice piped up from the back: 'Were you at the France–England match?'

Lancaster laughed.

At the end of March, Lancaster received confirmation that he had been handed the permanent post through to the 2015 World Cup. He was on his way home to Leeds from Twickenham. He delayed giving the good news to his wife Nina straight away because the washing machine was broken and the kids had been playing up. He eventually told her in bed.

4

Who Is This Lancaster Bloke Anyway?

I am not in the roll of common men.

Henry IV Part I, Act 3, Scene 1

Stuart Lancaster grew up on the family farm at Culgaith in the shadow of Cross Fell, the highest point of the Pennines. It is a rugged part of the world, wonderfully picturesque when the clouds part in summer but exposed to the English winter's sharpest stabs. When the grey roof is drawn across, it can be bleak and forbidding. The houses huddle together for protection.

While tourists flock west to the Lake District, the footfall through Culgaith village is quieter. There are a couple of B&Bs but this is not the Cumbria of Wordsworth's poetic daffodils. The Northern Pennines are harsher and its villages unshowy, resilient and self-sufficient. If a backdrop helps to shape a personality then Culgaith helped to do the job for Lancaster.

The farmhouse where he was brought up with his two brothers and sister was a stone monument to solidity. A hundred yards from the village's one oak-beamed pub, it stood sentinel against the elements, looking across the fields towards the Eden

Valley below. Across the river, the railway line and the A66 a Center Parcs stands where urbanites play at living in the great outdoors; back on the farm it was the real thing. Lime Tree Farm was a busy mixed farm of dairy, beef and sheep and Lancaster was part of the workforce. A farm is a living workplace and there were always jobs to be done. Hard graft was the daily currency.

As Lancaster told the *Cumberland Herald* – the paper he chose for his first interview after taking on the England job: 'Being brought up on a farm was a fantastic life. You got used to being outdoors and learned what hard work is. It's tough but it keeps you grounded in a lot of ways. Cumbrians are a down-to-earth lot anyway. They tend to be honest and hardworking with great integrity and great values.'

For all his immersion into country life, he was never instinctively drawn to becoming a farmer. That was more his elder brother Stephen's bag. Sport was Lancaster's thing and his DNA was promising – his maternal grandfather had been a scratch golfer and Scottish champion and both his parents were handy squash players. Self-reliant, he would spend his down time alone out in the farmyard, relentlessly hammering a tennis ball against the wall or kicking a football around.

Until the age of ten, Lancaster was playing junior football as a left-sided midfielder for the neighbouring village of Langwathby, dreaming of being signed up by Leeds United. His friends at junior school included John Holliday, who went on to play professional football for Carlisle United and Mansfield Town, and England wicketkeeper Paul Nixon with whom he would eventually play cricket for Cumbria Schools.

Life and ambition changed when he was packed off to board at a small Cumbrian public school – St Bees – where his father

John, and the actor Rowan Atkinson, had gone before him and where rugby union was the winter game of choice. It was a significant marker post in Lancaster's life – he was only ten and it was sink-or-swim time. Being sent away at such an early age is daunting. It can traumatise children. Yet difficult though the first few days were, there were no tear-stained pillows or attempts to escape. He thrived on the opportunities boarding-school life offered.

It helped that his elder brother was there – his presence providing a degree of comfort and familiarity – but Lancaster enjoyed his remote surroundings from the start. He loved the sense of independence and the requirement to stand on his own two feet. He loved the house rivalries and the dorm raids. And he adored the comradeship and competitiveness of rugby.

St Bees, with its red sandstone buildings set against the green hills to the east and the Irish Sea to the west, was a community in itself. It had to be – it was a long way from anywhere. St Bees Head was the most westerly point in the North of England and marked the start of the Coast to Coast Walk across the Pennines to Robin Hood's Bay.

School rugby played a central part in the community. For big matches, it would not be just parents lining the touchline; the villagers would turn out to watch, too.

The school itself was steeped in tradition – it had been founded in 1583 and had its own Eton Fives court – but had begun to dip a toe into the modern world by the time Lancaster arrived. It had opened its doors to girls in 1976 but they were of significantly less interest to him than rugby.

The first international match Lancaster saw was as an eleven-year-old on a school trip at Murrayfield when Scotland played France. He played against Stewart's Melville College in the morning and then ended up being transfixed in the afternoon by the bobbing blond mane of Jean-Pierre Rives, tearing into rucks and tackles.

Lancaster would watch the school 1st XV play against other northern public schools such as Giggleswick and fierce rivals Sedbergh who tended to use St Bees as a doormat and dream of one day being part of the side that beat them.

He would return home to the farm during the holidays and slot back into life at Culgaith – playing for the village cricket team, fixing gates and helping with the milking on the farm, but increasingly St Bees became his life. And life at St Bees meant rugby.

He started out as a prop but by fifteen he had moved into the back row. He was relatively small but a fine ball player, very fit – he had been sufficiently driven to do extra training sessions on his own from the age of thirteen – and had a tactical awareness beyond his years.

Tony Rolt, the Master in Charge of Rugby at St Bees, clearly recalls their first meeting when Lancaster was about to go into the Lower 6th Form. 'It was pre-season training and he turned up late with a guy called Stuart Reid,' said Rolt. 'I sent them around the pitch a few times. I told them that we're only on this planet for a short space of time and I didn't want to be waiting too long for them.'

Being barked at by the coach was an inauspicious start to a relationship which would go on to be one of the most important in Lancaster's rugby career. Forgiven, Lancaster joined an out-standing group who would go on to lose only one match all season – inevitably to Sedbergh, where the likes of Will Carling and Will Greenwood had started out. It was their twentieth successive defeat against their local rivals. The notable triumphs included a supremely obscure victory against Yugoslavia under-21s in Split on tour.

Lancaster fitted in well on the pitch – he was a smart player – but it was away from the actual matches that he stood apart from the crowd. In training, even though he was a year younger than most of his team-mates, he was the one who would be asking the questions. 'He didn't accept they should do something just because they'd been told to,' said Rolt. 'He would ask quite searching questions. It wasn't that he was in any way difficult or opinionated, he'd just want to know why. I was quite happy to sit down with him and tell him: "Stuart, we're doing this because..."'

Rolt was used to rugby players simply obeying orders but Lancaster, who had enjoyed his first taste of club rugby at Penrith by then, was clearly different. Impressed, Rolt chose him to captain the side in his final year.

His leadership ability was recognised off the pitch, too. Even though he was not an out-and-out academic, he was appointed head of school. At a school such as St Bees, it was more than just a title. There was plenty of responsibility involved. It had practical implications like organising a team of prefects and attending meetings with the head teacher that required Lancaster to speak up for himself and others. It was a taste of operating outside his comfort zone and a useful illustration to him that if he pitched the right message to the right audience others would take notice of what he said, whatever their status. It did not matter to Lancaster that others were supposedly his superiors. He had a common-sense authority which made others listen. Even his teachers. His willingness to speak up and to question made them think, too.

'When he was captain I had to take account of every training session I was doing to ensure I could justify why I was doing it,' said Rolt. 'There were players around him – Howard Graham [England Sevens] and Stuart Reid [Scotland] – who went on to play at a far higher level – but they didn't have the insight into the way the game was being played that Stuart did.

'I've been fortunate to coach some outstanding players but for the most part they just took what I was giving them without bothering to question it. He was one of the few schoolboys I have ever coached who was actually analytical. Even then his attention to detail was remarkable.' It was like having an extra coach – only one who was eighteen with a mop of bog-brush hair.

'His leadership skills were outstanding. He didn't stand any nonsense on or off the pitch. He had a very fixed view on what he wanted from his players and I was more than happy to take a back seat as far as that was concerned,' said Rolt.

On occasion it was hard to tell who was the teacher. Lancaster was also a good enough opening batsman to represent Cumbria Schools and took captaining St Bees at cricket seriously. When he spotted Rolt taking sevens' rugby training on the cricket square he was indignant. 'He came out and gave me a monumental rollicking,' said Rolt. 'He wasn't rude. It was just he had seen something he thought wasn't right and had felt the need to challenge it which is what he's like. I had to hold my hand up and admit I was in the wrong.'

Being picked as captain for every team he played for was an honour but it meant sticking his head above the parapet and that was to cost Lancaster. Having led Cumbria Schools at rugby, he was then picked for the North at 18-Group level and offered the chance to captain the region.

'I tried to persuade him not to take the captaincy – it is a poisoned chalice to be made captain at that level – but he had his own mind and he accepted it,' said Rolt. 'He played one game, they lost to the Midlands and he got dropped. He was as good as anyone else in the back row that day but the captaincy went against him and he didn't get any further. That was the end of his school representative career.'

It was a major personal setback and it hurt. Being told you're not good enough always does. It was the first evidence that he would end up being a nearly-but-not-quite rugby player.

Lancaster's response was interesting. He did not go into his shell, quite the opposite. He was resilient enough and possessed a sufficient well of inner confidence to bounce back with some outstanding performances for St Bees, where he was leading a team who were punching pounds above their weight. With Lancaster driving the side on, St Bees were knocking off their rivals left, right and centre. The annual grudge match against Sedbergh was looming and there was even optimistic talk that the demoralising run without a win in the fixture could come to an end.

Then, disaster struck. Lancaster picked up an ankle injury in the run-up to the game. 'He was desperate to play and I was desperate for him to play. At that level he was a cut above many others because of his ability to read the game,' said Rolt. 'I couldn't get him to a physio, so I rang one of the parents who I knew pretty well. He was a vet. I said to him: "I've got this guy who has to play unless his injury is life-threatening – can you do anything for him?" So he came down and gave him an ultrasound. All the time he was comparing him to a horse. Stuart was laid on this table with his eyes agog wondering what I'd let him in for. But he managed to bolt him back together.'

Passed fit to run in the biggest race of his life, Lancaster did something highly unusual on the day before the game. He felt that if Sedbergh were to be beaten, St Bees would not only have to play to the upper limits of their ability but also be better prepared than their opponents. So he approached his teacher and informed him he should expect visitors that evening.

'He told me that the fifteen players needed to get together the night before the game so they all came to my house. We sat in the lounge and talked about what we were going to do,' said Rolt. 'That evening was a revelation for me in terms of the importance of people talking off the pitch. Stuart was at the forefront of that. He was totally instrumental in terms of gelling that side.'

You can probably guess the rest. In front of what seemed to be the entire population of the village that Wednesday afternoon a meticulously prepared St Bees side, who appeared to be willing to swim the length of Windermere for each other, finally laid the Sedbergh ghost to rest. It proved early on to Lancaster that there were few limits to what a bonded team wearing a jersey they took pride in could achieve. He still has the video of that match.

Cumbria feels a long way from Twickenham for many reasons – cultural, financial and agricultural – but mainly because it is a long way away. Stand on the top of England's highest mountain, Scafell Pike, and you are much closer to Edinburgh than London. It is definitively England still but the boundaries are beginning to blur. Although Lancaster was English born and raised, his mother, Ann, hailed from Dumfries, which gave him a Scottish qualification.

Unwanted by England at representative level or even by the North, Lancaster played for the Anglo-Scots under-19s throughout the 1988/9 season. He was picked to make his Scotland debut at the end of the season in a side who included future internationals Doddie Weir, Graham Shiel and Stuart Reid, his old St Bees' team-mate. Lancaster's one match for Scotland under-19s ended in a 29-13 victory over Italy at Ayr.

If truth be known he felt little attachment to the thistle but international rugby was still international rugby. 'I was hugely honoured to pull on the jersey,' said Lancaster. He promptly gave it to his mum.

Lancaster was at Leeds Metropolitan University at the time, having embarked on a Sports Science degree. His future wife was on the same course. He went on to play for Scottish Students for a season while he was there, lining up against England in one game. The Scots lost.

Andy Nicol, who went on to captain Scotland, was part of the same Scottish Students' team. He remembers Lancaster as the sort of player who never stood out but who did invaluable work in making the team tick.

Scottish Students were coached by former Lions stand-off John Rutherford, who remembered Lancaster as an 'honest' player – faint praise which might explain why he missed out on selection for the Students' World Cup. Nearly but not quite once again. If Lancaster was going to make it to the top in rugby it looked increasingly unlikely it would be as a player.

Lancaster did not know it at the time but the clues were all there that coaching, rather than playing, would be his path of least resistance. He was inherently fascinated by the nuts and bolts of the game.

He was, recalled Rutherford, a forensic analyst of the game – someone pre-programmed to become a coach one day.

When his old teacher Tony Rolt, who by then had moved on to Trent College, mentioned the England age-group sides would be coming to his new patch in Nottingham during the

RFU's National Youth Week, Lancaster's antennae were tweaked. He asked if he could come along. 'He stayed with our family that week. He spent a lot of time there just standing and watching other coaches conduct their training sessions,' said Rolt. 'That was when I thought: "Hang on, there's a bit more about this guy than the others." He was only twenty-one.'

The thought of improving others appealed. Rugby union remained an amateur game at the time and Lancaster decided his professional future lay as a PE teacher. At the end of his degree course, he enrolled on a year-long graduate conversion course.

His early attempts to land a job were unsuccessful. He was sufficiently overconfident in his own ability to apply for head-of-department posts before he had even done a day's paid teaching. Undeterred, he kept on aiming high. To fill the time until someone said yes, he took a job driving a truck with a huge promotional rugby ball on the back around the country. It was his first experience of working for the RFU.

The teaching break – not as a departmental head – finally came with a post at Heysham High School in Morecambe where he cut his teeth for a year. Heysham made for an interesting contrast to St Bees – it was a state school with much more modest facilities – but for Lancaster it made for a priceless grounding. It was an early test of his ability to motivate others. Running cross-country in the rain did not instinctively appeal to everyone.

It also gave him a first taste of coaching rugby union – and refereeing. He would take charge of the school side in the morning before racing 100 miles across the Pennines to play for Wakefield in the afternoon. Lancaster had, typically, aimed for the top in choosing Wakefield who were at the time the leading club in Yorkshire. But the reality was he spent as much time in the second team as the first. He was quick, super-fit and had great hands but his modest size counted against him as a forward.

Living in Kendal and playing for Wakefield was not ideal so when a teaching post came up at Kettlethorpe High School in Wakefield he jumped at the chance. There, he coached both codes of rugby – league was the popular one; union was kick and clap. The fact that 'sir' played for Wakefield did not cut much ice among his pupils. Now if it had been Trinity that would have been another matter.

The established power of league in the urbanised areas was one of the reasons Yorkshire had never produced a super-club to rival a Leicester or a Northampton, despite its proliferation of rugby union clubs. It had enjoyed plenty of success at county level and produced countless internationals but, with professionalism on its way, Yorkshire needed a club big enough to compete at elite level with the established giants.

While Wakefield gave it a go, they never had the finance to mount a serious challenge. A merger between Headingley and Roundhay in 1991 to form Leeds was a more viable solution. It was a contentious move – certainly at committee level – and a lot of history was jettisoned but with the prospect of a windfall from the sale of Roundhay's ground, the Leeds project went ahead, a new club was formed and Lancaster found himself at the bedside for the birth. He had moved to Headingley the previous season after three years at Wakefield in search of regular first-team rugby but no sooner had he arrived than Headingley ceased to be.

Leeds were a Fourth Division club still trying to build an identity but in a rush to make it to the top. The combination of cash and naked ambition made them an inviting target for their

Yorkshire rivals who took great delight in knocking them down a peg or two and frustrating their best-laid plans.

The bigger picture of providing a team to take on the rest of the country was lost in the score-settling. Leeds were a big-city club with big ideas but were unable to separate themselves from the rest. They were getting nowhere fast so, with the gates of hell opened and rugby union turned professional, the solution they came up with was to spend big.

Leeds lured Wales legend Phil Davies north to become their director of rugby but while he carried the aura and vision to drive the club forward off the pitch he was near the end of his playing days and he needed a leader on it. Step forward Lancaster, a cool head at a chaotic time.

'When I arrived at Leeds there were a few stalwarts of the club around and Stuart was one of them,' recalled Davies. 'He was always very rational and a very deep thinker about the game. He understood it. That's why I made him captain. He led by example but he was also very good at bringing others into play. He realised no one person had all the answers. That's a key thing about leadership.

'He was a very good captain and a very good No. 7 in the Neil Back mould. He was a very intelligent footballer who would understand when to kick, when to drive and when to build momentum. He was a smart rugby player.'

As rugby union stumbled blindly into its new professional world, Lancaster received his first contract offer from Leeds. It was worth a princely £3,000 for a season. It was a training contract which enabled him to keep his job as a teacher and join the squad for evening, or early morning, sessions three times a week.

Union was still testing the water when it came to paying players and there was some confusion over what was expected in return. The game's amateur drinking culture was still alive and well and professionalism – or in Lancaster's case semi-professionalism – basically translated as a few extra quid to spend at the bar. The Leeds players used to play home games on a Sunday and then head out for a ferocious refuelling session in the city. Lancaster wasn't one of the hard core but at that stage of his life he was no puritan either and, sociable sort that he was, he used to hold his own.

That was rugby: a tough game followed by a few pints. The beer and the mateship were an intrinsic part of the game's fabric.

As he was a part-time pro, Lancaster would avoid the really heavy-duty session which occurred after Monday morning training. That would see the full-timers on the payroll spending the rest of the day on the Otley run which was not, as the name might imply, a cross-country jog but a Headingley pub crawl.

As they moved slowly up the leagues, Leeds edged towards a more professional outlook and a fully professional squad. If a player wanted to be part of the new era, increasingly he had to be available for daytime training sessions. Lancaster was nudging thirty and had a settled teaching career but when Leeds came with an offer for him to combine a rugby contract with a development role which involved establishing a junior scouting network and setting up an under-19s team he decided to go for it. He took a year's sabbatical from Kettlethorpe School.

He might not have done so if he had been on just a playing contract. He liked to be busy and professional players did not appear to be that busy but the chance to shape and coach a new team for a club he had grown to love appealed strongly. The off-field role went well – Lancaster pulled together a team who reached the National Colts final – but the on-field part of it was a dead-end.

Training-session accidents happen from time to time and it was Lancaster's luck to be on the receiving end of one which wrecked his season during one forwards' session. Tom Palmer, of all people, was the unintentional perpetrator. 'We were doing a rucking drill. He stepped over one of our forwards on the floor and I challenged him with the tackle bag. His back foot slipped, he fell awkwardly and did the splits,' recalled Palmer.

'He was obviously in some pain and had to go off but we didn't realise quite how serious it was until he'd gone for his scan. He'd torn his hamstring off the bone. I said sorry but there was no malice in it and he understood that. It was just one of those things.'

Lancaster started one first-team game that season. By the time he was fit to return Leeds had made the decision to release him.

Lancaster had helped Leeds rise from the fourth tier of the English game to the brink of the Premiership. They would finally make it the following season – again for him a case of nearly but not quite. He had become the first man to play more than 100 games for the club. But this was a professional business now and sentiment meant little. Lancaster was deemed surplus to requirements. The timing was terrible with his first child on the way.

Dejected, he prepared to go back into teaching at Kettlethorpe and to combine his old job with a player-coach role, lower down the league ladder with Huddersfield in the sixth tier of the English game. But on the day he was due to meet the club to sign the contract, his wife Nina went into labour. By the time he was able to reschedule, he was a father to Sophie and life had been turned on its head. Suddenly it struck him that the responsibility of being a teacher, player-coach and father as well was too much. He turned down Huddersfield.

Sometimes things just work out. Leeds were awarded an academy licence by the RFU a few days later and Davies, who had told Lancaster there would be no playing contract for him a few months earlier, rang him to tell him he was the man he wanted to run it.

Lancaster decided to give it a shot and told Kettlethorpe School he would not be returning after all. He had a team to build and a destiny to fulfil. His playing days were over, so was his time in teaching. At thirty, he was heading towards the job he had been made for all along.

5

The Coaching Road

Presume not that I am the thing I was

Henry IV Part 2, Act 5, Scene 5

Wayne Shelford, the All Blacks great, was once asked to describe the role of a rugby coach. Shelford was a hard man, hard enough to return to the pitch after having his scrotum stitched and losing four teeth in his second Test for New Zealand, and he made no apologies for his answer. 'The coach has got to be their friend, their mother, their father,' he said. 'And he's got to be their enemy at times.'

When Stuart Lancaster set about coaching the Leeds Academy he did so with a clear idea of the standards he wanted his players to meet. Whether it was punctuality, dress code or commitment, the bar was set high. If they failed to meet those standards, they would know about it. He did not want to be the players' enemy but if he felt they needed it he would be. Lancaster was unapologetic about his tough love. As he saw it, he was helping to instil the discipline which would make the players successful professionals one day.

In Lancaster's five years in charge, the Leeds Academy pipe-line produced players of the quality of Danny Care, Luther Burrell, Rob Webber and Calum Clark, all of whom would go on to be part of his England squad.

'I know what he expected of me as a fifteen-year-old and it hasn't changed much now with England,' reflected Care. 'I'm still as scared of him now as I was back then. He still gives you that look when he's not happy. He's a very proud bloke we want to play well for. I learned pretty quickly what was unacceptable in his regime. It's the way Stuart is.'

Burrell, too, had drilled into him as a teenager by Lancaster the life lesson that easy street led nowhere. 'He was similar to how he is now. He's a very straight-up-the-middle bloke. He's got a certain way of doing things and that hasn't changed. He demands that players train hard, he's very strict with the boys and the lads really respect what he's about,' said Burrell.

Leeds, having reached the Premiership at last, were locking horns with the very best in the country. But despite their local reputation as a moneybags club and the spending on players which had coincided with the arrival of professionalism, the financial reality at the club was very different from a Leicester or a Bath.

On small crowds, theirs was a make-do-and-mend set-up in comparison. Buying in the best talent to compete with their Premiership rivals was not an option so the academy was a vital resource. It was Lancaster's job to deliver players capable of coping with top-level rugby for director of rugby Phil Davies.

'What I wanted was players who were holistically developed – players who understood what it took physically, mentally, technically and tactically. Players who understood the culture of hard work,' said Davies. 'Rugby union in Yorkshire was sometimes more of a white-collar game but we tried to put a real hard blue-collar work ethic into a city club. We needed a big team spirit, a work ethic and a jersey that meant something. Rugby is physical, mental, technical and tactical but what bolts it all together is the culture around it. It was something Stuart and I spoke about – trying to create an identity that people in Yorkshire could relate to.

'They could relate to Yorkshire grit, hard work and team spirit and we all bought into it. Stuart drove it through the academy and I drove it at first-team level and we were relatively successful. His philosophy was very similar to mine – give young people an opportunity and make sure they understand who they are playing for and what the jersey on their back means. It was what we tried to build Leeds on from the beginning.'

Lancaster made a point of picking on character as much as ability but he did not always get his selection right first time. Sifting through the hundreds of kids playing rugby in Yorkshire was an imperfect science and sometimes players slipped through – good ones.

'He turned both Luther and me down!' laughed Care. 'I still have the first letter he ever sent me saying I wasn't good enough to train with the Elite Player Development Group. My dad kept that and framed it so I remind Stuart about that now and again.'

When Burrell was also rejected as a fifteen-year-old, his mum, Joyce, sent Lancaster an outraged email. 'I kept telling her not to send it but she did,' said Burrell. Sharp parental elbows prevailed and the coach agreed to take a second look. He relented and took Burrell on.

Care and Burrell joined a set-up which Lancaster had constructed along similar lines to the Leeds Rhinos Academy. The Rhinos had a tried and tested system of producing and nurturing rugby league talent and it provided a useful template. The two clubs were run by the same Leeds Rugby umbrella organisation, shared Headingley Stadium and also the training ground at Kirkstall. It offered Lancaster the opportunity to study closely the methods of Tony Smith, the Australian who guided the Rhinos to two Super League titles and a World Club Challenge victory during his four years in charge. He wasn't shy about knocking on Smith's door.

'Our offices were only about fifteen metres apart and I'd often come in after a training session and have a tea or coffee with him and talk about our respective situations,' said Smith, who subsequently moved on to more success with Warrington.

'I got on particularly well with Stuart. There was always a mutual respect there. We had similar philosophies about coaching and teaching. He was always welcome in our environment at the Rhinos and he took that opportunity up whenever he could. He came to our training sessions and our team meetings. He was always looking to learn and add to the attributes he already had. He's a very well organised and thoughtful man and he was always seeking to improve his players – which is what coaching is all about.'

Rugby league had grown apart from rugby union in their century of separation but there were obvious crossovers, too, and as it had been professional for a lot longer there were lessons to be learned for a coach open to new ideas.

'Not all coaches have the ability to take something from one sport and adapt it to another. While there are a lot of similarities between our two codes, there are a lot of things which are vastly different as well,' said Smith. 'But with Stuart, he was always asking the reasons why we did certain things. It wasn't just "What are you doing?" it was "Why". That's real coaching.

'He certainly wasn't a copycat in any way, shape or form. He wanted to understand the principles of why we were doing something to adapt it to his sport.

'It might sound a bit boring or analytical but those were the sort of discussions we'd get into. They were very stimulating for both of us. While he got a lot from us, I got a lot from him personally as well because our discussions made me back up some of my opinions.'

After the best part of a decade in education, Lancaster had a PE teacher's manner when it came to coaching but he was far from some one-dimensional disciplinarian. His inquisitive nature led him down some different paths. On one occasion, he gave a seminar to a group of northern coaches in which he told them that rugby union should be coached by playing mini-games to provide as close an approximation as possible to situations players would encounter in matches. That all made perfect sense. But the coaches were surprised to learn the words he quoted had come from the Dutch Football Coaching Manual. 'He was always looking to improve. His thirst for knowledge was phenomenal,' said Phil Davies.

Lancaster added in ideas from other academies he visited such as Leicester Tigers and Arsenal Football Club and created an environment which quickly came to be regarded as a leader in the field.

When the RFU came to audit every academy in the country, Leeds scored highest. That wasn't to say they were the best team in the country – results suggested otherwise – but when it came to nurturing and delivering elite-end players the Leeds Academy was the place to be.

So what was Lancaster doing inside it that made the academy function so effectively?

At the same time as he was improving the academy players under his command, Lancaster was also embarking on a journey of self-improvement, diligently working his way through the RFU coaching exams. He passed each in turn until only one remained.

The Level 5 award had only just been constituted and was really intended for top-level coaches and ex-international players. It was for high achievers to assist them in climbing yet higher. Of the first intake of 12, ten places had already been filled by established coaching figures like Gary Gold, then at London Irish, and Jon Callard, at Bath, when Lancaster threw his hat into the ring.

By rights, this was out of his range. It was a punt. But aim high and you never know what can happen… after two interviews Lancaster, in his direct, persuasive way, had convinced the RFU he was worth a place. It was to be his coaching awakening.

As part of the Level 5 award, each candidate had to write a 10,000-word thesis. Lancaster's was entitled: 'An Analysis into the Effectiveness of Changing My Coaching Behaviour to Create Mentally Stronger Individuals and a More Cohesive Team.' The title could have been snappier but the content was fascinating. In it, Lancaster chose to reveal the skeleton of how he would one day run England.

The coaching philosophy he was employing at the Leeds Academy would develop but as an insight into a Lancaster environment it was instructive.

Distilled, this was it:

1. Create a culture in which players feel valued.
2. Develop players in such a way that they think of the greater good of the team over the individual, yet they understand

and trust that the coach will balance the team and individual interests.

3. Focus on the performance, not the result.

4. Empower the players to take responsibility for their own and the team's development, yet make them understand the bottom line, i.e. the head coach has the final say.

5. Educate the players to allow them to understand the coach's philosophies and to have a greater understanding of their own personality and the impact that has on team cohesion.

6. Over the season there should be a balance between coach-led and player-led sessions.

7. There will be a no-ego culture.

8. Players will be coached to give out positive rather than negative energy.

9. Where possible, players are to be consulted on team strategy.

10. Players will be encouraged not to humiliate defeated opponents and to appear gracious in defeat.

11. The working environment must be challenging to create mentally strong individuals and a collective team.

12. Be honest...without being naive.

13. Keep consistency in approach; do not allow standards to slip as the season progresses and therefore allow people to become complacent as the novelty of the new season wears off.

14. We are all in it together...mutual accountability.

Lancaster-land was a place where selflessness and high standards on and off the pitch were non-negotiables. It was not a place for big-time Charlies. It was also clear that while players were given leeway to contribute, the coach was ultimately the boss.

The Level 5 course was extremely wide ranging and exposed the coaches both to rugby theory and leadership training from a variety of other worlds.

They listened to talks from explorers, conductors and management gurus at the Ashridge Business School in Hertfordshire. They then tapped into the military, learning about the army's model of 'pop-up' leadership which, with its doctrine of post-engagement adaptability, bore a striking resemblance to rugby.

The RFU's thought process was to take ideas from other fields and transplant them into coaching in a rugby environment. Some were sceptical but Lancaster's mind was open and he started reading and researching leadership and management material more widely. He became human blotting paper. Anything relevant that he could lay his hands on was read and absorbed. In any coach's career, there is a take-off point where he suddenly knows this is who he was born to be and this was Lancaster's enlightenment. He found he enjoyed the process of discovery in a way other coaches did not and he threw himself into his study, using the Leeds Academy as his practical laboratory for the theories.

Lancaster, with all this new information at hand, sought to discover how far a coach's behaviour could tip the balance in an environment where talent was spread roughly evenly between competing teams. He wanted to know to what extent individual mental toughness and a sense of comradeship could make a difference and how far a coach could be responsible for shaping both. While his study revolved around the Leeds Academy team, the lessons drawn from it were applicable at any level.

Through a series of detailed questionnaires, he measured his squad's mental toughness at the end of the 2004/5 season. Then he deliberately altered his approach in pre-season training and in the early weeks of the 2005/6 season, after resolving to become less schoolmasterly and more supportive, took updated responses in the same spheres from across the team.

He met one-to-one more often with his players to talk through the transition from age-group to senior rugby. As a resilient character brought up on the self-sufficiency of farm life, he was not instinctively drawn towards discussing personal problems. 'Get on with it' would have been his own advice to himself. But having seen the positive effect that working with a psychologist had on one of his academy players, Kearnan Myall, who would go on to play for England Saxons, he began to realise that, with work in this area, some individuals could be improved considerably as rugby players.

Not that he was going soft: professional rugby is a pressured environment and Lancaster thought shielding his players from that reality would end up being counter-productive when they broke through to the first team. He continued to work them hard and expected a certain stoic acceptance in response – they were instructed to hide any discomfort they might be feeling – even when it came to the dreaded pre-season hill runs. But he subtly changed the calibration of his coaching towards an arm round the shoulder and away from a boot up the backside.

The results in his questionnaires showed a rise, not only in the players' scores for total mental toughness but also in the sub-sections of self-confidence, negative energy control and passion. The coach's change of emphasis was making a difference.

Over the same period he also measured his side's unity. Togetherness is an elusive concept in team sport. Those sides that have it tend to prosper, those who do not are more prone to splinter, but chasing it can be like catching water for a coach. While an adult rugby team might attempt to foster it through a long gargle together, prescribing something similar was not wise for a bunch of teenage would-be professionals. Coaches had to find another way.

Lancaster had read a team-building book called *The Spirit of Teams* by former England hockey coach David Whitaker which identified 23 key qualities that combine to produce high-performing sides. To assess how the Leeds Academy fared, Lancaster turned these points into a series of questions for his players and asked them to quantify how they felt the team scored when it came to togetherness. The base scores were high but he attempted to drive them up further by involving the players more in their own coaching.

As their input increased, the players were told to monitor and encourage each other constantly in training and work on their body language to make it more positive. Sessions were filmed to highlight good practice and expose poor practice. In one, a lanky young centre was caught cheating on a press-up drill. Luther Burrell was suitably embarrassed.

Releasing elements of control went against the grain for Lancaster but he could see the potential benefits. He tried to open up more about himself and his way of thinking too, so the players could understand exactly where he was coming from and what they were part of.

Even though Leeds were enduring a mixed season in terms of results in 2005/6, the second set of scores for mutual trust and respect, unity of purpose and all the other markers for togetherness were higher still. The changes in his coaching approach had been shown to bear fruit. It was a useful experiment, one which not only looked impressive in his thesis but helped to shape his own thinking.

He went on to ask his academy players for feedback on his

own performance as a young coach finding his feet in professional rugby union. He assured them the process would be
anonymous. It took a certain degree of self-confidence to
undergo this sort of analysis. Plenty of coaches would not have
wanted to hear home truths. Lancaster felt he should be made
aware of his shortcomings as a coach, as well as his strengths.
His view was that he had to know them if he was to confront
them. And Lancaster was also sure enough of himself to predict
he would not be slated by his players. He carried out the same
self-assessment to see if the marks married up.

In most cases, Lancaster was harsher on himself than his players were on him. While he felt he needed to be more precise
with some of his coaching and devote more time to improving
individuals, they did not perceive weakness in these areas. Their
view on him was overwhelmingly positive, as the following
responses showed.

Area	Average players' mark	Lancaster mark (out of five):
Training and instruction	4.4	3.8
Social Support	3.3	2.4
Autocratic	2.6	2.2
Democratic	3.8	3.2
Rewarding	4.2	4.4

Broken down further, the highest average score of all from
his players – 4.9 out of 5 – came in response to the following
statement: 'He sees to it that the players work to capacity'. He
remained a hard taskmaster but one who rewarded his players
for their effort.

He also scored highly in the following areas:

'Make(s) sure that the coach's role as head of the team is understood by all players' – 4.7

'See(s) to it that players' efforts as a team are co-ordinated' – 4.6

'Pay(s) special attention to correcting players' technical faults' – 4.6

'Give(s) credit where it's due' – 4.5

One area in which the players expressed concern was in their coach's response to them taking risks. They felt they would be blamed if things went wrong. Lancaster duly noted this as an area to improve on and also pledged to improve the way he spoke to his players. 'That's not good enough' became 'I expect you to do better' in post-match reviews. It was a small change but important. The emphasis moved to improvement rather than finger-pointing.

He also received a low mark from his team when it came to his closeness to them. To the statement – he 'expresses any affection felt for the players' – he scored only 2.6 out of 5. This time, Lancaster was delighted.

He wanted his rapport with his players to be strong but they also had to know there was a line which could not be crossed. No player was ever invited to his family home despite its proximity to the training ground.

What we learn through the eyes of his players about Lancaster six years into his coaching development was that he worked them hard and set them high standards. He was strict but fair, empathetic if deliberately distant and overpoweringly team-centric. He could sometimes lose sight of the individual in his over-arching desire for the group to progress. He was also an excellent communicator who ran a relatively democratic ship but who would ultimately have the final say.

It was a probing insight. As he acknowledged in his Level 5 paper, while he could tweak parts of his approach and alter his emphasis, he could not change who he was. This was the canvas on which England's future coach was painted. Lancaster passed the Level 5 with flying colours, convinced he had it in him to coach at senior level.

It had given Lancaster a great sense of accomplishment to see his fledglings fly but the experience had lit a fire in him to test himself and his expanding well of knowledge higher up. He was ready to take the next step – and events were about to conspire in his favour to give him the opportunity to do so.

Having won the Powergen Cup at Twickenham in 2004/5, Leeds had decided the time was right to bring some star quality to Headingley. They had taken a financial gamble by dipping into the transfer market and bringing in proven internationals like All Blacks' scrum-half Justin Marshall and Scotland hooker Gordon Bulloch. But the plan had backfired. With huge salary disparities, the team spirit the side had been built on had gone down the drain and so had the side's performances.

They had gone backwards rather than forwards. They had started the league season with seven successive defeats and, with relegation assured, Phil Davies paid the price near the end of the 2005/6 season. He was sacked. There was only one league game remaining and Leeds turned to Lancaster to take temporary charge for the game at Newcastle. It was a brief taste of Premiership management and a memorable one for all the wrong reasons.

Three days after guiding his shining academy graduates to the Yorkshire Cup with victory in the final against Wharfedale's senior team, Lancaster took the first team to Kingston Park. Rob Andrew's Newcastle side, comprised entirely of Englishmen, humiliated a bedraggled Leeds 54-19.

The day got worse. On the way back down the A1 the Leeds team coach broke down and then caught fire. If ever there was an image which depicted a season, it was that of a stranded Leeds squad standing by a smouldering bus, powerless to do anything about their fate.

The planned leaving party for departing prop forward Mike Shelley that night became more of a wake when the squad finally made it back to Leeds. The squad was splitting up, the side was going down and the bus was blowing up. Not the ideal circumstances under which to assume command. But Lancaster was determined not to miss the chance. When he was offered the position of director of rugby on a permanent basis at the end of the season he was not put off. He willingly accepted the hospital pass.

6

The Impossible Job

Uneasy lies the head that wears a crown

Henry IV Part 2, Act 3, Scene I

Leeds were in disarray. Relegation had led to a mass exodus, leaving Lancaster with only seven senior players on the books. New coaches cannot expect to land plum jobs but this was as challenging a baptism as it was possible to imagine, the very definition of crisis management.

It may have been a new job for him but there was no time for a learning curve. Lancaster had £1.5million to spend from the Premiership relegation parachute payment but the money would last only one year. He had to deliver immediately. If he failed, his senior coaching career was likely to be stillborn.

Gary Hetherington was the Leeds chief executive, a role he also held with the Rhinos. Lancaster was his appointment. 'He didn't have a gun to his head but everyone knew the importance of going straight back up,' said Hetherington. 'If we didn't we would have disappeared into the wilderness. That was the nature of the competition in those days.

'There was a temptation to go for someone with a proven track record but there was a bigger picture to consider. We'd been raped and pillaged and we found ourselves in a bit of trauma. We needed someone to steady the ship but also to put some standards in there, someone to rebuild a team and a culture. I had consulted Phil Davies on his successor and Phil was very insightful about what qualities we needed in the next man.

'It was more than a coach we were looking for, it was someone who understood the values of the organisation and its strengths and weaknesses. There was no better fit for that than Stuart Lancaster himself. He was the right man for the right time. He knew the club inside out, he had a quiet passion about him and we knew how thorough he would be so it had been a pretty straightforward decision to appoint Stuart but it wasn't without risk. He'd been a schoolteacher and run the academy but he'd never coached men before.'

Fortunately, there were barely any grown-ups left. One of the seven loyalists who remained was the Devonian second row Stuart Hooper, who had arrived from Saracens in the summer of 2003. Aged twenty-five, he was appointed captain of the motley crew.

'When we started pre-season training in June we had seven players and a coach who had only just moved up from the academy. All the best players had been signed by then and the season was starting in two months' time,' said Hooper. 'It was a very similar job in many ways to the one Stuart took on with England after the World Cup. We were in need of a real identity and it was an absolute credit to him in how he went about it.

'If we'd had a room of international stars, they might have said: "Who is this guy?" but because we were club men who had stayed we reacted well to him. It certainly never crossed my mind, as maybe the most senior guy there, that surely there must be someone better to do the job.

'He didn't have a huge reputation as a coach because he hadn't been involved in the coaching of the first team before then but I think that actually helped him. When you've been relegated, new ideas and a different perspective are a breath of fresh of air. What Stu did have was a very big reputation as a Leeds man. He didn't have any airs or graces; he said it as it was and he made us feel right from the beginning that we were in it together.

'What he spoke about straight away was signing players with the right character with a reason why they wanted to play for Leeds. And he did. It was a very hungry group of players.'

It was an eclectic team with an American, Mike MacDonald, an Argentine, Martin Schusterman, and an on-loan Samoan in Andy Tuilagi knitted in with locally-recruited players and others promoted from the club's academy. Pulling together a new group so quickly was not a straightforward task. The players hardly knew each other's names at first, never mind their games, but Lancaster's character-based signing policy at least ensured they were willing to put in the hours. They needed to.

'There was one training session early on which I remember vividly. The standard was just appalling,' said Hooper. 'We knocked it on the head and decided, among ourselves, to come back in the afternoon and do it again.'

The Leeds training base next to the River Aire was spread across two sections. On one side of Bridge Road, which turned into Kirkstall Lane as it wended its way uphill towards Headingley Stadium, was the changing room, gym and a couple of training pitches; on the other Abbey Fields where the squad was often put through its paces.

'Stuart brought in a system where we would all jog closely together to Abbey Fields as a team to train,' recalled Hooper. 'One day I said to the lads in the changing room: "Just make your own way over today when you're ready". It was the day after a game, I was still doing my laces up and I wanted it to be a bit more relaxed. We got over there and Stu was looking at me. "What's going on?" he said.

'"I told the lads to jog over when they were ready," I said. "That was 100 per cent the wrong decision," said Stuart.'

Lancaster's punishment was to send his players on a 4km run around the fields as an unpleasant alternative to the light group warm-up they had missed. 'At the time I was thinking: "What good's this going to do?" but when I look back I understand. It was about being a team and doing everything as a team,' reflected Hooper.

They might have resented their coach for a while afterwards but they felt duty-bound to respect him. He led the run every step of the way.

The stress on the collective that Lancaster had used in the academy was brought to the first team. He believed that, by emphasising the team and their cause above that of the individual Leeds could become more than the sum of their parts.

Leeds was not a club with a long history but Lancaster had been there right from the start and his attachment ran deep. His job was to transfer that loyalty to a new group of players.

'Stuart knew every single person who had ever played for Leeds which was a pretty powerful tool and he tapped into that history,' said Hooper. 'But, as well as being aware of what had gone on before at the club, there was also an emphasis on what we could create as a team.'

The Lancaster era could not have started worse with a home

defeat by London Welsh in the opening game.

There was not much wriggle room with only one team being promoted at the end of the 30-match season and another defeat at Bedford in their seventh game put the squeeze on. When a penalty with two minutes left condemned Leeds to another defeat at promotion rivals Rotherham on New Year's Eve, Lancaster came under intense pressure.

Leeds had naively tried to play rugby on a bog of a pitch which had needed the intervention of the local fire brigade to remove standing water on the morning of the game. As conditions deteriorated, so did Leeds and they were overpowered up front.

In the shadow of the single stand at Clifton Lane, Gary Hetherington collared Lancaster to express his concerns. This was a young coach feeling the bitter wind of reality blowing. It was the first time Lancaster felt his position was under threat.

If Hetherington had cut the thread who knows what would have happened to Stuart Lancaster. He might be a teacher now; or more likely a headmaster. But something told Hetherington he should keep the faith. Ten games – and ten wins – later, the decision had been vindicated. Leeds's victory at Otley, coupled with Rotherham's home defeat by Doncaster, had sealed promotion back to the Premiership with two games to spare.

'I'm very proud of the players, the coaching staff and everyone associated with the club,' Lancaster told the *Yorkshire Post*. 'It's a fantastic achievement. Given the situation at the start, it would rank as one of the best in the club's history.'

It was a promotion achieved with some panache. Leeds scored 126 tries that season.

'He had an idea in his head about how he wanted the game to be played and he had the ability to get that across. In essence, that's coaching,' said Hooper.

Leeds's promotion was, though, as much about the attitude as the style.

'No one in that squad, myself included, could have put their hand up and said: "I'm one of the best players in England," but because we had assembled this squad of players who genuinely cared about what they were doing, who were so passionate about playing for Leeds and for each other, we managed to get promoted,' said Hooper. 'Stuart made me realise just what you could get out of people.'

After winning promotion at the first attempt, Lancaster's staff appraisal that September made for interesting reading. 'Exceeds expectations' was the ticked box on his form – number two on a five-rung ladder, one below 'outstanding'.

Hetherington flagged up what he viewed as Lancaster's 'outstanding management skills'. He rated him 'a good communicator' who was clear and unemotional. He saw him as a 'fair, compassionate and honest' leader who 'recognised the importance of creating and maintaining team unity and a hard-working environment'. He was also regarded by his boss as a 'good delegator' who had a 'good understanding' of professional rugby.

Lancaster was marked by Hetherington in six broad areas in which he also scored himself. The numbers, almost identical from both boss and employee when broken down further, were high across the board. He rated perfectly in the role-model section and extremely well at developing people, communication and team working, where he scored ten out of ten when it came to 'openness to ideas' and 'inviting contributions from all levels'. His inclusiveness shone through.

The numbers for staff welfare and commercial awareness – his weakest suit – were also good but slightly lower. The dip in the commercial area was to be expected. He was only a year into his first job as a director of rugby and new to the wheeler-dealing and budget management involved.

The staff welfare marks revealed some deeper traits. There was a ten for 'treating individuals as people rather than employees' but a less generous eight for 'giving praise and recognition'. That emotional barrier he instinctively built between coach and player remained.

The belief that his players should man up and work as hard as he did was also reflected in two other scores in the section. There was an eight for 'identifying and managing stress' and a seven for 'implementing work/life balance solutions'. The off button was not something he was comfortable reaching for.

Viewed as a whole, the appraisal was overwhelmingly positive but his inexperience meant there were still unanswered questions about Lancaster as Leeds entered the Premiership. Hetherington spelled them out on the form. Under individual coaching ability, he asked 'Can you create a winning performance?' and 'Can you create an x-factor feature of team performance?' He questioned whether Lancaster might have 'too much loyalty' to senior players and coaching staff. He asked whether he had the 'ability to change direction and alter course' and to 'make tough decisions'. But in his conclusion he indicated that he believed Lancaster would ultimately answer those questions. 'As CEO I have total confidence in you and your actions and I see your status and influence rising for many years to come,' said Hetherington.

For Leeds and Lancaster, there was no time to rest on their laurels. Their return to the Premiership was an almighty challenge.

The problem for any side coming up, apart from the disparity in standard, is the lack of time to prepare for the big league. By the time promotion is confirmed the best players have all been snapped up by other clubs. Leeds desperately needed additions in order to compete but, on a budget under half of that of most of their Premiership rivals, they were never going to be able to bring in the cream of the crop.

Lancaster had to shop at the bargain end of the market and sometimes be prepared to cut corners. The circumstances surrounding the signing of the Rotherham captain Joe Bedford, a former Leeds Academy boy, amounted to tapping up.

'When he got the first team job at Leeds I got a phone call to say that Stuart would be interested in meeting with me to sound me out,' said Bedford. 'He knew I was under contract at Rotherham but I went to see him anyway and he said: "I'd love you to come and play for me at Leeds next season – what do you think?" I suppose maybe it was tapping up but I said: "Yeah, brilliant." I was only twenty-two but he made me vice-captain and his first choice scrum-half. It was the first time anyone had put total faith in me.' Tapping up, while commonplace in rugby, was still against the regulations.

Players from National One, however they were acquired, were all Lancaster could realistically afford. The Premiership was a mismatch on paper and the coach knew it. Somehow he had to brainwash his cut-price collection into believing they were capable of trading blows with teams packed with internationals.

'We went on a pre-season camp with the Marines down in Exmouth – Stuart loves his players to be fit – and he sat us down in a meeting room and did this PowerPoint presentation,' recalled Bedford. 'Our first three games were against Gloucester, Harlequins and Saracens. He put their squads up on the screen and told us these were the players who we would be playing against.

'Then he picked out a few players in the squad and asked each of us: "Are you afraid of your opposite numbers?" Obviously, we all said no. He was making us aware of the challenge but making us realise they were just players like us and talking them down so we weren't going into those games with fear. We never went into one game that season thinking we were going to lose and that was down to Stuart.'

But lose they did. Lancaster did not have a great team at his command. Or much luck. Within half an hour of the opening game kicking off he had lost two of his key signings – flanker Hendre Fourie, for half the season with a ruptured bicep, and stand-off Alberto di Bernardo, with a broken hand.

Fourie, a South African who would go on to play for England, was another summer arrival from Rotherham but had almost slipped through the net because of the rookie coach's global naivety.

Lancaster had been searching for a foraging open-side flanker and been tipped off about the strong No. 7 operating down the M1 but had been put off when he saw a No. 6 on his back.

'He didn't want to sign me at first because I preferred to wear the No. 6 jersey that open sides wear in South Africa and so he thought I was a blind side,' said Fourie. 'Joe Bedford's dad worked at Headingley and he had to tell him I was just wearing a No. 6 shirt and that I was actually an open side!'

With Daryl Powell, a rugby league coach, working along-side him, Lancaster tried to come up with a formula which would make his limited side competitive. He put in endless hours at his Kirkstall office, analysing his own side, studying opponents – anything to find a way for Leeds to gain a toehold in the division.

'The boys wouldn't be in until 8.30 a.m. but he'd be in at 6 a.m.,' said Bedford. 'Sometimes I'd go shopping at Morrisons just across the road at 6 p.m. with my wife and the light would still be on in his office. He was a workaholic.'

Detail, he decided, was the key to survival and he went out of his way to load the players with information. Sometimes too much information. 'He was a young coach and he was really adamant about getting his point across. We had a lot of long video sessions,' said Fourie.

Lancaster loved a meeting. And sometimes a meeting about a meeting. It was the one bone the side had to pick with their meticulous coach. 'We did spend a lot of time in meetings. He was a teacher who had become a coach,' said Bedford. 'Maybe he evolved in that respect afterwards but what it did mean was that we were organised. You'd never go into a game thinking "Where should I be?" He was very methodical and he never left a stone unturned.'

Leaving well alone is a hard lesson for a coach to learn and that season was when Lancaster was taught that less can be more. 'He's not too pig-headed that he won't listen – he learned what he had to get better at,' said Hooper.

He was not afraid to be told how he could improve. The printed schedule the players received at the start of each week always included a group meeting at which they could air any grievances. 'A lot of coaches might shy away from that – they would rather not know – but Lanny wanted feedback all the time to get a feel for what has happening in the squad,' said Bedford. 'It wasn't just the senior players, it had a couple of academy lads in there, too, and maybe someone who hadn't been picked very often to get a sense of what he was feeling, too.'

Leeds beat Worcester in October and Newcastle in March at Headingley and made it to the quarter-finals of the European Challenge Cup, but that was it as far as success went.

As the defeats piled up, Lancaster tried psychological tricks to maintain the fiction that the side was competitive. 'We did this thing where we would sit down opposite a team-mate for ten minutes and just tell each other what they were good at,' said Bedford. 'I did one with Tom Biggs and came out of the room feeling a million dollars. I was thinking: "Wow, is that what he really thinks?"'

Ultimately, though, Lancaster was trying to solve an impossible riddle. 'The reality was that we just weren't good enough because the quality of players in the Premiership was much higher,' said Hooper. 'It was pretty tough but we never gave in and that is the test of a team. All you want is to look your team-mates in the eye and know they gave it their best crack. We did, but the other teams were just better than us.'

Lancaster shuffled his limited resources around, giving a first Premiership start to Burrell in the penultimate game of the season against London Irish, but the outcome was always the same.

'He was in at the deep end because he had a mediocre squad, a lot of injuries early in the season when it was crucial we put our foot in the Premiership door and no resources to bring new players in. It must have been really difficult for him,' said Fourie. 'He was a young coach and you could see the pressure was getting to him a little bit.'

As the inevitable relegation approached, frustration occasionally got the better of him. 'He probably lost it once or maybe twice that season,' said Bedford, who started every Premiership game. 'When he did, we knew he was upset more than angry. It was because he cared. He wouldn't get angry if we dropped a pass or made a bad decision – it would only be if we weren't at the races that day.'

Leeds's fate was sealed at Kingsholm three matches from the

end of the season when they lost 39-16 in a game which saw Luther Burrell play his first full 80 minutes in the Premiership. 'The reality is that we have been relegated. Personally, and as a team, that is very disappointing,' admitted Lancaster afterwards. 'However, I don't think that there was anything more we could have done this season to avoid relegation. We found out late that we had won promotion and we have been catching up all season.'

Lancaster had dedicated his every waking hour to keeping Leeds up and he had failed, but it would have needed a world-class levitator to keep Leeds up – not a rugby coach.

'We gave it our best shot every single game but came up short. We just didn't have enough quality and that came down to finance, not Stuart,' said Bedford. 'He was always going to come out on top in the end, though, because he lived the motto of "hard work makes dreams come true".'

Relegation meant there were decisions to be made. The players were chewing over whether to stay and so, too, was the coach. The RFU had approached Lancaster with an offer to become the head of their elite-player development, a position which involved overseeing the England age-group and sevens sides and the regional academies.

Leeds did not want him to go; Lancaster, who had another year on his contract, didn't really want to leave the club he loved but if he wanted to progress he had to accept the RFU offer. He went to see his chief executive.

'I was pissed off because they had come in for him through the back door rather than the front and I said to him he needed to think carefully because it was an academy job, not the England job,' said Hetherington. 'We didn't want to lose him but if it's something someone really wants to do we're not going to keep him here kicking and screaming.'

Lancaster wrestled long and hard with the decision – he had preached loyalty to his squad – but he reluctantly made the call to leave. It cut him in half. Breaking the bond with his club and informing his players proved to be searingly painful.

'He gathered us in a meeting room and when he told us he was going to leave for the RFU job he was really emotional. He cried,' recalled Fourie. 'It showed how much he cared and his love for Leeds as a club. But the opportunity in front of him was so massive he'd have been stupid to turn it down.'

The resolute Lancaster in tears was not a sight any of the players ever expected to see but leaving proved intensely moving.

Lancaster rang Henry Paul and Jonathan Pendlebury, players he had signed for the following season, to tell them he would not be there when they arrived and his exit was made public before the final game of the season against Wasps.

'I was here when the club was formed sixteen years ago and I have given my all as a player, as captain, as academy manager and as director of rugby,' said Lancaster.

'I can think of no other role I would have left the club for. However this is a once-in-a-lifetime opportunity. It allows me to work and coach at the top end of the international game developing senior and young players alike to play for England.'

He left for Twickenham at the end of the 2007/8 season with a heavy heart. It had been a short but turbulent period in charge of Leeds. He had probably crammed five years' worth of experience into two roller-coaster seasons, but it was time to spread his wings.

7

National Service

Put forth thy hand, reach at the glorious gold
Henry VI Part 2, Act 1, Scene 2

Kevin Bowring is sitting in a café in the Gloucestershire village of Nailsworth. Behind him, stones bulge out of its thick white, uneven walls, lending the place a rustic authenticity. The light from a warm late summer's day floods through the window. This is one of English rugby union's heartlands – the nearest Premier League football team is 70 miles away.

Bowring, a man of Neath, is employed by the RFU as their head of elite-coach development. There is a certain irony that the man English rugby employs to polish its finest coaches is Welsh – and was Wales's first professional national coach – but knowledge knows no national boundaries and the English game was happy to bring Bowring on board when the position was created in 2002. He has been part of the Twickenham set-up ever since.

Bowring pours himself a cup of strong coffee from a cafetière and begins to reminisce about Stuart Lancaster. Specifically, about the time he was offered one job by the RFU but talked his way into another.

Traditionally when candidates are interviewed they try to sell themselves for the advertised position; Lancaster being Lancaster, he decided to aim for something bigger when he went to meet the RFU to discuss the post of head of elite-player development. Having been headhunted, he felt in a strong position so he came up with an alternative suggestion which would enable him to remain a front-line coach.

'At the interview Stuart sold the idea of coaching the Saxons. It was an interesting idea,' said Bowring, who was on the interview panel. 'He wanted to coach the Saxons to enable him to link the senior team with the elite players coming into the set-up that he would know from his elite-player development role. He would be the connection.' Bowring laughs now at the cheek of it. But the RFU bought Lancaster's pitch. He was given the dual position he wanted.

With his swept-back grey hair and lecturer's jacket, Bowring, an elegant sixty, gives off a faintly professorial air as he sips his coffee. The appearance is appropriate for one of Lancaster's two *éminences grises*.

The other is Bill Beswick, a bespectacled, quietly spoken Mancunian four years Bowring's senior, who made his name as Steve McClaren's psychologist when he managed the England football team. A former coach to the England basketball team, he acts as mind man and cultural guardian to the England rugby squad as well as working in football and swimming.

If Bowring, Wales's coach for three years in the late nineties, is Lancaster's rugby guru, Beswick, a grass-roots rugby supporter at Winnington Park in Cheshire, is the man he turns to for guidance on team-building matters. Both act as Lancaster's mentors. Bowring winces slightly at the word – and delivers an alternative he prefers – but he accepts the premise.

'Bill and I would be Stuart's thinking partners,' he said. 'We're the people who he thinks out loud with, people who ask enough questions so that when he makes a decision he is sure it is the right one for him to make because he's accountable for it. He's humble enough to call on us but he does it less and less because he is growing in knowledge, experience and maturity in the role.'

Bowring has worked with every national coach from Sir Clive Woodward onwards but he has formed a special relationship with Lancaster. They go back a long way. Further even than that Saxons interview. 'I first met Stuart through the academy managers' network. We were trying to set up the academy process at the time – they hadn't been going long at that point,' recalled Bowring in his Welsh lilt.

'The academies were all slightly different according to the needs of their area. I remember him talking about the rugby league model because he was working closely with Stuart Wilkinson, the academy manager at the Rhinos, and really taking an interest in what Tony Smith was doing there. He was one of the respected academy managers who was listened to because he talked common sense.

'What stood out about him on reflection was what I can only describe as his growth mindset – his appetite for learning, his hunger for development and continual improvement, his thirst for knowledge and his reading around subjects.'

Beswick's link with Lancaster also stretches back to his Leeds days, although not quite as far as Bowring's. Beswick first encountered him in 2006 at a Six Nations' coaching course at France's base in Marcoussis just outside Paris when Lancaster had just taken over as director of rugby at Leeds.

There were six coaches from each nation present, of whom Lancaster was comfortably one of the least well-known or experienced. As the host, Beswick asked if anyone would care to share his coaching philosophy with the rest. There was an awkward silence. It was Lancaster who broke the ice.

'Over the weekend he consistently had the courage to make interventions, which I liked,' said Beswick. 'He wasn't cowed by people of perceived greater status in coaching.

'One of my sessions was a workshop on profiling player roles and Stuart was leading and reporting on that. What he said made really good sense. This young man was engaged, involved, focused, quick and went to greater depth than other coaches. He understood. He got it. His thinking was more advanced than other coaches. And it wasn't just one workshop. I deal with a lot of coaches and instinct tells you when you've got something special. I made the comment to Kevin: "You've got a future coach there".'

Lancaster once said, in one of his more mystical moments, that when a coach is ready for a mentor, a mentor will come to him, but there was an outside hand at work in forging his relationship with Beswick.

'Kevin very cleverly put us in a taxi together to go to the airport from Marcoussis, then rang us individually to ask how we had got on with each other,' said Beswick. 'In my business you need to be able to build a relationship on a personal level before you can get into any real productive engagement. I wanted to see what kind of man he was.

'On that taxi ride I gained the feeling that he had a restless mind. He had no vision of coaching England then – he was too humble for that – but he had a curiosity. He was interested in what I did and what it could tell him. Some of his questions to me were very perceptive. I thought he could handle the pressure of high-performance coaching. If you are seeking excellence you are constantly under pressure – it's extremely demanding and you have to be comfortable with yourself and be able to deal with yourself. But I thought: "This man can do it".'

Back in the UK, Bowring dipped into his RFU coaching budget to arrange quarterly meetings between Lancaster and the figure who was to become his guide. In coaching terms it was Obi-Wan Kenobi meets the young Luke Skywalker. Except without light sabres. They wouldn't have been allowed in the chapel of the Manchester YMCA where Beswick took Lancaster for their first session. 'I've been a YMCA board member for many years so normally I can get a room but the only room available was the chapel. Stuart looked up, saw where I was taking him, and said: "It's not that bad is it?"'

Beswick was high church when it came to elite coaching and team building, having studied in the USA and worked at the cutting edge of football. He was a generation older than Lancaster but there proved to be a natural kinship between the two. 'My job was to give Stuart a more rounded education in high-performance coaching and to introduce him to the world that I had experienced in many years of working with top coaches and top teams,' said Beswick.

'I wanted him to understand what made them top coaches and what made them top teams. We'd spend three hours together and it would go like that because he is a very engaging man and very curious. One thing I noticed was that he didn't take many notes but when I said something which hit home, he'd stop me and write it down. If he wrote it down, he would never forget it.'

The sessions were interesting preparation for the world Lancaster would one day inhabit. He was asked to play the role of a national football manager or an NBA head coach and to think his way through real problems and come up with appropriate solutions.

'I had no concept – and Stuart had no concept – that he would end up as England coach but I decided I would stretch him,' said Beswick. 'I'd say to him: "OK, you're head coach, here's a scenario, take over". He'd run through it, then I'd tell him how it was actually dealt with. It was fascinating work and very enjoyable.

'The examples were from all sports. I think one of the issues we have in this country with our coaches is that they get too insular in their own sports. I'm a great believer in cross-fertilisation. I talked to him about issues with the England football team and the British basketball team and lessons from American coaches. I'm a great student of coaching and all the people I've worked with who are now coaching at the highest level are fascinated with lessons from America.'

Each time they met, Beswick would hand Lancaster a coaching or management book to read and absorb. He would also arrange for Lancaster to spend time at Premier League football clubs such as Newcastle United where another client of his, Steve Round, was the assistant manager. 'I wanted him to meet a different circle of people to extend his learning,' said Beswick. 'It was about extending what was a very curious mind and making him think in a more analytical way about high performance.'

Talking his way into the Saxons job gave Lancaster a team on which to practise the theory he had been learning. The role Lancaster fought for had previously been farmed out to existing Premiership coaches as a part-time role because of the relatively small fixture programme. Steve Bates had been the last incumbent but had given the job up to concentrate on his day job at Newcastle Falcons.

It was a far from straightforward position given its transient nature and the diametrically opposite groups of players who found themselves parachuted into a squad hand-picked by England's team manager, Martin Johnson. As well as the elite youngsters on the way up, it required Lancaster to deal with the discarded players on the way down.

When Johnson named his first squad in July 2008, he relegated 12 players to the Saxons, including Ben Kay, Mike Tindall and Joe Worsley, all of whom had World Cup-winners' medals. The squad also included big names like Nick Easter, David Strettle, Mike Brown, Danny Cipriani and Steffon Armitage.

There was no shortage of talent in the squad, but no shortage of resentment either. The combination presented an immediate challenge for Lancaster when the second-tier squad met up at Twickenham. He had never coached at national representative level, he had just presided over Leeds's relegation and there he was, tasked with persuading Test players who did not know him from Adam that his voice was worth listening to.

He knew if he failed to win them over on day one he would not win them over at all. He noticed the sceptical looks on the faces as he introduced himself. As he carried on, he saw several players slumped in their seats clearly wishing they were somewhere else.

Lancaster stopped. 'If some of us don't improve our body language we ain't going to be getting along very well,' he barked.

Point made.

Lancaster decided to split the squad into small groups and sit them down to discuss and write down what was good about

England rugby and what it could do better. He put the axed players in their own section and sat in on their discussion. The exercise allowed the players whose noses had been put out of joint a chance to vent some steam and, because Lancaster contributed as well, it allowed him to convince them he was on their side in trying to help elevate them back into the senior team.

'Rugby players are so sceptical – particularly English ones – but the thing that impressed me straight away were his people skills. One of the biggest problems in rugby is coaches who say "Right, we do it my way". With Stuart it was a conversation,' recalled Kay.

'The difficulty for him was that he was used to dealing with younger players; that sort of coaching is very different from dealing with seasoned older players. With younger players you can be analytical and classroom-based but there can be a bit of scepticism with older players about that. But Stuart handled that well just because of his people skills.' The mistrust Lancaster had sensed began to melt away.

'There was a little bit of that but it wasn't as though the lower-down England teams had been run by a load of superstar coaches before,' said Kay. 'It helped that Johnno was there setting the scene. A lot of us really trusted Johnno and we knew he wouldn't have been putting him up there if he didn't feel confident in him.'

If Lancaster had then proceeded to show himself as an imposter as an international rugby coach, all the management tricks in the world could not have saved him – credibility in the fundamentals of the job underpins everything – but a sharp session at Twickenham that first day demonstrated he knew what he was talking about and that working under him could be productive and enjoyable. The players were brought onside.

Kay, Tindall, Worsley, Easter, Brown, Cipriani and Armitage all went on to play for England again.

'The Saxons is a difficult job because often selection is imposed upon you and you only have a limited amount of time but Stuart did it particularly well,' said Bowring. 'He sold it as a way back for the players who had come down from the senior team and a first step on the ladder for the lads on the way up. By helping the team to achieve their goals they would help themselves to achieve their objectives – whatever they were.'

There was little in the way of profile with the job but there was room for controversy. For all its afterthought status internationally, A-team rugby was still international rugby and could still attract international incidents.

In his first full season in charge Lancaster refused to allow his Saxons team to take the field against Ireland A at Donnybrook because the ground was frozen. Both the Irish coach Michael Bradley and referee Jérôme Garcès wanted to play the game but Lancaster pulled the plug during the warm-up on safety grounds with the crowd already filtering into the stadium. With no opposition there was no game. 'We would have liked to have played it,' said an unimpressed Bradley.

Four months later, the Saxons embarked on their end-of-season trip to North America to contest the Churchill Cup. It was Lancaster's first extended period with the squad and he was excited to see what he could achieve with them. He discovered some interesting home truths before they had even set off.

'We had talked a lot about cohesion – task cohesion where a team knew where it was going on the field in all situations – and social cohesion where a team played for each other, not with each other. He was very keen on those two items,' said Beswick.

'On his first Saxons tour the team flew out to Denver. As the players boarded the plane, they turned right into premium economy. Three of them turned left into first class. They had upgraded themselves. Stuart was appalled.'

Lancaster had not announced the make-up of the squad until a fortnight after the end of the domestic season, which was a big mistake. The players had switched off, hit the beach and the pub and returned in less than perfect condition which, for a tournament played at altitude, was bad news. They almost lost their opening game against Argentina's second string.

The more he saw of some of the squad's attitudes on the trip, the less impressed he became. 'There were one or two individual player relationships he struggled with. Some of them did not meet his standards,' said Beswick. 'There is always debris in high-performance sport and the Saxons was an early lesson in where he was going to set the bar. He set it very high. He has less tolerance than many of the football people I've worked with. His personal standards reflect in his professional standards. He expects honesty and integrity from people.'

England reached the final of the Churchill Cup but Ireland A exacted painful revenge for the refusal to play earlier in the season by thrashing them 49-22 in Denver.

Lancaster learned some hard lessons that day about the power of emotion. They were ransacked by an Irish side revved up by captain Neil Best. The Saxons were blown away.

'It was a critical moment for him on his coaching journey,' said Bowring. 'There are some learning incidents which drive people not to want to go through the same experience again. They learn from it and are better prepared to deal with it. There's a little part of him which can't wait to avenge events like that.'

The following season beach time was banned and the squad

were sent to train in altitude chambers instead. England won the Churchill Cup. He won three in all with the Saxons.

Those players who had worked with him at club level saw a subtle change in him as a coach at this higher level. His standards were still exacting and his planning detailed but there was less of an issue with players staying awake in preparation periods. Lancaster still liked a meeting, but as Hendre Fourie found out when he was called up in 2010, they were a lot shorter than during his Leeds days. Having less time with the players meant using it more efficiently.

'He learned about how long practice sessions should last and about priorities – what players must know, what they should know and what they might know before they take the field,' said Beswick. 'He tried things out. He had his ideas and he applied them. Some of them didn't work but a lot of them did, which gave him a lot of confidence.'

Bowring, who also coached at A-team level with Wales, assesses Lancaster's time with the Saxons as invaluable. 'The difference in international coaching is that you have a higher level of player for a shorter period of time and you have to gel them in that short period of time, connect them as people and give them a common purpose,' he said.

'The life cycle of the team is short. The process starts again when the next Saxons team is named because half the team will have changed. It was important for him to see international rugby, albeit one level down. And during those years he was also a fly on the wall of the England senior coaching team.'

Sitting in with Martin Johnson and his coaching team gave Lancaster an insight into the much greater pressures of working with the national side. The attention and the stakes were infinitely greater. But nothing he saw in that environment convinced him that caution was the correct policy when it came to running England.

Where Johnson was drawn to experienced players he knew and trusted, the dual role Lancaster held with the RFU enabled him to see fast-tracked youngsters close up in the Saxons. He knew they had talent and how well they were being conditioned for Test rugby.

Rugby union at top level was changing, a point identified by Lancaster's predecessor in the role, Conor O'Shea, and England needed to keep up. In his elite-player development role, Lancaster was in charge of identifying and developing potential future England internationals from the age of thirteen upwards, as well as overseeing the management of the national under-18s and under-20s sides. It was his responsibility to deliver a conveyor belt of players who would ultimately be capable of delivering a successful national side in the future.

The factories where they were to be produced were the 14 RFU-licensed academies around the country where the work was being done to produce the next generation of internationals. The directive from Lancaster to them was that the RFU wanted a generation of players who could fit into a new way of thinking.

They needed to be able to fill the traditional mould – forwards who could drive and backs who could win collisions and chase kicks – but they also needed to be comfortable on the ball whatever the number on their shirt. The national representative sides were encouraged to adopt an attacking philosophy which saw an emphasis placed on self-expression. The old staple of the catch-and-drive was ditched in favour of a more imaginative approach. It was even seen as acceptable to lose Test matches at under-18s and under-20s level in pursuit of the greater goal of player development.

Such idealism hardened by the time it came to junior world championships but the skills they had developed in the enlightened environment brought results. During Lancaster's time, England were runners-up to New Zealand at under-20s level three times in the IRB Junior World Championship. The seeds sown in Lancaster's four years in the position bore even greater fruit when he moved on, as England won the title in 2013 and 2014. He was sure this was a generation who could take the national side forward.

A number of talented players made a mark on him. In 2009 Courtney Lawes and Ben Youngs were involved. In 2010 Joe Marler was an ever-present in the England under-20s side, playing all ten games in a team which also included Christian Wade. In 2011, Joe Launchbury was England's players' player of the Junior World Championship in a line-up featuring Owen Farrell, Mako Vunipola and George Ford – the IRB junior player of the year. They all had something in common. Every one of them was a ball-playing athlete as well as a rugby player.

Lancaster saw at first hand the talent being developed through the academies, talent which the Premiership clubs were increasingly willing to blood. In part this was down to necessity. The high-end overseas players who once made for England had been diverted to France because of the riches on offer there. But there was also a growing recognition that players were physically and mentally ready for top-level rugby at a younger age. Inexperience was no longer a barrier to playing Test rugby; nor, in Lancaster's mind, to coaching it.

When the senior England job became available in 2011 he felt he knew enough about the problems of a decaying old guard – and more importantly the ready-made solutions he had seen at national junior level – to confirm his candidacy.

By selling himself as the connecting point between the country's most promising young players and the national side when he had asked for the Saxons job, he had given himself a unique vantage point. It was time to make the most of it. Lancaster was, as ever, willing to shoot for the top.

'As part of his Saxons role he was able to sit in on senior coaching meetings as an observer. He'd seen the issues which were besetting the national team. It was struggling,' said Beswick.

'Turning round the team became a very topical debate for us. When he told me he had a chance of the job, by and large I was in favour – I felt he was strong enough – but I told him I needed to think about it. I pointed out the pressures but he was up for it – he felt excited by it, energised, challenged. He'd seen what was happening with England and he felt he knew how to change it.

'It wasn't ideal timing in his career path – working for a top club first for five or six years would have been a greater grounding – but at the same time I couldn't see anyone else around who was English who should be doing it. I'm very much an advocate of an English coach for an England team.'

Beswick, who had seen his client and close friend Steve McClaren pilloried as England football manager, did harbour private doubts. If it had gone wrong for Lancaster, the backlash would have been painful. But all the hours they had spent together had convinced him Lancaster could make a success of the role.

'He was the best man for the situation,' said Beswick. 'It was a very, very brave appointment by the RFU because the media pressure was for a foreigner with a track record. But it was a very good decision.'

8

California Dreaming

Exceedingly well read

Henry IV Part I, Act 3, Scene 1

When Stuart Lancaster embarked on his whirlwind overhaul of England's national rugby union team, he had a clear idea of how he wanted it to look – uncannily like the San Francisco 49ers' American football team.

Bill Beswick's parting gift of a book after each of their meetings had provided Lancaster with a groaning table of transatlantic food for thought over the years. He had absorbed the teachings of the American basketball coach John Wooden, who had led the UCLA Bruins to seven consecutive US collegiate titles in the late sixties and early seventies, and the legendary gridiron coach Vince Lombardi, the force behind the powerhouse Green Bay Packers side of the same era.

He had been intrigued by the thoughts of Chicago Bulls basketball coach Phil Jackson and his star player Michael Jordan in that dominant side of the nineties. But nothing compared to the influence of a title Beswick gave to Lancaster in 2011. It was to have a profound influence on him and the way he was to run England.

The Score Takes Care of Itself was a book on American football chronicling the teachings of the 49ers' visionary coach Bill Walsh but, flicking through the pages, Lancaster quickly realised the symmetry with rugby. The parallels with his own thinking were striking, too.

Rugby, like gridiron, was an impact sport with specialised units which all had to function for the team as a whole to succeed. It, too, demanded bravery and sacrifice when a side could stand and fall not only by its talent but by the players' commitment to a cause and attachment to each other. It was not so much the similarity of the canvas which struck Lancaster as the paints Walsh applied to it. He was obsessed with the quality of the environment in which a team operated; Lancaster was, too.

He already had a picture in his head of what a successful sports organisation would look like but Walsh articulated it so clearly and in such detail that his words, published after his death in 2007, became Lancaster's bible.

The nearest Lancaster had come to life in California was flipping burgers in San Diego's SeaWorld over three summers on the WorkAmerica scheme during his student days, but he saw in the great coach's teachings a lot he could relate to. They became some of the foundation stones of the team-building theories he would employ with England.

If a coach was looking for the ultimate transformation model, Walsh's time with the 49ers embodied it. Walsh was the head football coach of the 49ers from 1979 to 1989. During those ten years he took the worst team in the National Football League to three Super Bowl championships. No team won more games in that decade. His legacy was a side who went on to win two more Super Bowls in the six years following his retirement.

At the heart of everything Walsh taught was something he called the standard of performance. This was the base level of professionalism which acted as the foundation for an organisation's success.

His primary focus, he explained, was never on winning games but rather on persuading everyone, starting with himself, to live up to his performance standard. Fall short and the team would fall short; achieve it and the results would flow automatically as a by-product.

The 'standard' involved building an inventory of skills which would improve execution in training and matches. But it was an all-consuming approach which extended way beyond the football field. Walsh demanded excellence from every person in his organisation. Regardless of the job, he wanted it done to the best of that person's ability.

When Walsh took over, coaches, players, back-room staff, marketing executives, scouts and groundsmen received specific detailed instructions from him on what was expected of them. All the way through to the receptionists. In an hour-long presentation to them he outlined their role in upgrading the 49ers. Among their two pages of bullet points, was the requirement that all telephone messages, however trivial, had to be answered inside 24 hours. The public had to know how professional and connected the organisation was. If it was detailed for the receptionists, for the players the directives, delivered in four one-hour sessions, were all-encompassing.

Respect for each other and for the opposition was prioritised – there was to be no showboating after touchdowns, no posturing, no cheap shots and no fighting. Hazing – the humiliation of new players through anything from head shaving to physical assault – was outlawed. The rookie was to feel as highly valued as the star player. There was to be no hierarchy of importance.

Players were expected to be punctual, refrain from swearing in public areas and to treat fans and media with politeness. There was a dress code in the dining areas and sitting down was not acceptable on the practice ground. Shirts had to be tucked in.

Elevated expectations extended to how kit should be treated. Anything that bore the 49ers' emblem had to be shown respect. Practice helmets were either worn, held or put on the locker shelf. They were never thrown or sat upon. Equipment was not to be left lying around.

When a player followed the rules that underpinned the organisation, he was marking his commitment to it. If a player did not sign up to Walsh's principles that was fine. But he would have to leave the 49ers.

Lancaster saw in this outline the shape of what he believed an elite rugby squad should look like. It was not one he recognised in the England side he inherited.

Standards were critically important to Bill Walsh. He stressed the importance of maintaining them in defeat as well as victory. It mattered enormously to Walsh that his team should retain their dignity in all circumstances. Losing happens in sport but when his 49ers lost they were expected to stick to their principles and not unravel.

They had plenty of practice over his first two seasons. The 49ers were starting from the lowest of bases and it took into a third season to turn around their fortunes. But even with results continuing to go the wrong way in years one and two he observed, behind the scenes, how his moral methods and work ethic were bringing about a change in how the players perceived themselves and the team.

As Walsh put it: 'Champions behave like champions before they are champions.' They began to take pride in being part of the group and viewing themselves as members of a first-class, professional organisation. Because they felt connected to it, they each felt an ownership of it. In turn that brought about a change in attitude. They became self-starters who wanted to add to the environment. And when one individual raised his level of work-rate and sacrifice, the man next to him tended to do so as well.

Eventually the alteration in outlook translated into victories. From 14 defeats in 16 games in 1979 and 10 in 16 in 1980, they won the Super Bowl in 1981. The signs were there towards the end of Walsh's second season when they came back from 35-7 down at half-time to beat the New Orleans Saints in over-time to record what was then the biggest comeback win in NFL history. A team built on sand simply could not have done that.

The boulder had been pushed to the top of the hill. The following season it came crashing down the other side with the dominant Dallas Cowboys taken down in the NFC Championship game and the Cincinnati Bengals defeated at the Super Bowl. One of the most remarkable turnarounds in American sport had been engineered. The 49ers had the first Super Bowl in their history and were on their way to NFL pre-eminence.

It could not have happened without Walsh. His belief was that everything had to start from the top. To extract the standard of performance he wants from his squad, a head coach has to live his message. 'Do as I say and not as I do' is a non-starter as a doctrine.

The way Walsh saw it, the behaviour of the coach translated itself into the team's characteristics over time. When implemented in its entirety by a leader, Walsh was convinced his philosophy would transform any organisation from a low-expectation environment to a high-performance culture.

This was his 17-point template for success. A head coach must:

1. Exhibit a ferocious and intelligently applied work ethic directed at continual improvement.

2. Demonstrate respect for each person in the organisation and the work he or she does.

3. Be deeply committed to learning and teaching, which means increasing your own expertise.

4. Be fair.

5. Demonstrate character.

6. Honour the direct connection between details and improvement – and relentlessly seek the latter.

7. Show self-control especially where it counts most – under pressure.

8. Demonstrate and prize loyalty.

9. Use positive language and have a positive attitude.

10. Take pride in your effort as an entity separate from the result of that effort.

11. Be willing to go the extra mile for the organisation.

12. Deal appropriately with victory and defeat, adulation and humiliation.

13. Promote internal communication that is both open and substantive.

14. Seek poise in yourself and those you lead.

15. Put your team's welfare and priorities ahead of your own.

16. Maintain an ongoing lead of concentration and focus that is abnormally high.

17. Make sacrifice and commitment the organisation's trademark.

The package would never bring a head coach victory in every game – Walsh calculated that 20 per cent of every match is down to luck or the match officials anyway – but he stacked the odds with his standard of performance. 'I never wavered in my dedication to installing – teaching – those actions and attitudes I believed would create a great team, a superior organisation. I knew that if I achieved that, the score would take care of itself,' he wrote.

Walsh believed he had drawn up the formula for creating a long-term winning team in a high-performance environment – which was exactly what Lancaster wanted with England. It was to be his road map.

Walsh's original thoughts on coaching were recorded in another book, first published in 1998 but now out of print, called *Finding the Winning Edge*. Lancaster tracked down a copy in the United States. It is a fascinating, in-depth manual on sports management, almost dot-to-dot-like in its level of precision on how to create a successful team. More seeds were planted in a fertile mind.

In it Walsh breaks down and runs through a head coach's responsibilities from selector and tactician to man manager and time manager, combining the minutiae of the moment with the grand expanse of the long term.

The balance between hands-on micro-management and distant macro-management is hard to achieve but crucial. Walsh likens it to appreciating a piece of art. Stand close to the piece and the texture and fine detail becomes apparent; stand back and the full picture becomes clear.

Given the choice, Walsh recommends standing too close. A head coach should involve himself in the nitty-gritty or risk losing his grip on the essentials, he believed. For him, that meant choreographing the West Coast Offense which became the 49ers' calling card.

When it came to selection, Walsh took a pragmatic view. He advised every head coach to strive to be as good as he could be at this important role but accept he would never be perfect. His advice was to pick players with character and an ability to think on their feet and individuals who could work with others – not bull-headed know-it-alls. He put a big cross against players who would not buy easily into a head coach's philosophy or whose negative energy might sap the group culture.

As they grew into the dominant force of American football in the 1980s, the 49ers had their superstars – quarterback Joe Montana, running back Roger Craig and wide receiver Jerry Rice among them. The increasing priority placed on personal statistics in American football, the rise of agents and the knock-on effect both had on a player's value in the marketplace conspired against the team ethic Walsh was attempting to prioritise.

Walsh's antidote was to put time into creating an environ-ment at the 49ers strong on work ethic where every player appreciated the roles of his team-mates. Montana, Craig and Rice had to appreciate they were cogs in a bigger wheel. His iron rule was that the blocker was just as important as the catcher or the thrower in a touchdown play. The big names understood the importance of the lesser lights in their – and the team's – success.

Lancaster could relate to that. The tight-head prop who kept the scrum square for the try-scoring set play was just as impor-tant as the winger who finished the move. The landscape of his England side, like Walsh's 49ers, had to be egalitarian.

It seemed every word Walsh had written on the shape of the

49ers' team environment was written with the reconstructed England in mind, too.

When Lancaster discovered Walsh was also a guest contributor for *Forbes* magazine in the 1990s, he contacted the publishers in New York to have all the articles he had written for them sent over to him. The back issues make up a formidable library.

On 29 March 1993, Walsh wrote on one of his favourite topics, planning. Nothing, he declared, is more important to an organisation's chances of succeeding than preparation. The leader's job is to plan for every eventuality which may arise in a game – or a season.

Before the start of the 1987 campaign, a threat had been issued by the unions that the NFL players might go on strike. Most teams dismissed the possibility; Walsh did not. He ordered his head of scouting to search for players who could fill in if the strike went ahead and kept in touch with others who had been cut in the summer from his squad because they already knew the 49ers' system.

When a 24-day walkout was called, most teams were thrown into chaos. San Francisco were ready and waiting. They had their replacement team and won the three games played during the strike.

That season, the 49ers topped the NFC West. The margin was one victory. As Walsh put it: 'Having planned for the worst, you can do a lot more than hope for the best.'

Planning was his mantra. Training was scheduled to the minute – as were matches. Walsh would pre-script as many contingencies as possible before a match to reduce the number of off-the-cuff decisions he would have to make in the game. The team would know the first 25 plays they would use before they took the field.

'The less thinking people have to do under adverse circumstances, the better. When you're under pressure the mind can play tricks on you,' he wrote.

'When things get tense in a football game I want to make decisions clinically because I've thought them through beforehand rather than take an ad-libbed, seat-of-the-pants approach. Being able to go with a well-rehearsed plan is far better than depending on heroics which work better in fiction than in real life.'

He would inevitably have to deliver some instinct calls – all coaches do – but all the homework minimised the number of them he had to make and increased the chances that the decisions he did make were good ones.

While the stop-start nature of American football lends itself much more to coach intervention, the theory held true in rugby, too. Go through the theoretical scenarios beforehand and a coach is in a better position to respond to them if they become reality. In the hubbub of games, Walsh used to imagine a soundproof glass booth around him so he was able to make calls with perfect clarity.

Walsh's opinion was that players did not respond on the field to his great speeches – they had forgotten them by the time of the first impact. What they were most inspired by was his calm and accurate decision-making under pressure. If a coach looks in control, the team has increased faith that he is control. It is a state which proves beyond many professional sports coaches with livelihoods on the line.

Walsh was nicknamed 'Genius' by the American media – he had a Master's degree from San Jose State University – and there was also something of the five-star general about him. He was a keen reader on the American Civil War and the Second World

War. The tag he preferred, though, was 'teacher'. When all is boiled down a coach – be it in rugby or American football – is a teacher and the player is his pupil – albeit a vastly overgrown one. He was preaching to the converted with Lancaster.

Walsh's view was that information is power and that a player can never have too much of it. Knowing the system – not just their own role in it – helps individuals to function as a team. His instruction to coaches in imparting it was to be organised, employ technology and to assume athletes have a maximum 20-minute attention span.

Walsh said he never wanted his coaches or players to feel too comfortable. Although he viewed ranting and raving for its own sake as counter-productive, he saw the value of an occasional explosion as a shock tactic. He once forced the 49ers players off the team bus to deliver a road-side rev-up on the way to a game in New York because he sensed a flat atmosphere.

Conversely, Walsh was not averse to using humour now and again to lighten the mood. He dressed up as a porter ahead of Super Bowl XVI to surprise the team when they checked into their hotel and once had his assistants dress as a pimp, a hooker and a dealer when he was delivering an anti-drug message to the squad.

The coach's job was to assess the temperature of the organisation and respond accordingly. He recommended being personable to players but not overly familiar. After all, the likelihood was that he would have to drop most, if not all of them, at some point. Walsh's advice was to use straightforward language with players but not 'their' language. 'In' phrases, he believed, sounded false coming from a member of an older generation.

Walsh was already forty-seven when he first took charge of the 49ers, having served a long apprenticeship as an assistant with the Oakland Raiders, Cincinnati Bengals and San Diego Chargers before taking up a head coach post in college football at Stanford University. Having sat on both sides of the fence, Walsh knew the assistant coach relationship was not a straight-forward one for a head coach to manage. Specialists were often frustrated head coaches themselves which could cause friction and each one would be pushing for his own field of expertise to be prioritised, bringing inevitable pinch points.

He believed it was essential for individual remits to be clearly defined to minimise the potential for division.

He recommended allowing room for debate until the point when a decision is made, then no leeway whatsoever. After that the back-up team had to be 100 per cent loyal. Anything less and the situation could become corrosive.

The sheer depth to which Walsh goes in his writings is mind-boggling. He offers advice on managing the media, rela-tionships with rival coaches, the danger of pleasure after a victory disappearing and being replaced by relief... just about anything a young head coach could possibly think of and much more besides.

Distil the many messages down to their basics, though, and the lesson which shines through is that meticulous planning, hard work and above all non-negotiable high standards can turn around any sporting environment. 'Every organisation has a cultural conscience that takes it forward year after year,' he wrote.

Listen to the audio version of *The Score Takes Care of Itself*, a copy of which happens to reside permanently in Lancaster's car, and it is hard to miss the correlation between the guiding prin-ciples Walsh employed with the San Francisco 49ers and those Lancaster used as England's leader.

Pick out any of Walsh's 17 points and traces of them can be found in Lancaster's early stewardship of England. This was no coincidence. The Walsh Way was the Lancaster Way.

Take No. 1 – the ferocious work ethic.

In a Test week Lancaster would always be up before his players, often hitting the gym at 6 a.m. before attending to the matters of the day. Keeping himself in good shape kept him sharp mentally, gave him time to think and if it had the by-product of impressing his charges, then there was no harm in that either. He was habitually punctual – unlike the previous regime – and meticulously organised. Every hour in the A4 Collins diary, which accompanied him like a guide dog wherever he went, was filled.

How about No. 7 – showing self-control under pressure?

There is a spoof clip on Lancaster's laptop which shows a football manager and his assistant railing against the players, referee and the world in general from their dugout as a game unfolds. The assistant parrots the manager in increasingly animated fashion until they have completely lost control. As a coach, Lancaster views it as a useful template – for how not to conduct yourself.

It was true that he had needed two stitches in a cut finger after punching the roof of the coach's box at Murrayfield celebrating Charlie Hodgson's try in his first match in charge, but the only emotion the lens was allowed to see was positive. An almost imperceptible shake of the head was the maximum show of disappointment. Lancaster proved a waste of time for the hungry camera seeking an explosion from the coach during matches.

Or No. 11 – going the extra mile?

Lancaster made it a priority to pay regular visits to club

coaches to rebuild collapsed bridges and accumulate the inside information essential for him to make accurate selection decisions. If that meant undertaking a 600-mile return journey from his home in Leeds to see Rob Baxter, the Exeter director of rugby, and calling in at Gloucester on the way back, so be it. Keeping the club coaches informed and onside was a major part of the job in his view.

No. 12 – deal appropriately with victory and defeat, adulation and humiliation?

In his public dealings, Lancaster never seemed overly high after a win or low after a loss. It was hard to tell the difference in Lancaster as he spoke to the media after the defeat by Wales in his first Six Nations or the crushing win over Ireland which rounded off the tournament. There was a reassuring levelness about him in interviews which those behind the scenes saw replicated there.

It wasn't that he was disconnected – he was clearly under the skin of the England project – but he seemed able to put the outcomes in their appropriate boxes. It was partly because he had mentally prepared his responses – Walsh-like – to the differing scenarios of a good, bad or indifferent performance by his team.

Lancaster would bristle at the suggestion that he merely copied Walsh's blueprint. Spend time in his company and it is obvious he is his own man with his own mind and ideas. But he would also acknowledge he found much in the Californian's theories with which he could identify. Reading – and listening to – the American's words had the effect of crystallising and clarifying his own thinking.

Just as Walsh inherited a failing organisation which had lost its sense of direction, so did Lancaster. Both the 49ers and

England had senior-player cabals who had lost the true meaning of what it meant to wear the jersey. Lancaster's remedy mirrored that of Walsh – instil a standard of performance on and off the field which would deliver success as a natural by-product.

Underpinning those changes was the cultural revolution Lancaster set in motion aimed at re-establishing the England jersey as something to cherish and the rose as a badge of honour.

9

The Jersey

But if it be a sin to covet honour,
I am the most offending soul alive
Henry V, Act 4, Scene 3

When any new player joins Stuart Lancaster's England he is required to stand up in front of the rest of the squad and explain what it means to him to represent his country. The task requires him to think about the honour which has just been bestowed on him and set it in the context of his own life.

It is not just new caps who go through this. Players rejoining the squad after long-term injury also do so. For them it is a case of reaffirming their vows.

Billy Vunipola, the Saracens No. 8, went through the ceremony as a twenty-year-old. 'It's quite a special tradition they've started and one I think is very good,' he said. 'It's not hard to do. The rest of the squad aren't going to sit there laughing at you because it's a journey they have been on too so they can relate to it.'

Some choose to talk about how it represents a childhood

dream fulfilled or a triumph over adversity; others prefer to talk about the tremendous pride for their family. For many, articulating their innermost feelings is a highly emotional process and not one which might normally be associated with the alpha-male world of a physical-contact sport. Love – of family, of jersey or of country – is a very personal emotion. Talking about it requires an abnormally high level of trust within a group.

It is not hard to imagine the sniggering from the back if England's 2011 World Cup squad had convened for such a gathering. The off-field excesses in New Zealand had exposed a group of senior players who were living by their own rules. They might, at skin level, have felt proud to wear the England shirt but they had lost its deeper meaning.

When Lancaster took over as England interim head coach, armed with the wisdom of Bill Walsh and the limited experience of coaching the Saxons, he did not have the luxury of time. If he had won 12 per cent of his games in his first year in charge as Walsh had, he would have been out on his ear, so he had to implement phase one of his cultural revolution in a hurry. He did so by focusing on the power of the reason why.

Lancaster addressed this point in a revealing presentation to a gathering of the Leeds Rugby business network at the city's Marriott Hotel in December 2014. 'It was an unbelievable honour to be given the role of England head coach but I felt there was a piece missing. Some of the players had lost the reason why playing for England was special. I wanted to bring that back,' he told the spellbound suits in the room.

'A lot of people, when they build teams, talk about what they are going to do and how they're going to do it. They never talk about why working for a team is special. A lot of people forget why working for a team or organisation is special. I remember as a teacher going to training days and I was desperate for the head teacher just to put all the paperwork to one side and say "let's just talk about why we all want to be here. It's about getting kids better and motivating them." But he never did that.

'What we talked about constantly was reinforcing the reason why playing for England is special. We put it at the forefront of the players' minds.'

In standing up and telling their team-mates what representing England meant to them, the players were articulating the reason why.

Lancaster uses the image of three concentric circles. The outer circle contains the word 'what', the circle inside it the word 'how' and the smallest circle in the middle the word 'why'. It is an England Rugby version of what the management guru Simon Sinek has christened 'The Golden Circle'.

In business, most companies start from the outside and work their way inwards. They work out what they are going to do, decide how they are going to go about it and then, almost as an after thought, think why. The really high-performing exceptions start from the middle with why.

Sinek uses Apple as an example. Apple's 'why' is to challenge the status quo and think differently. It informs everything they do. From there flows 'how' – by making products that are beautifully designed and user-friendly – and 'what' – cool computers and smartphones. The spin-off, as opposed to the aim, is massive profits and global domination.

For a sports team, the instinctive response to the question of why is to win. But winning should be the spin-off of a purer driving force – those feelings players such as Billy Vunipola articulated when they stood in front of their team-mates. The honour of wearing the England jersey, the pride he has in representing his family and the determination he has to repay them for their sacrifice. By focusing on why representing England was special, Lancaster was starting at the heart of everything.

'As soon as I came on board, after the World Cup, I knew I had to get the players' attitudes right. They needed to think about the shirt and what it means,' said Lancaster. 'We had to get back to basics and to make sure the players were passionate about playing for England and filled with pride. It sounds simple but I think it was forgotten along the way.'

Lancaster gained traction straight away in that critical first week together at Weetwood Hall in Leeds with his demands for an improvement in behaviour and his restoration of pride in the rose. The players he had chosen wanted to be part of something they could be proud of.

Writing to each player's parents ahead of that first squad camp in Leeds and asking them to express their pride at seeing their son playing for England was intended to bring home the point that they were not just representing themselves. Asking the parents to contact the players' formative rugby coaches to articulate their feelings, too, spread the net a little wider.

To remind them further of their connection to the grass-roots game where they started – and their continuing responsibility to it – they walked out at Twickenham against South Africa alongside an under-12s player from the club where they had first played as juniors.

They were expected to be ambassadors, playing by the RFU's core values – teamwork, respect, enjoyment, discipline, sportsmanship. It was part of the dramatic overhaul in outlook away from 'me' and towards 'we' that Lancaster set in motion when he became England coach.

Lancaster has another diagram which explains his entire

development plan for England in one simple pyramid. It is divided into six horizontal layers. They read, from the bottom up, as follows: culture, identity, higher purpose, behaviours and standards, ownership, player leadership.

The top one is the point at which a mature team takes control of its own destiny, having first taken ownership of itself, policed itself, become respected and realised who it was.

Culture – the squad's behaviours and beliefs – is the structure's lowest, and widest, brick for a reason. It is the foundation stone on which everything else is constructed. Without it the whole edifice would collapse. 'I set about trying to rebuild that. You have to get the cultural foundations of your team and organisation right first, otherwise under pressure it will collapse,' said Lancaster.

'You can look at examples in other sports – or maybe us in 2011. When the heat comes on it falls apart very quickly. Corridor conversations take place, players start falling out with each other, coaches start doubting what you are doing and before you know it you are in a firestorm that you can't deal with. You need to have a very strong foundation to build a team on. And I think that probably took a year, if not longer.'

The launch base for the environment he strove to create – one of trust and openness, humility and honesty – was picking individuals who he thought would measure up to his exacting standards. They were not necessarily the best players.

'The start point to getting the right culture was getting the right people and that meant selecting on talent and character. I'd much prefer to have B+ talent and A grade character to start with than the other way around,' said Lancaster. 'Once we got the right people on the bus, we started talking about what it meant to play for England.'

Lancaster's policy from the start militated against the gifted maverick. If there were question marks over a player's willingness to conform he would have to work harder to earn a place in the England squad.

Lancaster's first squad in 2012 was patchy in terms of world-beating quality but strong on team players – grafters who would buy into his redesign. Nick Easter was excluded, so were the Armitage brothers and, while age and overseas employment provided a convenient explanation, they bore the look of square pegs for round holes in Lancaster's Roundhead England. The swallow-diving Chris Ashton was included but he was asked to think hard about his signature try-scoring celebration and to decide whether the Ash Splash was about the team or himself.

Forging an instant team spirit with such a new group was not straightforward but Lancaster had done it before when he took over at Leeds. He presented to them a cause they could all buy into and set up a working environment they looked forward to joining. The energy the newcomers brought helped disguise the inexperience of everyone involved.

Finishing second in the Six Nations' Championship with a completely new team melded from the fires of chaos was vindication of his policy and his selection approach.

Lancaster showed he was willing to give second chances to repentant sinners if they bought in. Danny Care was restored to the squad after his Six Nations exclusion for the summer tour to South Africa in 2012.

England lost the series 2-0 having been steamrollered early on at Johannesburg in the second Test when they shipped 22 points in the first 18 minutes. However a 14-14 draw in the third Test at Port Elizabeth spared them a series whitewash and allowed a young team to fly home with honour. Care was man of the match.

Before the tour the players had been shown cuttings of how

the World Cup misbehaviour had been reported. They were then told they had a choice of how they wanted to be remembered as an England player. There were no incidents involving any England player reported.

The back-room situation changed on that trip when backs' coach Andy Farrell, who had only been on loan to England, returned to Saracens. Mike Catt was brought in as a stand-in, effectively on trial. Lancaster was pleased with his contribution – one of his quirkier coaching methods was to whack tennis balls miles into the air for the restart catchers to pick off above their heads – and, when Farrell returned for good in the autumn after the RFU agreed a compensation fee with his club, Catt was kept on in an expanded management team for the autumn series. It was one which provided the first examination of the solidity of Lancaster's building blocks.

After a routine win over Fiji, England were outplayed by the Wallabies the following week and slumped to a disappointing defeat. The Springboks were next up. It was to be a bad day at the office.

A freakish try from Willem Alberts, which arrived when Ben Youngs' fly-hack bounced off wing J.P. Pietersen via Ben Morgan and into the Springbok behemoth's hands, put England up against it with time running out. England, four points adrift, were awarded a kickable penalty but with only three minutes remaining logic suggested they had to kick for the corner and try to drive the mighty Springbok pack over their own line. After some very obvious dithering, captain Chris Robshaw ordered an annoyed Owen Farrell to kick for goal instead of going after a try. He kicked the goal but England could not salvage the game and lost by a point.

Hammered in the media, who were already in the mood for

blood after defeat by Australia the previous week, England – and their captain in particular – were suddenly feeling the pinch.

Robshaw had spent the night awake worrying what the response from his team-mates would be to his blunder on his return into camp.

'I make the calls and, at the end of the day, it was all on me. The mix-up was the first time I'd experienced such negativity towards me and made me realise just how much my head is on a stake as captain,' admitted Robshaw in *Behind the Rose*, the history of the England team through the ages.

Robshaw turned up at the start of the next week at Pennyhill Park with a feeling of dread in his stomach but the collective closed ranks around him. One by one his team-mates came up to him and told him not to worry; they would win the next game. He was overwhelmed by the squad's support. They were all in it together. The failure was shared. And they would put it right against the All Blacks at the weekend.

If ever there was a time for self-belief to waver it was then. After back-to-back defeats at Twickenham, they had the finest team in the world lying in wait for them. But with Robshaw at the forefront, they delivered the finest England performance since Woodward's side won the 2003 World Cup, shredding New Zealand to pieces.

England's record 38-21 demolition of an All Blacks side, who had gone through the year unbeaten up until that point, announced Lancaster's side to the world. The glue had held.

Culture, in the context of a sports team, refers to how its members go about doing things. Most organisations, in trying to build their culture, tend to use props or rituals to re-enforce it.

There were some existing rituals in place in the England squad.

A tasselled red cap was given to every debutant, for instance, and a new boy had to sing a song after his debut. Some were better performers than others. Jonny Wilkinson wrecked 'Wonderwall' by Oasis as an eighteen-year-old on the team bus; New York-born Alex Corbisiero brought the house down in the home dressing room with an off-the-cuff rap on his first appearance.

Lancaster wanted something much more substantial at the heart of England rugby. He centred on the shirt. And a white shirt, too.

After seeing England take the field in an abomination of a kit against Australia, Lancaster issued a decree. No more purple – the colours of the St George's flag only. 'I had a big fall-out with the commercial department about wearing a purple shirt,' said Lancaster. 'They said that it was going to sell well. I told them that I didn't care; we're not wearing it. It is a white shirt and if we have to wear an away shirt, it is a red shirt. We only wear white or red now.'

John Mitchell, a New Zealander charged with coaching England's forwards in the early days of the Woodward regime, once spoke with awe of the purity of the white jersey hung up in the Twickenham dressing room. Lancaster persuaded his players to view it in the same way. It was less about the actual cloth itself than what it stood for.

'It's a special moment when they receive it before an international as it represents many things – those that have supported the players on their path to becoming an England player, former internationals who have worn the shirt before them, all those who are involved in and support the game and the English nation as a whole. That pride in wearing the shirt is massively important to the players,' said Lancaster.

The two Youngs brothers were brought up on the family

farm in Norfolk knowing what playing for England should mean. Their father, Nick, won six caps as a scrum-half for England in the eighties. One jersey may have been baggy, the other sprayed on but the red rose on the chest made them one and the same.

'When I speak to my dad that shirt is still part of him. I don't think it ever leaves you. He's part of that club forever, which is very special,' said Tom, the elder by two years. 'It's all about digging into what the shirt represents to you. It's about thinking about all those people who sacrificed a lot for you to get into that position – that can be parents driving you around the country when you were little or coaches who have really helped you along the way. When you put that shirt on, everyone who has played their part is wearing that shirt with you. It's understanding what you wearing it means to them as well.'

Just as Bill Walsh's 49ers would never abandon team kit on the floor, neither would Lancaster's England. 'You respect the shirt. You wouldn't see anyone chucking it around,' said Tom Youngs. 'You'd never see one lying around on the floor. It would always be folded up nicely.'

The shirt was the emblem of their togetherness.

England back row Tom Wood first wore it as a twenty-four-year-old against Wales in the 2011 Six Nations' Championship. 'The shirt is important to us as a team,' said Wood. 'We always talk about the idea of handing the shirt on in a better state and the fact that we are custodians of it only for a short time. We want to fill the shirt with belief and confidence for the next guys, show them the path if you like, and pave that for them so that they can walk in an England shirt that bit taller.'

An England team is a naturally discordant entity. International players spend comfortably less time with each other than with their clubs and those club rivalries can run deep. Players naturally gravitate to those they know best. The Leicester contingent within England was particularly tight when Lancaster took over.

It can take time to build trust between players who have been at each other's throats for their clubs a few days beforehand. Sometimes, as in the case of Brian Moore and Graham Dawe – two rivals for the England hooker's jersey who refused to speak to each other – that point never arrives.

So every time the national squad assembled, Lancaster would have the players back in their England training kit working together on the pitch as quickly as he could. He wanted them to click out of club mode and back into England's way of thinking as soon as possible. Injury absences made for a constant churn of players but working hard together immediately put them on common ground.

The new players coming into the England set-up were required to be open. When they first arrived in the squad they were asked to divulge three pieces of information about themselves that others might not know to help thaw the ice.

The faith Lancaster had in English rugby's upcoming talent meant that very often these were young players. They were treated as equals. Old-school rugger-bugger bullying was outlawed – there was no 'back seat' culture on the England bus. Players could sit where they wanted. They were also encouraged to contribute in team meetings from the start, not defer to seniority. Everyone had a voice.

Ultimately, though, there are only 15 positions available in a starting line-up, 23 in a match-day Test squad. Premiership first choices end up as bench-warmers with England or, even worse, holding the tackle bags at training before being sent back to their clubs midweek, surplus to requirements. It is an inevitable source of friction.

The trick for Lancaster was to create an England environment where the bigger picture took precedence over individual ambition. It went against the naked selfishness which often propels professional sportsmen – but he put a lot of time into making it work.

'I constantly look for things that take energy away from the team or that could cause damage to the culture,' he said. 'It could be an incident off the field, it could be negative media, it could be a person that's been dropped who doesn't like it and who has begun to change the mind-set of one or two of the players around him because he's not that happy.'

He was not alone. Bill Beswick headed a group of three observers, which included operations manager Tom Stokes and media manager Dave Barton, which checked for areas of stress in England's cultural framework.

Past England coaches might have thought of bacteria at the mention of culture but Wood viewed the relentless emphasis on it as essential. 'Where coaches can often slip up is that they focus so hard on results and the rugby detail that they forget that it is the strength of the group which underpins all that. Some coaches try to tag culture on the end with some gimmicky things – some entertainment or a few beers – but that's not really how it works,' said Wood. 'You need those strong foundations first and from that comes the tightness, the togetherness and a real trust in one another. When you respect each other and work hard for each other because you don't want to let your team-mates down – that is where the performance comes from. When you get to that stage you govern yourselves. You don't need any set rules or code of conduct because everyone knows the craic. You self-police.'

So the players also began to monitor the environment through a leadership group which met with Lancaster early in a Test week. It was an indication to Lancaster that the players had begun to build the England environment for him. The penny had dropped.

Wood was one of its members. 'The group don't necessarily talk about performance or the detail of the current game. It is more about standard-setting and taking ownership of the team. We set the trademarks of the team and the standards we want to live by,' said Wood.

As an example of the required behaviour inside Lancaster's England, the attitude towards litter was illustrative. 'Tidying the changing room was something that has traditionally been there in rugby but we had gone away from it a bit in the professional era,' explained Wood. 'Within a professional environment we are well looked after. We have protein shakes made for us after training and sometimes even shaken for us. If people then chuck the bottle at the bin and it bounces out on to the floor and just stays there, or they do the same with tape and strapping and then walk out and expect someone else to come and clean up after you, then what does that say about you? Nowhere else in the world is that acceptable but it became a bit of a habit within most rugby environments.'

If a player has not tidied up after himself he will be reminded by his peers to do so. If he has already left, they will do it for him just so long as the environment is left how they found it. It comes down to self-respect.

'We're a team that talks about humility and hard work and we should live it,' said Wood. 'Most rugby players are kids to a large extent. They've come straight out of school into a rugby academy and had everything done for them from nutrition to kit to sponsorship deals. Things come easy. It's not until you sit back and look at it and think, "That's a disgrace", that you begin to change.

'If a team wants to talk about its high standards, its attention to detail, its humility and work ethic, then to disrespect whoever is making you the protein shakes or giving you the water bottles is wrong.'

Lancaster's junior team at West Park Leeds had a rule which stated that drinks bottles had to be put back in the rack after they had been used. The point? In respecting the equipment, the player is respecting his team-mates – he doesn't want them to be drinking from a dirty bottle. So why not England?

'It is that kind of personal pride we want. We don't need someone to come and sweep up after us and take care of us – we take care of it ourselves,' said Wood.

'If we can trust each other to put our stuff in the bin and respect our environment, then we can trust each other to do our line-out homework and the extras we need on fitness and weights and taking care of our diets – the one per cents that make the difference on game day. It's not about crippling discipline that has everyone on edge all the time worrying about what they are doing, it's about having high standards and everyone being mindful of that. It makes a big difference.

'It is just a mind-set thing but it goes a long way. It is a case of living and breathing it and making sure you are a shining example of it so that when new guys come into the team they can see that straight away, respect it and get on board.'

How do Dave Attwood and Dave Wilson dutifully sweeping up England's training base to leave it spotless after the team have used it help them to win games? It doesn't – directly. But indirectly Lancaster was convinced, like Bill Walsh before him, that the ripple effects of such diligence, such devotion to the team environment, did have an effect.

It was not mere decoration. This was the base of the pyramid on which England was being rebuilt. 'I've studied great coaches and great teams and looked at what they believe and how they operate and there's a consistency about the best. The best are the ones that have the strongest culture, those who have a team ethic and a desire to work hard for each other,' said Lancaster.

'It's important in any sport but I think in a sport like rugby where you need a huge level of personal commitment and that commitment has to work through the team you can't have a strong team without having a strong culture.

'I would say it is what I think about most. I think about it more than scrums and line-outs and rucks and mauls.'

HIGHEST OF THE HIGH

England 38 New Zealand 21 – 1 December 2012 Twickenham, London

If New Zealand have more of the ball during a game they win. Simple as that. Come to think of it when New Zealand have less of the ball during a match they still tend to win.

So how was it that with 48 per cent of possession, England managed to inflict such a jarring defeat on an All Blacks side unbeaten in their previous 20 matches? Pressure.

Pressure in defence where they harried and hounded the world champions into mistakes they would never normally make, pressure at the breakdown where England won 13 turnovers and pressure in attack where New Zealand missed 18 tackles.

Physical pressure, too. Where once it was Englishmen

running scared of an adopted South Seas Islander, this time it was New Zealand who were unable to handle the physical presence of an East Midlands Samoan. It was Manu Tuilagi playing Jonah Lomu as the All Blacks were routed.

Tuilagi scored the third of three second-half tries in what was England's first victory over the All Blacks for nine years.

England had gone into the game with their backs against the wall following successive defeats to Australia and South Africa but the response was breathtaking. And the noise…this was polite old Twickenham transformed into a seething bear pit.

'We'd lost two games against Australia and South Africa, people had turned a bit and were questioning where we were going but the energy the crowd gave us against New Zealand was unbelievable,' Stuart Lancaster told a huddle of newspaper writers at Twickenham that evening.

'For me, as a coach, it was the highest point so far because we had played the world champions, coming in unbeaten in twenty, and had put in a performance that had beaten a hugely talented and experienced team fair and square. You feel the need to get the win to show people the clarity of what we are doing. But then I had never doubted the direction in which we were going.'

The pre-match criticism had served as fuel for the fire for a side who had quickly grown into a close unit. 'We were getting a lot of stick but it brought us together. You could feel it during the week. There was a great buzz around everyone,' recalled hooker Tom Youngs.

'Chris [Robshaw] was getting a bit of stick about his decision-making and it was about looking after him and keeping him upbeat. It was a week where we were thinking "what have we got to lose? Let's just go out there and throw everything at it." The atmosphere at Twickenham was one of the best I've ever experienced. It was unbelievable and things just clicked out there. It happens sometimes in a game of rugby where everything goes your way – the bounce of the ball, decisions – and we could just feel it that day.'

England came out at Twickenham like a side possessed. They rocked New Zealand from the start, squeezed them at the scrum and hammered them in the tackle and at the ruck. By the interval they had built up a 12-0 lead from Owen Farrell's kicking. Another penalty just afterwards made it 15-0.

'It was all about line speed in defence and we created some havoc there. They were spilling balls, which was very unlike New Zealand. They were struggling to get any rhythm in their game. We were piling the pressure on them,' said Youngs.

The All Blacks were too good a team simply to stand aside and allow this to happen to them. Converted tries by Julian Savea and Kieran Read cut the lead to a single point and swung the momentum New Zealand's way. Suddenly it looked a very different match.

'They just came at us – boom, boom, boom – and we were thinking: "Jesus, how do we stop this?" We had to regroup quickly,' said Youngs. 'But we told ourselves not to panic because we were still in the lead.'

England did not falter. They did not crack. Their

self-belief did not desert them. Instead they rolled up their sleeves and hit New Zealand hard again.

Brad Barritt's one-two with Tuilagi brought a try for Barritt to give England the initiative again. Then Tuilagi made a big hole in the New Zealand defence to put Chris Ashton over for another try which he celebrated with a euphoric swan dive. 'I had no intention of doing the Ash Splash and I really had no idea of where it came from!' said Ashton later. Lancaster let that one go.

Moments later, England were over again with Tuilagi intercepting Read's pass and sending Twickenham into ecstasy.

Sir Clive Woodward rated it England's finest performance since they won the World Cup; his 2003 scrum-half Matt Dawson called it England's greatest win of all time at Twickenham. While that was debatable, it was statistically England's biggest margin of victory against New Zealand – and indisputably their finest display under Lancaster.

The All Blacks tend to be hard to impress but not on this occasion. Only once in their 109-year history had they lost by a bigger margin. Dan Carter called England 'brilliant' and their coach Steve Hansen, on the wrong end of his first defeat as head coach, elevated England into the top bracket of world rugby. 'There were two teams out there capable of winning the World Cup. They should be proud of what they have achieved,' said Hansen.

England: Goode; Ashton, Tuilagi, Barritt, Brown; Farrell, B. Youngs; Corbisiero, T. Youngs, Cole, Launchbury, Parling, Wood, Robshaw, Morgan.

Wakefield's Caldy Sevens-winning squad in 1991. Lancaster, back row, second from right next to coach Jim Kilfoyle in a team which also included England wing Jon Sleightholme (front left)

Behind the Iron Curtain with St Bees prior to facing Yugoslavia under-21s in Split. Lancaster is front row, third from right with future Scotland international Stuart Reid back row, fourth from left in a line-up led by England Sevens player Howard Graham. Coach Tony Rolt, Lancaster's first rugby influence, is on the back row, far right

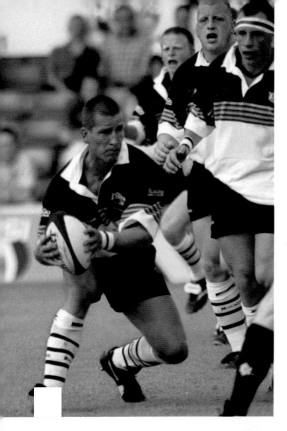

Lancaster as a ball-playing
back row for Leeds

The start of the coaching road

'Have we got 15?' Spelling it out to the Leeds loyalists

Landing promotion at the first attempt,
Lancaster celebrates at Headingley

The England pack on ploughing duty in the Pennyhill Park scrum garden

Singing the national anthem before his first Six Nations' match as England coach against Scotland, the country he played for at youth level

Deep in thought as England prepare to play at Twickenham

The brains trust. From left England's coaching team of Mike Catt, Graham Rowntree, Lancaster and Andy Farrell at Pennyhill Park

The captain. Chris Robshaw has taken his share of criticism but Lancaster has stuck resolutely by his man

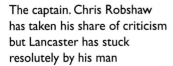

The work ethic. Lancaster mucks in during England training

Joe Launchbury wins lineout possession against New Zealand en route to England's spectacular victory over the All Blacks at Twickenham in 2012

The jersey. Pristine England shirts awaiting the players in the redesigned Twickenham dressing room

Chris Robshaw shows off the Hillary Shield later that stunning day

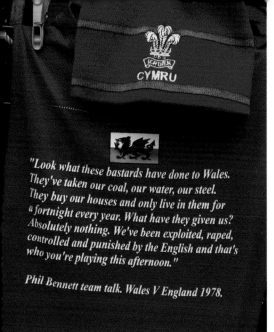

"Look what these bastards have done to Wales. They've taken our coal, our water, our steel. They buy our houses and only live in them for a fortnight every year. What have they given us? Absolutely nothing. We've been exploited, raped, controlled and punished by the English and that's who you're playing this afternoon."

Phil Bennett team talk. Wales V England 1978.

Incendiary Welsh merchandise available outside the Millennium Stadium ahead of the 2013 Six Nations' decider

Playing against a nation – Wales fans turn up the heat on England

England's players feel the pain as their Grand Slam goes up in smoke and so does the championship

England's management show what it means to win at the Millennium Stadium in the dramatic 2015 Six Nations' opener

Jack Nowell holds off Rory Kockott to cross for England's seventh try with five minutes left against France at Twickenham

So close. England fall one converted try short of the title after one of the most extraordinary days in the championship's history

The inner circle. Stuart Lancaster looks on as his England squad gather together in training during the 2015 Six Nations' Championship

Man on a mission. Stuart Lancaster marches down the Twickenham tunnel

Replacements: Joseph for Tuilagi (66), Burns for Farrell (64), Care for B. Youngs (68), M. Vunipola for Corbisiero (66), Paice for T. Youngs (72), Wilson for Cole (72), Lawes for Launchbury (66), Haskell for Morgan (57).

New Zealand: Dagg; Jane, C. Smith, Nonu, Savea; Carter, A. Smith; Woodcock, Mealamu, O. Franks, Retallick, S. Whitelock, Messam, McCaw, Read. **Replacements:** B. Smith for Dagg (71), Cruden for Carter (64), Weepu for A. Smith (64), Crockett for Woodcock (66), Coles for Mealamu (62), Faumuina for O. Franks (52), Romano for Retallick (48), Vito for Messam (63).

Referee: George Clancy (Ireland).

10

The England Plan

When we mean to build
We first survey the plot, then draw the model
Henry IV Part 2, Act 1, Scene 3

In January 2013 the England squad was shown a plan that was as comprehensive in its scope as any of them had seen before. It outlined what would happen every day of their lives as England players until the date of the Rugby World Cup final on 31 October 2015.

The calendar covered everything from coaching and conditioning to analysis, training science and medicine. The man who had drawn it up was called Matt Parker. By his own admission, he knew nothing about rugby.

When he took the England job Stuart Lancaster was asked by the RFU if he would consider having a manager above him to help with the workload. His answer was that what he actually needed was someone below him – a strategist who could help shape the long-term way ahead for the team. He wanted someone who was capable of pulling together the different strands of elite-sport preparation and plaiting them into a strong enough rope to drag the team in the direction he wanted them to go.

As Bill Walsh had noted, planning is essential to the wellbeing and prosperity of a team. It provides a framework to work within and stability under stress and Lancaster was a fully paid-up member of the spreadsheet-appreciation society.

He had the vision of where he wanted England to go so for the detail Lancaster turned to Britain's most successful sport at the London Olympics – cycling. Parker had made his name as lead coach with the British 4,000m team pursuit squad, extracting a staggering nine-second improvement from them in 18 months. They took gold at the Beijing Olympics in 2008 and broke the world record. After that he worked with Bradley Wiggins for two years, pushing him to an unexpected fourth place in the 2009 Tour de France before heading back to the track to oversee the London medal avalanche. When Parker was brought in by Lancaster as head of athletic performance, it was a leap into the unknown.

'I don't have any background in rugby,' he explained, standing in front of a big screen in a conference room at Pennyhill Park on which is depicted the outline of England's World Cup plan.

'I played a little bit at school, as most people did, but not having a background in it means I had no preconception about the right way of doing things. I was never going to come in and say straight away: "This is how we prepare for a World Cup". It fitted with Stuart evolving the culture and the team.

'I wanted to use my experience of high-performance environments and delivering under pressure to come up with a plan to produce our best at a home World Cup. I've been through three Olympics, including a home Olympics. I felt this was a challenge I couldn't turn down. There aren't many opportunities that come up like working with England Rugby at a home World Cup.'

Once Parker was on board, Lancaster presented him with his vision of what a World Cup-winning side would look like – how many caps it would contain, what its average age would be, what its conditioning and tactical requirements would be. Then they worked backwards together to fill in the blanks as to how the side might arrive there.

Backwards planning was new to English rugby but not to Parker, who had used it in British Cycling. Set the time you believe will win the team pursuit gold at the next Olympics and work out the selection and training schedule which will allow you to arrive there.

The 2015 Rugby World Cup was the first target but not the end point. Parker's remit was to co-ordinate all long-term performance planning. Away from the glare of the spotlight, he is already working on the path through to 2019 in Japan.

Parker is an unassuming, low-key figure who happily slips into the background but he has a mind for detail which appealed to Lancaster. Originally from Staffordshire, he studied physiology at Glasgow University and initially headed into the NHS before joining the Institute of Sport in Manchester. He worked in swimming, squash and athletics before making his name in cycling.

When he joined England Rugby, Parker was put in charge of a high-performance team which included five medical staff, two analysts, two strength-and-conditioning staff, a sports scientist, a psychologist and a nutritionist. England was thankfully not the Third World sporting set-up he had feared. The players already had an app on their RFU-issue iPads which gave them access to video footage of previous England games, upcoming opposition and instructions from the conditioning staff. And the analysis the players themselves would routinely undertake in camp was well ahead of what he had expected.

'When I was in cycling no one was talking about rugby at all so when I came in I expected it to be a bit further back but there were a lot of good people doing a lot of good work,' he said. 'The key for me was getting it all on the same page and relating it towards delivering the game plan – it's one of the big challenges in many sports.

'Our job as a performance team is to be world class with an ambition to be world leading so the players have everything in their tool box to perform. The coaches tell us what each player's job is and everything we do is aligned to prepare him to do it. Every day it's making sure we have this mental checklist of maintaining our standards and keeping everything as sharp as it could be.'

British Cycling had thrived on the theory of marginal gains – picking apart preparation into its constituent parts, seeing what could be improved and then putting it back together again. It entailed aerodynamic helmets, hot pants to keep thigh muscles warm between races and alcohol sprays for tyres to improve traction. England wanted Parker to transfer that attention to the nuts and bolts of their environment. In rugby it was less about the gadgets than finding minor improvements in the training regime which, when put together, could make a difference. It was about bringing order to a game of chaos.

'Marginal gains was a philosophy. Details are important and you need to look at the details in everything you do on a day-to-day basis and work hard at them,' said Parker. 'You look at the environment, you look at the game plan the coaches are looking to deliver and its demands and then you put a plan together. My natural style is to go about my business in a quiet way, ask questions and problem-solve. It's not often one thing comes along which gives you a 10 or 15 per cent jump in performance. There was Dick Fosbury and the Fosbury Flop in the high jump, McLaren and the F-duct in Formula One [the driver-controlled system which altered the airflow and dramatically reduced drag to gain a speed advantage down the straight] but not many others. While you are chasing the big leap you can miss the day-to-day details, the little one per centers.

'Have you presented the information clearly to the players so that they have understood it? Have they real clarity about what you want from a session? Do they know how to prepare themselves for the session? Do they know how to recover best afterwards? Have you worked with them on an individual basis afterwards to make sure they are set up for the next one? Are we being accurate in a session? Are they using good technique? Are they doing it at the right times?'

Rugby union proved a more complicated environment to work in than cycling. The injury count was higher, the number of athletes greater. Emotional swings also appeared to govern performance to a greater degree. While an avenging England side on the rebound was able to summon up an extraordinary performance in beating New Zealand, they were unable to match Wales's intensity after five successive wins in the 2013 Six Nations' Championship decider three-and-a-half months later.

England rode the wave of their show-stopping win over the All Blacks at the start of the championship to set up a Grand Slam shot against Wales but the ripples, which had been continuing with steadily decreasing force, came to a complete standstill in the decider.

The ferocity which a Wales team more experienced in games of such magnitude brought to bear was telling. England were blown apart 30-3 at the Millennium Stadium. It requires perfect timing to reach the emotional peak on game day but they were taught a devastating lesson in harnessing emotion and channelling it into a match-winning performance.

'No stone was left unturned to make sure we got a performance out there. I just think that when you haven't been to a place and experienced what it is about it is difficult to try to replicate that,' reflected James Haskell.

England thought they were ready for everything Wales would throw at them but, clearly, they weren't.

The mental readiness of the England team during the build-up to a game is assessed by the psychologist Bill Beswick. He helps to monitor the squad during the week to ensure they are on track. 'I look at body language. I look for buzz, enthusiasm, energy, eye contact, purpose, and I judge where we are in terms of mind-set for the week. It is different on a Monday to a Thursday. If I feel it necessary, which very often I don't, I'll wander over to Stuart and suggest a recalibration,' said Beswick.

The working week for a home Saturday game follows a similar pattern each time. The squad gathers on Sunday evening at Pennyhill Park ahead of a nine o'clock meeting on Monday morning where the previous week's game will be reviewed and the scene set for the week ahead.

After weights, the squad will head out on to the training field for a training session split into two groups with the backs overseen by Andy Farrell and Mike Catt and the forwards drilled by Graham Rowntree before coming together for a team session in the afternoon. This session is always directed by

Lancaster. It is where he shapes, hands-on, the side's direction for the week ahead.

His assistants take control on Tuesday, the heaviest training day for the players, with a team training session either side of lunch. These will cover the moves the team will use at the weekend and the tools they are likely to need against a specific opposition. The morning session will also include work in their units when Catt helps the forwards with their skills.

Wednesday is a day off. International rugby is an intense environment and a fallow day during the week for an outbreak of normality is a mental – as well as physical – restorative. The squad reconvenes on Wednesday evening ahead of Thursday morning's team meeting and training.

Friday is captain's run morning at Twickenham when the players run through a few basic plays on the pitch before an afternoon off for their own personal preparation.

Threaded through the week will be opportunities for the players to pay their personal visits to the analysis suite to bone up on the opposition or their own training.

The computers are in the hotel but the rest of the work is done at a gleaming new on-site training centre set back from the long, tree-lined drive at Pennyhill Park, away from inquisitive eyes. The complex, which was part of a £3million overhaul of their England training facility, includes a spacious gym and a 40m x 40m 3G indoor pitch. Its specific purpose is to enable England to align their training much more closely with match situations than previously.

The proximity of its different areas allows England to combine draining physical lifting with hand–eye co-ordination work, mirroring rugby's blend of brute force and dexterity. Forwards move from indoor weights sessions straight outside into the area Rowntree refers to lovingly as his 'scrum garden' – an outdoor artificial surface conspicuously low on hardy perennials and herbaceous border plants – for short, sharp workouts on the scrum machines. Fifteen minutes on a Tuesday; 15 minutes on a Thursday. But with muscles screaming.

GPS equipment and heart-rate monitors fitted into the players' training kit monitor their output so as to ensure they are being stretched but not overstretched.

Professional rugby union has gone full circle since its painful birth pangs in the mid-nineties. The amateur era had seen the authorities actively legislate against excellence. International Rugby Board regulations had banned teams from training together more than 48 hours before a game.

When the amateur walls were torn down and players were suddenly relieved of the demands of day jobs, the temptation for coaches with players suddenly available for 24 hours a day was to train them for 24 hours a day. They were flogged. Gradually, the onus changed to shorter, but much more intense sessions, with the spare hours filled with analysis and rehabilitation instead.

'All the training is at the intensity of what you'd expect at a Test match,' said prop Dan Cole.

For Chris Robshaw, it is not so much the physical strain this puts on the players as the mental stress which is beneficial.

'We try to simulate pressure during training,' explained Robshaw. 'Whenever we train we do so at intensity so that the mind's not thinking as clearly as it would if there was no pressure. You need to be able to react and think in the correct manner when the pressure's on and we practise that. We don't hang around talking about things for a couple of minutes. We just go "there, there, there, back, OK you've done that, run back there, do this. OK you've dealt with that now you have to get out of this situation". You don't have two minutes thinking "what shall we do here?".

'It is about replicating things under the most intense pressure. Of course there's nothing quite like a Saturday but you need to build it up so that when you are there you hopefully know how to deal with it.'

James Haskell has trained in environments in France, Japan and New Zealand in his globe-trotting career and he found Lancaster's England set-up to be the sharpest and most challenging he had worked in. 'The attention to detail is persistently there. Everything is very calculated. You don't feel there is any box ticking when it comes to training. There is an ultra-high level of professionalism,' said Haskell. 'Everything has a purpose. The standards are consistently pushed. You never feel settled.'

That is the aim, according to Parker. Bespoke training sessions for matches. 'It's very easy to fill your training with junk,' he said. 'We will train for an hour and we try to make it very specific so the players understand why they are doing each part and that it fits the detail of the final plan.'

The devil is in the detail and every training session is filmed. Line-outs, scrums, backline moves are broken down in the analysis room where the numbers are crunched by England's video analysts Duncan Locke and Mike Hughes and the footage broken down for the coaches and players to study and assess.

'We review every session we do,' said Owen Farrell. 'The thing with our sessions is that they're not massively long so you can't repeat, you move on. If I've got something wrong I might grab someone who plays outside me and say "let's have a look at that after training". We'd sit there and watch training together. Sometimes taking a step back and having a look at it from a distance rather than being right in it on the pitch is massively beneficial.'

England, with Parker on board, were constantly on the look-out for an edge. Christian Cook, a Kiwi physiologist who had worked with the All Blacks and for UK Sport ahead of the 2012 Olympics, was introduced behind the scenes as a consultant to help with the strength-and-conditioning programme.

One of his fields of expertise is the interaction between hormone levels and performance and in particular the science of recovery, to which England paid particular attention. Mobile cryotherapy chambers – deep freezes on wheels – were brought in to the England camp. After games, players would stand in the nitrogen-cooled chambers for periods of up to three minutes at temperatures of -135 degrees C. It served to reduce inflammation and joint pain and help players sleep – the most important component of all in recovery.

A partnership was set up with a research laboratory nearby owned by GlaxoSmithKline. England players were sent there to have their sweat levels tested and the results used to determine hydration requirements and lengths of recovery sessions before being sent on to the squad's suppliers to help with the design of the World Cup kit.

For players who had experienced the previous regime, such as Bath's genial Geordie prop David Wilson who had made his England debut in 2009 in the Martin Johnson era, the scientific emphasis represented a shift in thinking. 'It is different to what it was like before. Stuart brought the right people in with the right experience and created the right environment for us to play well. We have everything we need,' he said.

'There is a lot more sports science involved in areas like

training methods and nutrition which makes us more aware of the one per centers which could make the difference in a close game.'

It is a smart environment and a computer-savvy one but, for all the lure of marginal gains, something much more basic lies at England's heart. 'It's not a science project. You can overdo it and start thinking you are cleverer than you really are and adding stuff in because you want to see it, not because it is the right thing for the players,' admitted Parker.

'Performances are based on hard work, commitment and the talent of the players. If you don't have that, there's not much point adding the rest. There's no point adding 5 per cent if you are 20 per cent off. The culture and the work ethic is what will define a winning team. Our training culture is very simple – hard work, discipline, honesty.'

When England won the Rugby World Cup in 2003 they needed extra time. When New Zealand lifted the trophy in 2011 they did so hanging on by their fingernails in the last seconds. They had to push right the way to the 80th minute. Success demands individuals prepared to go the extra mile. It is ultimately up to England's players how hard they drive themselves – and how far they push each other.

When Parker unveiled his performance chart to the England team he also outlined to the players an image of what a winning team should look like. It is a photo of the England team, arms around each other, as the national anthem is being played at Twickenham, overlaid with five phrases:

1. Clear direction
2. Good people
3. Performance plan

4. Relentless pursuit of excellence

5. Winning culture.

Good people? Parker, by his own admission knew little about the rugby, but he saw in some of those Lancaster had chosen echoes of the relentlessness which characterised Wiggins and Sir Chris Hoy.

'The commitment to training on a day-to-day basis is that of a team that wants to be the best in the world,' he said. 'You need good people. We want to be the best in the world so we need players who are committed to being the best in the world themselves. Every great athlete I have worked with has wanted to be the best. It isn't just about winning; it's about wanting to be the best in the world.'

Parker persuaded Wiggins – a Wigan rugby league fan – to visit the England squad to impart his knowledge of what it took to reach the very top. His testimony was rendered all the more compelling to the players because of his frankness. He confessed to squandering his early chances before realising how much of himself he had to give to his pursuit of greatness if he wanted to fulfil his potential.

'Bradley Wiggins was pretty inspirational. We took a lot from him,' said Wilson. 'He made us understand what it actually takes to be the best. He was a normal guy who had worked so hard to get to where he did.

'He was completely honest about what he did wrong earlier on in his career and why it hadn't worked out and then all the sacrifices he made to make sure that it did in the end. You can relate to people like that.'

While guest speakers with Olympic gold medals such as Wiggins and yachtsman Ben Ainslie turned the heads of the players, it was a talk by a cricketer which made a lasting impression on Lancaster.

Andrew Strauss, the former England captain, visited the squad at the start of 2013 to pass on his thoughts on how his side had made it to the top of the world rankings. However, he also made a point which struck home on the folly of failing to set extended goals.

While England's cricket team had created a detailed plan on how to become number one in the world and achieved it, they had nothing left to strive for once they had climbed their Everest. And so they fell off a cliff. His advice to the rugby team was not to limit the scale of their ambition even to something as monumental as winning a home World Cup.

It underlined to Lancaster the importance of looking beyond the next training session, the next match, the next series and the next World Cup. So while the outward plan ran to the 2015 World Cup final, the real plan had no end goal. It was something altogether more esoteric and less measurable – continuous high performance.

Parker, the man who joined the dots, knew what that felt like, having worked in the medal factory that is British Cycling. His assessment was that the England environment under Lancaster looked very similar.

'What he has instilled in the culture of the whole group, not just the playing team, feels like high performance,' said Parker. 'That's critical for sustaining success at the highest level.'

When you mention continuous high performance in rugby union, there is one team which springs immediately to mind. If England's intricately planned revolution was to take them to the very top they would have to deal with New Zealand.

LOWEST OF THE LOW

Wales 30 England 3 – 16 March 2013, Millennium Stadium, Cardiff

The Grand Slam – the greatest prize the Six Nations' Championship has to offer. Tantalisingly close for England after four wins out of four. Just one more hurdle to clear. Wales. At the Millennium Stadium.

England arrived full of hope...and departed empty-handed, the victims of a brutal mugging.

Stuart Lancaster had never played in a game of such magnitude and never coached in one with so much on the line. That day he learned the power of patriotic fervour and the polarising effect of the really big occasion.

His lieutenants – Catt, Rowntree and Farrell – had first-hand experience of such occasions and had done their best to prime the players on what was coming but, in the end, they were swamped by a tidal wave of red.

'When we lost at the Millennium Stadium, we weren't just playing against fifteen players; we were playing against twenty-three players, the Millennium Stadium and a nation. The power of that force against us was huge,' admitted Lancaster afterwards. It was, he said, the lowest point of his coaching career.

There could hardly have been more on the line. A Grand Slam for England, the championship for Wales in a final-round shoot-out which doubled as a trial for Lions selection ahead of the 2013 tour to Australia.

Warren Gatland, the Wales and Lions coach, has unguardedly mentioned that having too many Englishmen on a Lions tour is not a good idea – that was never going to be a problem after England were outplayed man for man by his rampant side.

Two-thirds of the England starting line-up had never played in the Millennium Stadium before and they were taken aback by the febrile atmosphere which drove Wales that day.

England are a prize coconut on a shy to most of the teams they play against and however much Lancaster had improved their image at home and abroad, they were still wanted men with a bounty on their heads when they arrived in Cardiff. Wales, on their own patch, needed no motivation beyond the sight of the white shirt to energise them.

The fact that they could deprive England of a Grand Slam and steal the title themselves if they won by at least seven points only added to an explosive mix. Wales went bang; England's dreams went up in smoke.

'If I'm honest there was a little bit of inexperience at play. It was the first time some of us had played at the Millennium Stadium,' said hooker Tom Youngs. 'The pace for the first forty minutes was just unbelievable and my lungs were burning. They were feeding off the crowd.

'We absorbed so much pressure, we survived a series of pick-and-gos on our line and we thought we'd come through it but then there was more to come. We just couldn't get the ball – they controlled it very well.'

It was only 9-3 to Wales at the break but England were creaking having blown an early chance when Manu Tuilagi knocked on.

Outmanoeuvred after the break at the scrum by Adam

Jones, who had Joe Marler, Mako Vunipola and referee Steve Walsh right where he wanted them, England went off-script for the first time under Lancaster as the game began to slip away. They lost their direction as they fell behind to the first of Alex Cuthbert's two tries. By the time the wing went over again, the stadium was shaking and England were gone. Cries of 'easy, easy' rang from the delirious Wales fans.

'You're tuned in to what is happening on the pitch and trying to block out the atmosphere but when you go twenty-five points down with a couple of minutes left and there's no chance of winning you just want the referee to blow the whistle and to get out of there,' said Tom Croft, whose final-minute fumble and sliced kick into the stands summed up the frustration. 'We compounded error on error – when we made one mistake, we panicked and then made another – and they just ran away with the game.'

Wales, carried along on a crashing tide of euphoria, took the title for the second season in a row.

'It was nice to score the tries but the forwards were the guys that won it for us. They bullied England,' said Cuthbert. 'I felt in command from the word go. It was just a matter of time before we broke through and when we did we were clinical. It was definitely the best Welsh performance I have been a part of.

'To win it like that against England when both teams were striving for the trophy was an amazing feeling.'

Man of the match Justin Tipuric rubbed it in. 'England had a good Six Nations but when it really came to it, man for man, they were not as good as Wales. The bubble has been burst,' he said.

As Wales celebrated, Chris Robshaw gathered the England team into a huddle on the pitch and told them to absorb the euphoric scenes they saw around them. To take it in. To feel the pain. To remember the day.

They could hardly have forgotten it. 'It felt horrendously flat afterwards in the changing room. It was one of the worst feelings – all we wanted to do was just go home,' said Youngs. 'We went back to the hotel and virtually all of us sloped off to bed.'

It was not just the Grand Slam that had gone.

'Not only had we thrown away a chance of a Grand Slam but we'd thrown away the Six Nations as well,' said Croft.

Little emphasis had been placed on adapting to a changing situation mid-game and playing for the narrow defeat which would have at least brought the Six Nations' title. While raising the trophy at the Millennium Stadium as a defeated side would have been a hollow feeling, it would still have been England's first championship of the Lancaster era.

England had made huge strides under the new regime but they remained a grand design in progress. As Robshaw subsequently admitted: 'I don't know if we were quite ready for a Grand Slam game and for them a championship game in the heart of Wales. Did we panic a bit? Yes, we did – and I'd include myself in that.'

Wales: Halfpenny; Cuthbert, Davies, Roberts, North; Biggar, Phillips; Jenkins, Hibbard, A. Jones, A.W. Jones, Evans, Warburton, Tipuric, Faletau.

Replacements: Shingler for Roberts (75), Hook for Biggar (75), L. Williams for Phillips (75), James for Jenkins (61), Owens for Hibbard (52), Coombs for Evans (70), S. Williams for Warburton (75).

England: Goode; Ashton, Tuilagi, Barritt, Brown; Farrell, B. Youngs; Marler, T. Youngs, Cole, Launchbury, Parling, Croft, Robshaw, Wood.

Replacements: Twelvetrees for Goode (64), Flood for Farrell (67), Care for B. Youngs (64), M. Vunipola for Marler (44), Hartley for T. Youngs (52), Wilson for Cole (72), Lawes for Launchbury (52), Haskell for Wood (67).

Referee: Steve Walsh (Australia).

11

Know Your Enemies

As greatness knows itself
Henry IV Part 1, Act 4, Scene 3

New Zealand's ability to dominate rugby union consistently is, when you think about it, freakish.

They have a smaller playing population than Ireland yet the All Blacks are arguably the most successful international team in any major sport, maintaining a win rate above 75 per cent throughout their existence. Not only that but they seem to be getting even better. Between winning the 2011 World Cup and June 2015 they lost only two Tests out of 42.

In the summer of 2013, while the Lions were playing in Australia, Stuart Lancaster boarded a plane and went to find out their secret. If England were going to learn from any of their rivals it might as well be from the best.

The English, being an island race, have a propensity to look inwards. It can be a source of strength when wagons need to be circled but also a weakness. It is a big world out there and there is a lot you can miss if you are staring at yourself.

Lancaster, having played all his rugby in the north of England, and been brought up in the English coaching system, had a very narrow world rugby view when he took over as the national team's coach. He had visited the bars of their Six Nations' opponents in his earlier days but never the changing rooms. He had never even set foot in South Africa when he assumed the position. Rarely can a Test coach have been as green about his rivals.

Lancaster accepted this and confronted it head-on. He made it his business to find out what made England's opponents tick. Before each Test, he would commission a scouting report not only on the opposition players and coaches and the venue for away matches but also a dossier on their prevailing rugby psychology.

In the case of South Africa, he indulged in a reading blitz which saw him swallow whole the autobiographies of Jake White, Victor Matfield, John Smit and Butch James before the side toured there in the summer of 2012. He also flew out himself to the country prior to the tour to check out England's bases and get a first-hand feel of rugby's place in that society.

On his way out to New Zealand a year later, he stopped off in Australia. He visited the New South Wales Waratahs and three leading rugby league clubs – Sydney Roosters, Melbourne Storm and the South Sydney Rabbitohs – to see what made their environments special. Then he called in on Aussie Rules side the Geelong Cats, from whom he borrowed the idea of the positional legends boards which sit in the Twickenham dressing room.

Searching abroad for ideas was an approach Sir Clive Woodward had used to his advantage during his time as England coach. Woodward, whose own thinking on how the game should be played was shaped to a great degree by his time as a player in Sydney, paid visits to the Denver Broncos American football team from where he transplanted the idea of big back-room teams and specialist coaches which was to become commonplace in rugby union.

He employed a South African visual skills coach, Sherylle Calder, later used by golfer Ernie Els when he won The Open at Royal Lytham in 2012, to expand his squad's peripheral vision, sending them for regular laptop workouts in her virtual eye gym.

He even suggested a joint World Cup warm-up camp with France in 2003 to share knowledge. The offer was turned down by his startled French counterpart Bernard Laporte. Woodward was wide open to new ideas from overseas.

Lancaster, too, was interested in how other countries went about their business, but New Zealand rugby and the legend of the All Blacks fascinated him above all else.

When he flew out in 2013, they were the world champions, the world's top-ranked side and on their way to becoming the first team in the professional era to go through a calendar year unbeaten. He had arranged to visit one of the grandees of New Zealand rugby, Sir Brian Lochore, to pick his brains about the Kiwi conveyor belt of success.

Lochore was Mr All Blacks. He captained them in 18 Tests, coached them to the 1987 World Cup and had also served as team manager. If anyone knew what made them tick, Lochore did.

Lancaster asked him two simple but fundamental questions. 'Why are New Zealand so good?' and 'What is your perception of England?'

Lochore was honest in his second answer – the word 'arrogant' did rear its ugly head – but his first answer was much more detailed. What he said served to deepen Lancaster's commitment to his English cultural revolution.

When confronted by their extraordinary statistics, it is easy to fall into the trap of assuming that everything has always been rosy in the All Blacks' garden. Flick through the history books and there aren't too many fallow periods.

Lochore, however, was one of the eight men convened in a room in Wellington as recently as 2004 to deal with a major crisis at the top of the game in New Zealand. When he talked about the backdrop to that crisis summit, it was one which sounded familiar to an Englishman such as Lancaster.

By New Zealand's standards the All Blacks were on the slide that year. True, they had won a home series against the world champions England but it was an England side that had tipped over the edge with Martin Johnson and Neil Back retired and Jonny Wilkinson, Jason Robinson and Phil Vickery injured. Successive defeats by Australia and South Africa in the Tri Nations were a more accurate reflection of where the All Blacks stood. In both games an alarming lack of leadership arose when the team had come under pressure. It was not so much the results which hit home – although the 40-26 drubbing by the Springboks at Ellis Park was a shocker – but what was happening behind the scenes.

A court session took place in Johannesburg after that defeat which appeared to show a team that had gone off the rails.

The performance had been poor enough – if South Africa's Percy Montgomery had not missed 13 points with the boot New Zealand could have been in record-defeat territory – but what followed looked more like something out of an unruly amateur club on tour.

The huge amounts of alcohol consumed in punishments left drunken players strewn all over the team hotel and its grounds, throwing up into the shrubbery. Some had to be helped to bed. As an advertisement for an elite sporting organisation it stank. There was a total disregard for the squad's reputation. 'There was a social occasion that I was appalled to be part of,' admitted the All Blacks coach Graham Henry, a former headmaster.

It was New Zealand's England 2011 World Cup moment – a very public signpost that something had gone badly awry inside the organisation.

On the return from South Africa, an emergency meeting was convened in the New Zealand capital. Eight people were in the room. The head coach Henry, his assistants Wayne Smith and Steve Hansen, captain Tana Umaga, vice-captain Richie McCaw, team manager Darren Shand, sports psychologist Gilbert Enoka and Lochore.

It is hard to overstate the significance of the occasion. Henry said it was the most important meeting in his eight years with the All Blacks; Smith described it as their 'coaching epiphany'.

They discussed the fact that New Zealand seemed to have lost the idea of who they were playing for. The Springboks seemed to have a greater sense of nationalism and pride in their jersey.

The All Blacks were, as always, a skilful and technically proficient group of rugby players but their moorings had loosened. Urgent action was needed to restore the heart of the All Blacks and rebuild an environment which would bring the best out of the players, not the worst.

The group met for three days and by the end of it had completely overhauled the All Blacks. 'That's when we got really serious about the leadership in the team,' said Henry. 'That was the start of changing the culture.'

The motto which was to underwrite the renaissance of the All Blacks was written by Lochore. It was, simply: 'Better people make better All Blacks'. The coaches were to prioritise picking individuals of good character and making sure the New Zealand environment was one in which they would learn and grow. The bad apples were out.

For those who remained, New Zealand's rugby wise men worked out that they needed to be given a purpose and then have it continually drilled into them. That meant revisiting their proud history and underscoring the one thing which united every man who had pulled on the black jersey. The jersey itself.

The iconic jersey and fern came into being on the New Zealand Natives' marathon tour of Britain in 1888. Rugby had been introduced 18 years beforehand by Charles John Monro, the son of an Edinburgh doctor, who had learned the game at Christ's College in London and brought it to Nelson on his return. It quickly caught on among both the settlers and the indigenous Maori population.

The Natives – a predominantly Maori team – played a mind-boggling 107 games on their tour of Britain of which they won 78. Right up there with the usual Kiwi global strike rate. They wore the black of Wellington with a white fern and preceded their matches with a haka – 'Ake Ake Kia Kaha' – which transfixed the crowds on the tour.

The success of the trip whetted the appetite for a national side and at the first meeting of the newly formed New Zealand Rugby Football Union, Tom Ellison a Native's tourist, who was to become the first New Zealand captain, proposed the tourists' colours be adopted. New Zealand duly wore the shirt when they played their first official international match in 1893 and have done ever since.

From the start, rugby was a unifying force in a rapidly

changing country. Once the Originals had toured Britain, France and North America in 1905, the black jersey attained a revered status.

Those All Blacks tourists, who lost only to Wales in their 35 matches, went down as an important marker post in a wider New Zealand history.

At a time when a young nation was searching for an identity, having chosen not to become Australia's seventh state four years earlier, pride in a rugby team who had put the country on the map abounded. Thousands turned out in Auckland to greet them when they returned from California. New Zealand historian Jock Phillips called the tour 'a defining element of the national consciousness'.

From the early success of the 1905 Originals' tour, the game proved a powerful tool for nation-building and it continues to serve as a loudhailer for a small country a long way from anywhere. It is hard to think of another country where national identity is so closely linked to the identity of a sports team. Rugby became a vehicle for New Zealand to punch above its weight and the black jersey became a symbol of who Kiwis were. It simply meant more to a greater percentage of the population than in any other country.

The obsession can be unhealthy. The national mood-swings when things go wrong for the All Blacks are irrational but the pressure to perform helps maintain the remarkable standards. 'We're driven by personal meaning, and a huge part of that personal meaning is to do with expectations and the scrutiny that surrounds the jersey,' explained Smith.

'Coaches and players in the All Blacks see it very much as a stewardship. When you've got the jersey, where you've got the position for a short time, there's a huge source of pride there to try and hand on ... your jersey in a better state or at least as good a state as what you received it in.'

It was that understanding of why they were there which had gone amiss in 2004. The All Blacks sought to re-establish it through a series of workshops with Enoka which were intended to help provide a clearer picture of what it meant to be a New Zealander and to wear the black jersey.

It entailed confessional sessions, role play and history lessons which provided the clarity they needed. All very touchy-feely; all very un-macho All Blacks. But it worked. The players developed a much greater appreciation of who they were as All Blacks.

On the back of it a new version of the traditional 'Ka Mate' haka – 'Kapa O Pango' – was created to portray their identity and the increased Polynesian make-up of the side more accurately.

The debate over whether the All Blacks' haka gives New Zealand an advantage in intimidating opponents before kick-off is as old as the hills. Look back at footage of the haka in the 1970s and early 1980s and the only danger to rival teams would be the possibility of laughing themselves to death at the shambolic Morris dance unravelling in front of them.

But ever since two of the side's Maoris, Wayne Shelford and Hika Reid, taught their Pakeha (non-Maori) team-mates how it should be done on tour to Argentina in 1985, its symbolic impact grew. From 1987 onwards, it began to be used before home Tests as well as on tour.

The new, bespoke version created after the cultural reawakening caused controversy because of the menacing throat-slitting gesture at the end which the All Blacks explained away as nothing more sinister than 'drawing the breath of life into the lungs'.

Whatever it evokes, it served to provide an example of the other key outcome of the Wellington debrief – giving the players more responsibility.

While it might have sounded counter-intuitive to give a group who could not be trusted more trust, there was logic at play. If the players had something of their own that they could buy into then they were more likely to make the sacrifices the team needed.

The All Blacks' rethink involved trying to develop the players as independent problem solvers. Full-time professionalism had served to create a brain-dead generation who could respond to orders but not think on its feet. The New Zealand management wanted to change that. Players were encouraged to lead balanced lifestyles with outside interests away from rugby – Richie McCaw earned his pilot's licence, Conrad Smith completed a law degree.

A leadership programme was devised by Enoka which was intended to encourage self-reliance, self-belief and mental toughness. The centralised command structure, which clearly was not working, was dissolved and a wider group of leaders developed with different individuals put in charge of off-field and on-field matters.

Initially the devolution of ownership was rigid with 11 players, voted in by their peers, assigned to lead different aspects of the team's activities. Each leader was assigned two or three team-mates to mentor. The leadership group would meet twice weekly, the first time with management present, the second time without. Minutes were even kept when they met at first. It was well-meaning but a little bureaucratic and clunky.

'It was always the philosophy...to dual-manage the All Blacks. But how we did that changed,' explained Henry, in

Otago University professor Ken Hodge's 'A Case Study of Excellence in Elite Sport'. 'When we first did it they all had portfolios of responsibility. They had all these cabinet ministers running around... and we'd meet a couple of times a week, and they'd feed back on their [responsibilities]. It was a step in the right direction, but it wasn't the ideal.'

Over time the leadership group shrank to ten and met less formally for a chat over lunch or a word after training but the principle remained. The players had to be central to the running of the All Blacks.

Rules were established by them, for them, on subjects such as alcohol limits, with binge drinking outlawed as out of keeping with the lifestyle of a modern professional sportsman. When it came to the rugby the players would do more of the analysis on the opposition and even deliver tactical talks. All Blacks had to be answerable to themselves.

'We thought that was the best way of developing a rugby side,' said Henry. 'The more confidence you can give them in leading the team, in making decisions on the field, the better they're going to play.'

The approach did not guarantee success over 80 minutes – Henry almost lost his job when the 2007 World Cup ended in tears in Cardiff against France at the quarter-final stage. But the NZRU's subsequent independent report into the exit was broadly supportive of the path they were on.

As well as predictably pinning some of the blame for the defeat on the referee – Englishman Wayne Barnes – the report highlighted the decision-making glitches which saw New Zealand press for a try or a penalty in the closing stages rather than go for a drop goal. 'The team failed to ensure the right decisions were taken at crucial moments,' it read.

But instead of claiming that all the investment in player leadership had been a waste of time, it concluded the approach was spot-on. New Zealand had, the report said, been holed beneath the waterline by the injuries to their trained leaders which meant that only four of their ten were on the pitch at the Millennium Stadium in the decisive moments, with the absentees including their top two No. 10s, Dan Carter and Nick Evans.

Tellingly, the report backed to the hilt the premise of producing a team of players capable of making their own decisions. The process was accelerated.

The subsequent results spoke for themselves. In 2011 the All Blacks won the Rugby World Cup. For some countries that may have been the end of the journey. With the goal achieved, standards may have slipped and motivation dipped but the victories just kept on coming.

The intrinsic drivers within the restored All Blacks set-up remained as powerful as ever. The Wellington summit was the gift that kept on giving.

When Lancaster had finished his illuminating conversation with Lochore he visited a friend in Wellington and went along with him to an under-18s school match in which his son was playing. The game was televised. And there were 5,000 people watching at the ground. The standard was exceptional. Because virtually everybody plays the sport in New Zealand, rugby tends to have the choice of the best athletes. The top schools run academy-standard set-ups with daily training sessions and top-quality coaching.

England back row James Haskell played for the Highlanders in Otago in 2012. Rugby was all he saw around him. 'Rugby is their passion. Nobody says he wants to play football. They all want to be rugby players,' he said.

It starts from the cradle. In New Zealand, a kid does not go to the park for a kick-about; he or she goes to chuck a ball around. The same goes for the beach. Children leaving school pass a rugby ball about on the way home rather than kicking stones.

The 10,000-hours rule is hard at work. By the time New Zealand players join professional set-ups, their skill levels are already highly advanced and they are reinforced by the emphasis of the coaching. 'Where we tend to focus on size and power, in New Zealand everything is orientated round the ball and skills,' said Haskell.

And those professional organisations – the provinces and Super Rugby franchises – all push in the same direction. Unlike in free-market models such as England and France, where overseas coaches and players feature heavily and private owners care about their club first and country second, the provinces and Super Rugby franchises are on the same page as the national side.

The feeder teams are all coached by New Zealanders and stocked with New Zealand players. Key men can be rested, promising players given opportunities – all with the national interest at heart. The style of rugby played is broadly similar to All Blacks rugby, too.

From the playground to the Test arena, everything is geared towards the success of the All Blacks.

Rugby is a democratic game in New Zealand. It is not exclusively for one sector of society. The history associated with the team and the relatively small population of New Zealand make for a potent combination. Not only do Kiwis revere the jersey but they also tend to know someone who has worn it. That sense of heroes you can touch inspires the next generation on to become All Blacks themselves and continue the tradition.

When Dan Carter was a small boy growing up in rural Southbridge that was his dream. His father helped foster it by putting up a set of goalposts in the paddock. He went on to become the highest points scorer in Test history – and to inspire another generation of young New Zealand boys. The wheel continues to turn.

'It's every kid's dream to put on the All Blacks jersey for the first time,' explained Carter. 'There's so much history with the All Blacks jersey. A high standard has been set for more than a hundred years so when it's your turn to wear it, you want to add to that legacy. You're only borrowing the shirt. It's your job to leave the jersey in a better place than it was before you got to wear it.'

The honour of becoming an All Black brings with it expectations in a side which hardly ever loses. The public and the national team management are not shy to remind them of it either.

When journalist Oliver Brown stumbled unwittingly into the unoccupied New Zealand team room at the Royal Gardens Hotel in Kensington ahead of the 2013 autumn Test against England, he found the following words written on a whiteboard – 'We are the most dominant team in the history of the world'. Not rugby team. Team.

Pressure comes as the sidekick of such constant re-enforcement but also a desire to meet the standards of the past and raise them. Success becomes a self-fulfilling prophecy. The past helps to shape the future.

Every new All Black is handed a leather-bound book when he is first called into the squad. On page one is a picture of the 1905 Originals' jersey. On the next page is the 1924 Invincibles' jersey. And so on through the generations. It also contains words on past All Blacks' heroes, the team's values and principles and code of honour.

The rest is left blank. That is up to the new man to fill with his contribution to the All Blacks' story.

Sometimes the linkage with their forebears could seem out of keeping with a cutting-edge global sports brand. Once a week on tour the squad hold a 'clubhouse night' at which they are given leave to enjoy a quiet drink wearing their old rugby club jerseys. They have a quiz, hold a raffle maybe and generally chew the fat. Just like thousands of New Zealand rugby players before them.

At the 2011 World Cup they carried around a fake mahogany honours' board with the name and number of caps of every squad member on it and put it up in their hotel team room, complete with photos of the trophies they had won. Just like the traditional clubhouse board.

But keeping it real is part of the All Blacks' way. In James Kerr's book, *Legacy: What the All Blacks Can Teach Us About the Business of Life,* he refers to the tradition of the team sweeping the dressing rooms clean after matches. Notice the similarity to house-proud England under Lancaster? New Zealand were simply the benchmark on and off the field as far as he was concerned, a brotherhood like no other in world rugby.

Wayne Smith has played for the All Blacks and coached them. He knows what lies at the organisation's strongly beating heart and he is not afraid to put the bond of the All Blacks in most un-rugby-like terms.

Smith likes to read widely and doing so has taken him into the world of the ancient Spartans. 'They were hugely courageous warriors and they were always looking for what the opposite of fear was so that they could develop that in their warriors. They found it wasn't courage, and it wasn't bravery, it was love,' said Smith.

'That's about connections. So we selected the right people and worked really hard on developing better people who had strong connections, played for themselves, but also played for each other, and people they loved. And they clearly loved each other within the All Blacks. I think that was a real source of performance.'

Lancaster wanted to recruit Smith to his backroom staff. He met him in South Africa in 2012 to try to persuade him to join the England management team. As Lancaster saw it, Smith was a perfect fit for England. He knew the English game from his time coaching Northampton. He knew how to build a winning culture, having been the driving force behind the rise of the Crusaders. And he knew how to win a World Cup, having been part of Graham Henry's management team in 2011. He was also a pretty shrewd backs' coach.

Smith was impressed with Lancaster's vision for England and gave the offer deep thought but ultimately decided to stay in New Zealand with the Waikato Chiefs. The prospect of coaching against the All Blacks was just too alien. The waters of love run deep. In 2015 Smith rejoined the All Blacks management team.

In James Kerr's book he also tells of the rope the All Blacks hang on the changing room wall before each Test. It is made by Maoris and includes intertwined strands of different colours. There is silver to represent the New Zealand fern, black for the jersey and red for their blood. Within it are woven different coloured strings to represent each victory – white for England, red for Wales etc. The few defeats stand out in black.

The rope represents the link between each succeeding

generation of All Blacks. Always the emphasis is on the continuation of the line. Lancaster read the book and was fascinated by the story. He decided England needed their own verbal version of the rope.

12

Know Yourself

From this day to the ending of the world
But we in it shall be rememberèd,
We few, we happy few, we band of brothers.
For he today that sheds his blood with me
Shall be my brother

Henry V, Act 4, Scene 3

Not far from the bizarre green stickle-brick structure of Headingley Cricket Ground's Carnegie Pavilion stands Trio, a three-tiered bar complex. The restaurant which occupies the middle floor, with its Jenga-piece ceiling décor, bookshelf wallpaper, bowler-hat lampshades and open kitchen, has a lively ambience.

In late October 2013, an exclusive club gathered there to have dinner together. You could have heard a pin drop. The group comprised the England rugby union squad, who had been training at West Park that day, members of the RFU management board and a quartet of distinguished players from the past – Bill Beaumont, Fran Cotton, Roger Uttley and Mike Harrison. It was the past which was occupying all their attention.

The group was being addressed on the history of English rugby by a New Zealand lawyer and team-building expert called Owen Eastwood. His lecture was about rugby but that was just the starting point.

The players heard tales of England teams from the past, of great days at Twickenham and of glorious Grand Slams won, but they also heard about dark days. They sat and listened to stories of the 27 England internationals who gave their lives in the First World War including Ronnie Poulton Palmer, the captain of England's Grand Slam-winning side in 1914 who was killed on the Western Front in May 1915.

Ronnie Poulton Palmer

Ronnie Poulton Palmer was an impossibly dashing three-quarter in the manner of a yesteryear David Duckham who led his country to the Grand Slam in 1914. Thirteen months later, he was shot dead by a sniper at Ypres.

Born Ronald Poulton, in September 1889, he was introduced to the game at Rugby School. He went up to Oxford to study engineering and scored five tries in the 1909 Varsity Match from the wing.

It was as a centre, though, that he made his name first with Harlequins, then Liverpool and England. A scything runner who cut defences apart at will, he was generally regarded as the finest player in the world. His attacking flair was something to behold and, with his mop of blond hair, he was as near to a pin-up as early twentieth-century rugby possessed.

He was not only a brilliant player but a keen social reformer who supported boys' clubs and working men's clubs in the north and south of England.

Engaging and charismatic, he was also a great team man and a natural choice to become captain of his country.

He led England to the Grand Slam in 1914, scoring five tries in the tournament, including four in one game against France as England recorded their second Slam in successive seasons.

The quirky thing is that he did so as Ronnie Palmer. His uncle, George Palmer, was the co-founder of the Huntley and Palmer biscuit company.

When the wealthy business man died in 1914 he left a fortune to his nephew, Ronnie, but on the condition that he added Palmer to his name. Not surprisingly he did.

Nine days after war broke out in 1914 the RFU issued a circular advising all rugby players to join up. The England captain, who had joined the officer training corps at university, obeyed the call like countless others. Like many of those others, he never came back.

In May 1915 he was overseeing a night-time working party strengthening trenches when he pulled himself up on to the roof of a dugout for a better view of his men at work and was picked off with a single shot. He was twenty-five and the first officer of the Royal Berkshire Regiment to die in the Great War.

His last words were reputed to have been: 'I shall never play at Twickenham again.'

He had captained England in the 1914 Calcutta Cup match. Of the two teams who contested that match, 11 of the players lost their lives in the conflict.

Who knows what he could have gone on to achieve on a rugby pitch and beyond had his life not been cut cruelly short?

There were other tales, too, from the Second World War, including that of Russian prince Alexander Obolensky, who had fled the Revolution as a child with his family, shown himself to be a natural at the sport at boarding school and scored two remarkable tries as a debutant in the victory over New Zealand at Twickenham in 1936. Auxilary Pilot Officer Obolensky was killed in an RAF training accident in Suffolk four years later.

The stories were at the same time sobering and inspiring for a group chosen to share the same shirt. It made a deep impression on the young Englishmen in the prime of their lives.

Tom Youngs was twenty-six at the time – two years older than Obolensky had been when he died. 'It was about what guys who have played in the England shirt before us have actually done for their country, not just the rugby,' said Youngs.

'There were some great stories from World Wars One and Two which went well beyond what you could possibly imagine as a rugby player. It was very interesting because these were guys who played for their country too, so you have that connection with them.'

For Billy Vunipola – real name Viliami – a Pacific Islander born in Australia, whose brother Mako was also there that evening, it was another name which turned his head. James Peters. 'He was the first black player to play for England – 71 years before English football had its first black player,' said Vunipola. 'It just touched me because it made me think how accepting England rugby is with the different cultures coming in. People come here looking for opportunities and England are more than happy to help out.

'That is how my brother and I have felt since we have played. We have not had anyone say: "What are they doing playing for England?"

'It definitely made me feel part of the group. It made me feel accepted and acknowledged. It made me feel part of the England identity – that is why his story touched me more than anything else. He was someone I could relate to.'

James Peters

England's first black international had, by any stretch of the imagination, an extraordinary life.

Born in Salford in 1879, the son of circus performers, he could have made his name in the Big Top. He was a bareback rider as a boy and a talented acrobat.

His direction in life changed radically when his West Indian father, George – a lion tamer – was mauled to death in a training cage. What happened to his white mother, Hannah, from Shropshire, is unclear but James was packed off to Fegan's Orphanage in London.

He later moved on to the Little Wanderers' Home in Greenwich where he was introduced to rugby. By fifteen he was the team captain at the orphanage. As a ball handler with searing pace, he was a natural.

He continued playing the game at the Knowle club in Bristol when he left the capital to become a printer. His performances in two seasons there turned heads. Unfortunately so did his skin colour and several members resigned in protest at having a black player at their club.

Peters moved on to Plymouth where he became a carpenter in the naval dockyards at Devonport and his rugby reputation continued to grow.

'Darkie', as he was inevitably called, played county rugby for Somerset and Devon where his athleticism and handling as fly-half lit up the field.

On talent alone, an England call-up was inevitable but there was still resistance to picking a black man in some quarters at the RFU. However, desperation knows no racial barriers, and with England in a deep rut in 1906 they turned to Peters. He delivered.

Peters' half-back partnership with Adrian Stoop rejuvenated the team and inspired them to a 9-3 victory over Scotland at Inverleith which stopped a run of seven successive defeats. Peters scored a try in his next game – England's first international against France – but then events took a depressing twist.

Peters' presence in the Devon side who played the touring South Africans almost caused an international incident. The Springboks had to be talked out of their dressing room by the South African High Commissioner to play the game, such was the disgust they felt at sharing the same pitch with him.

The game went ahead but, fearing a repeat when England faced the South Africans in the final game of the tour six weeks later, the RFU, to their shame, left Peters out of the side. To appease the tourists Cornwall's Richard Jago was brought in at scrum-half with Stoop switched to fly-half.

The decision was based partly on money. Crystal Palace, which was to host the Test, was already a 40,000 sell-out and the RFU did not want a cancellation. Peters was recalled the following year but played only three more Tests with his England career ending invisibly in heavy fog at Ashton Gate, Bristol, against Wales.

Peters, a teetotaller, carried on playing rugby at club

level even after losing three fingers in a dockyard accident in 1909. He could not escape controversy, though. When rebellious clubs in the south-west were punished by the RFU for contravening amateur regulations and paying their players, Peters was one of those accused of accepting payment.

He was suspended and, disillusioned, he headed back to his native north-west to play rugby league – where he could be paid legally. He played for Barrow in 1913 and St Helens the following season, where he ended his career.

Peters could have been forgiven for harbouring grudges after the infamous Test against South Africa but, if he did, they did not involve the man who took his place. Having moved back to Plymouth after his rugby career was over, he and Jago became firm friends and met every week to play chess.

Peters died in 1954 and is buried in Plymouth.

The point was that England was not simply some white upper-class rugger club. True, plenty of Anglo-Saxon represent-atives of the establishment had played for England over the years, but a wide variety of other creeds and classes had too.

It was a particularly resonant point for a squad containing the Vunipola brothers – and Samoan-born Manu Tuilagi who, for the first part of his Test career until he became a British citizen, had to queue separately from his team-mates at passport con-trol. The message they were hearing was that England was welcoming and inclusive.

That evening at Trio brought further enlightenment to a group of players who had been part of England's cultural make-over. They already knew who they were representing when they played for England and why it was special but now they knew more about those who had gone before them.

Identity. It was the second level of Lancaster's pyramid.

The England coach had observed that while English society as a whole was shaped hugely by its history and heritage, English sporting teams appeared to lack such strong links to their past.

'One of the things which brought it home to me was the shirt presentation Peter Winterbottom did for the side on the night before the France game in 2012,' said Lancaster. 'Geoff Parling, who was our oldest player, was sitting beside me and he said: "who's this guy?" He didn't know one of the iconic England rugby players of the eighties. As for our twenty-year-olds, they didn't have a clue.'

Lancaster wanted his team to hear from these former players what it had meant to play for England in their time and also what it would mean to them as ex-internationals to see the side be successful now.

England's rugby players were continuing a famous line. They were part of a team that had first played together when Queen Victoria was on the throne. Yet few of the squad knew much about the brotherhood to which they belonged. 'There wasn't always a great understanding of why you play or the history behind it but understanding who was there before and what they went through makes the cause you are playing for even more worthwhile,' said Bath prop David Wilson.

During that 2013 autumn series, the squad also met George Hastings, one of the oldest surviving England internationals who had been born on 7 November 1924. The goalkicking prop had played in England's championship-winning sides in 1957 and 1958 and had toe-ended the equalising penalty against

Scotland which had helped England to retain the title. It was back in an era when England players were expected to bring their own shorts and were given one pair of socks for the season which shrank in the wash.

In many ways Lancaster's restoration mission was a return to a more innocent amateur age, to an era when the regulations meant playing for England could be about nothing else bar honour. With free kit coming out of their ears and a £15,000 match fee, times were very different. Lancaster was determined to ensure values weren't.

Lancaster is not naïve when it comes to money – he is from farming stock – but despite having one of the most important jobs in English sport, he does not even have an agent.

As he noted in a contribution to David Becker and Scott Hill's book *Secrets of Winning Coaches Revealed*, written when he was Saxons coach: 'I've been involved in some teams where I feel that money has blunted the hunger of the player. And what it's done is that it's made it easy for them to accept the lifestyle they've got, which is a very lucrative lifestyle. And they've forgotten all that detail of what got them to that position in the first place. You must be intrinsically motivated, not extrinsically, to be the best you can be.

'Yes, a big pay cheque is a nice bonus, but ultimately, as we all know, it's only short-lived anyway. And you know, after your ten years of playing rugby; you finish at thirty, and you've got another thirty years of employment to find. Your personality and character will be a big part of that.'

Personality and character were what he wanted in his team. And he wanted his squad to explore what classic qualities of the English character they needed to help the team win in the present day. 'One of the things we've struggled with is being front foot about being English,' said Lancaster. 'For lots of historical reasons we are called arrogant. I think that is unfair and you definitely can't throw it at this England team.

'We've become more front foot about it and we have worked hard on talking about the identity of what being English means. You have to have character to be an England player, a strong sense of purpose, never take a backward step, always deliver under pressure, have a level of commitment that is probably above and beyond what most people would expect and a resilience.'

Englishness can be a nebulous concept to pin down. It often takes an outsider to see it most clearly. As a Welshman, Kevin Bowring believed Englishness equated to a proud refusal to buckle – whatever the odds.

'The question is, what is the identity of being English? It comes down to that speech by Churchill – "we will fight them on the beaches". When backs are against the wall that's where that Englishness comes out,' said Bowring. 'The English aren't particularly comfortable talking about it – stiff upper lip and all that – and it sounds a little contrived, but that is who you are.'

Hardiness, perseverance, resilience – all those traits were demonstrated in spades to Lancaster in the victory over world champions New Zealand at the end of 2012. The contrasting experience of being spanked by Wales in the Grand Slam game a few months later underlined further to Lancaster the need to harness the power of England's own national identity. He had felt as if England were playing against many more than 15 Welshmen at the Millennium Stadium that day. He wanted England's opponents to feel the same force against them.

The link to the past was critical to that power, believed Lancaster. Bev Risman, a revered cross-code international who went on to become president of the Rugby Football League, gave the following answer when asked what playing for England was like in the fifties. 'Every time I played for England I felt we were better than the opposition,' Risman said. 'Together we would just refuse to take a backward step.'

English arrogance? Or a cussed refusal to be beaten? Two sides of the same coin? Whatever, Lancaster liked those words enough to put them in giant letters on their dressing-room wall at Twickenham.

Lancaster would never countenance arrogance – his England set-up reeks of humility – but neither did he want his players to be shy about the pride they felt in playing for their country. He wanted them to feel the power of their heritage. 'We've got an incredible history as a country and as a rugby team and I think it's important for our players to understand some of the history behind the team. It's important for them to understand what these guys did when they played. It brings a bit of perspective to the players about what playing for England really means,' he said.

Lancaster commissioned Eastwood to prepare a DVD which would tell the story of what it means to be English and what it means to English players to represent their country.

Those who spoke on it, of their pride in the shirt and of playing at Twickenham, ranged across the generations. They included the venerable George Hastings and John Pullin, the captain who led England out at Lansdowne Road at the height of the Troubles in 1972, the season Wales and Scotland refused to travel to Ireland. England lost and finished bottom of the championship despite Ireland, Wales and Scotland not completing their fixtures, but the reception they were given will go down as one of the most emotional in Five or Six Nations' history. As Pullin said at the post-match reception: 'We may not be any good but at least we turn up.'

Lancaster's back-row idol Peter Winterbottom also contributed to the film on his time with the England side in the eighties and Jeremy Guscott in the nineties. There were stirring words, too, from a more modern-day England hero in Jason Robinson.

The voiceover at the start spoke of the players' connection to the land, how they were rooted in it, at one with it almost, and how representing it was their duty. It was an emotive and powerful piece of imagery. When Hastings was shown it, he dissolved into tears. When the present-day England team and their partners viewed it, they felt similarly choked.

International rugby is an emotional game. While success relies on mental clarity and discipline, it has to be driven by an all-consuming inner fire. Pulling on the white jersey should be enough to ignite that fire but Lancaster sought to deepen the attachment.

England won their first two autumn Tests in 2013, taking down Australia and Argentina who they had also beaten that summer without their touring Lions. But there was to be no repeat of the previous season's victory over New Zealand. The world champions had their revenge 30-22 at Twickenham after pulling into an early lead.

It said something about the strides England had made that they were bitterly disappointed at allowing the chance of back-to-back wins over the All Blacks to slip through their fingers.

In international terms, England were still growing up. Consistency eluded them. Teams who have enjoyed sustained success in the international arena possessed many attributes, of which experience was one important part, but a clear understanding of just who they were was also vital, Lancaster believed. New Zealand had that knowledge; England were still gaining it.

When it came to the redesign of the dressing room, the

players were given a little helping hand. A curving white honours board was put on the wall, engraved with the name of every
player to have represented England, set against the background
of a ghosted image of Twickenham on match day.

Lancaster noted with interest how often the dressing room
traffic stops as the players are passing it.

'It is fascinating how people are drawn to that board. If
you've made it on to it you are in a pretty exclusive club and I
think it brings it home to the players,' he said.

The history wall, inscribed with the landmarks of great past
players and the trophies of victorious England teams, added to
the sense of pride.

The white positional plaques at each changing place, decorated with a simple horizontal red cross and headed 'One of Us',
reinforced the honour and responsibility at carrying on the
tradition.

When the hookers Dylan Hartley, Rob Webber or Tom Youngs
walked towards their red padded seat they were confronted with
a list of names on which read: Steve Thompson, Mark Regan,
Brian Moore, Peter Wheeler, John Pullin, Eric Evans, John
Tucker, Norman Wodehouse, Bob Seddon, Charles Gurdon.

'You see all the names of the guys who have played in your
position in the changing room and what legends they are and
you now have that shirt. You have to make sure you fill that shirt
and leave it in a better place,' said Youngs.

A patriotic paintbrush was applied in the makeover.
Everything in the dressing room was done out in either white
or red, including the baths. Action shots of the current team
were put up on the walls together with motivational phrases
hammering home the special honour of representing England
and the expectations that brought with it.

When defensive awards were instigated within the squad, England decided to name them after a true English hero who gave his life for his country – Arthur Harrison, naval officer and only England rugby player to win the Victoria Cross.

Three are handed out after each game. The Mick Skinner award for the biggest hit, the Richard Hill award for the best breakdown work and the Lewis Moody award for going beyond the call of duty – all bracketed in honour of Harrison.

Joe Launchbury is the son of a Royal Marine. His father, Steve, served with them for 27 years before becoming a school bursar at Christ's Hospital in Sussex. He loved the link. 'I thought that was fantastic,' said Launchbury. 'Being from a military background myself, it was nice that a few military themes came through. Unity and teamwork are common to both and what we are about.

'The defensive awards are something the boys have really, really got behind. It's a big thing and it means a lot to us. It's not just a token gesture. We get round on a Thursday and look forward to it. We've really bought into it.'

Arthur Harrison

Arthur Harrison was the only England rugby player to win the Victoria Cross.

Born the son of a Royal Fusilier, in 1886 in Torquay, Harrison chose a career in the Royal Navy. He was already a serving officer when the First World War broke out. At the time, the services supplied a constant stream of players to England of whom Harrison, somewhat belatedly, was one.

He had begun his rugby career at Dover College before moving on to the Royal Naval College at Dartmouth. He was twenty-eight and playing his rugby for the United

Services, Portsmouth, club when his country's call came twice – and with very different demands – in 1914.

Harrison's international rugby debut came less than six months before the start of the war. It was against Ireland at Twickenham in a match attended by King George V – the first rugby match the monarch had attended since his coronation four years earlier.

The King saw a 17-12 victory for England with Harrison, a tough and tireless forward, playing his part along with his namesake Harold Harrison from the army.

A match report in *The Times* declared: 'The English forwards, stiffened in the scrummage by the two Harrisons, did better than against Wales.'

He missed the next match against Scotland on navy duty but returned for the emphatic 39-13 victory over France which brought a Grand Slam. It was to be his second and last cap.

When the First World War broke out Harrison was deployed to the battlecruiser HMS *Lion* which, in August 1914, sunk the German ships *Köln* and *Ariadne* at the Battle of Heligoland. In all, more than 1,000 German lives were lost.

The following year *Lion* took part in the Battle of Dogger Bank and in 1916, the year in which he was promoted to lieutenant-commander, the Battle of Jutland after which Harrison was mentioned in despatches.

He continued to play in the odd rugby match when on leave for Rosslyn Park, to whom he gave his address as 'HM Torpedo Boat No 16, Portsmouth'.

Harrison was an up-and-at-'em player and an-up-and-at-'em man. When the request came for volunteers for a particularly dangerous mission on board HMS *Vindictive* he was at the front of the queue.

An armada of destroyers, submarines and ferry boats set sail on the night of 22 April 1918, their mission to sink three cruisers filled with concrete to block the Zeebrugge–Bruges Canal. This would prevent German U-boats penned in further down the waterway using it to move into the open sea.

Harrison's job was to take charge of a landing party whose task was to take out the German machine guns on a vital breakwater at Zeebrugge.

Vindictive sailed up close to the breakwater, straight into the firing line. Several officers were killed and Harrison badly injured as a shell burst nearby, knocking him unconscious and breaking his jaw.

He was taken below deck but when he came round he insisted on not only returning to the fight but leading it. He gathered his men together and led the charge across the ship's gangway on to the breakwater towards the German positions. They were horribly exposed. He was shot and killed, as were all but two of his landing party. He was thirty-two.

Harrison was posthumously awarded the VC for 'conspicuous gallantry'. His citation read as follows: 'Lieut.-Commander Harrison, though already severely wounded and undoubtedly in great pain, displayed indomitable resolution and courage of the highest order in pressing his attack knowing, as he did, that any delay in silencing the guns might jeopardise the object of the expedition – the blocking of the Zeebrugge–Bruges Canal.'

HMS *Vindictive*'s captain, Alfred Carpenter, who was

also awarded a VC, later wrote: 'Harrison's charge down that narrow gangway of death was a worthy finale to the large number of charges which, as a forward of the first rank, he had led down many a rugby football ground.'

The total cost of the mission was 188 lives but the objective was achieved and the canal was blocked. It was later described by Winston Churchill thus: 'The Raid on Zeebrugge may well rank as the finest feat of arms in the Great War and certainly as an episode unsurpassed in the history of the Royal Navy.'

Harrison's VC, presented to his mother in 1919, is on show at the Britannia Royal Naval College, Dartmouth.

A four-man heritage committee was established within the squad to foster the links with the past and make sure they were honoured. Tom Wood sat on it. 'The make-up changes with injuries and selection but we will meet two or three times during a series and check how things are going,' said the Northampton back row.

'We talk about any new traditions we might want to start or maintain – maybe on match day with new caps or if there's a match on Remembrance Sunday poppies on our shirts.' He added: 'It's really important to look back to see what other guys have done, see the kind of men that have worn the shirt before and what you've got to live up to. You carry this on to the field with you.'

Owen Farrell also sits on the committee. 'It's about educating ourselves in the history of English rugby and making sure everyone is aware of what a special shirt it is. I'm sure everyone is proud to pull it on for themselves and for their family,' said Farrell.

New call-ups to the squad were inducted by their peers to ensure the message continued to permeate. 'There is a senior group of players who take you to one side and explain the history behind the shirt and what is expected of you as a person and as a player with England,' said Ed Slater, the Leicester second row who joined the squad in 2013. 'Dan Cole and Chris Robshaw explained to me what it means to play for England. Coming from guys like that it means a lot because you have respect for those people.'

Higher performance requires a higher purpose. As Lancaster puts it: 'The more you have to play for, the better you play.'

Rugby union is a complicated game. Its book of laws weighs the same as *War and Peace* and is as easy to follow as a version of it in the original Russian. But when all the legal sub-clauses are stripped away, rugby union is essentially combat between two groups of 15 men to be settled by who tackles hardest, runs fastest and thinks sharpest.

At Test level, the differentials in skill and conditioning between professional sides with equal resources are so small that the outcome can often be a coin flick. Heads or tails? Succeeds or fails. Lancaster believed he could rig the toss. He thought he could do so by giving England's players a cause.

On his laptop, Lancaster has a file containing a graph. The vertical axis shows the level of a player's motivation; the horizontal axis his behaviour – how much he gives to the side he plays for. A line of five points on the graph shows how various different driving forces influence a player's commitment.

The lowest point on the graph is labelled 'me'. At that point, effort is discretionary. No one cares about anything other than himself. The team is going nowhere. In fact there is no sense of team at all.

The next point on the graph is 'those who care about me', which is reached when a player also plays for family and friends. 'By writing to the parents I was trying to tap into that subconscious motivation,' said Lancaster. 'The England shirt is a source of huge pride for the players,' he said. 'When we talk to the players about what it means to play for England a lot of them talk about family and friends and what they have done and the people that have supported them on this path to become an England player. All those people who have helped the player get to this point will all be sat at home or in the crowd supporting them and that's a big, big driver for the player.'

The third point is marked 'band of brothers' where camaraderie leads team-mates to play for each other. Their shared bond drives the players on to work hard for each other and the team will perform reasonably well. 'We're definitely there, even though in England it is probably more difficult than in any other country because of the twelve-club scenario and the inter-club rivalry,' said Lancaster.

Two points remain. The fourth is labelled 'the shirt', where the individual's main objective revolves around furthering the honour of the jersey they have inherited. All vestiges of 'me' have disappeared. If they play for the shirt itself, the physical manifestation of the lineage they are part of, the side will perform very well. 'Making the shirt the driver is the next point and something which the All Blacks do really well,' said Lancaster.

The final point is 'the cause' where individuals abandon all pretext of self. This was the point he was aiming for with England. 'The ultimate suppressor of self-interest is a cause where you are prepared to put your life on the line to fight for your country,' said Lancaster.

Rugby is not war, it is a game. Lancaster was seeking a state of mind – that adopted by soldiers going into battle – rather than an actual death wish. But if a team can deal in the currency of self-sacrifice it can achieve great things.

Desire and drive cannot be the be-all and end-all – talent and tactics clearly come into play – but if those scales are balanced they can make a difference. Rugby is a physical combat sport and if one team wants to win more often than another then the majority of times they do. It cannot be headless-chicken stuff – the mind must still control the body – but if a side can harness an intensity and bravery bordering on personal recklessness then they are hard to contain.

Test matches are decided when the last grains of sand drain from the hourglass. The side that is prepared to go deeper into their well of resolve in its most painful, lung-busting moments in pursuit of their cause will win.

It is a theory built on the emotional premise that love conquers all. Lancaster, as a sports science graduate rather than a romantic poet, puts a number on this. He believes that this level of cultural nirvana improves a side's performance by up to 15 per cent. At the very top end of elite sport, where outcomes turn on the smallest of margins, this is an enormous leap.

Sitting in Changing Room No. 1 at Twickenham, with all its psychological prompts, he spells it out. 'To win the top games you need a whole variety of different qualities – technical, physical, mental – but ultimately you need motivation. You need to think "What's the reason I am going to play for this team? Why is playing for this team special?" You need to pull that together and create an extra 10 or 15 per cent in a player that can take him to a place where he'll put his body on the line but also work harder than he has ever worked before. That motivation is not a little part of the jigsaw – it's a big, big part of the jigsaw and it's the difference sometimes between winning and losing.'

13

Holding Your Nerve

Out of this nettle danger we pluck this flower safety

Henry IV Part I, Act 2, Scene 4

It is 4 a.m. on 22 November 2014. The England head coach is lying in bed in his room, 'Newlands', at the Pennyhill Park. He is wide awake.

Stuart Lancaster normally sleeps soundly, if not for particularly long, but on this occasion his mind is restless and uneasy. Samoa, nominally the easiest of England's autumn Test opposition, lie in wait later that day.

The Samoans are in disarray politically. They are at war with their own Union. They had even threatened to call off the fixture a few weeks beforehand in order to highlight their grievances. Their preparation for the game has been haphazard but Samoa have some seriously dangerous individuals, hard-hitting players who are in high demand across Europe's top leagues.

As for England, they are coming into the game on the back of five successive defeats. With the World Cup ten months away, they are under scrutiny as never before.

England have never lost to Samoa before. They should win but...what if?

Lancaster has not transmitted his concerns to his team – he has been the same purposeful, demanding coach as usual – albeit one with a slightly more stressed countenance – but the pressure the run has brought on the side from outside has been weighing heavily on him. England, and Lancaster, are under siege. 'Shit,' he thinks to himself. 'I hope we win today – or else it's not going to be a very good day.'

Kick-off at Twickenham is still 16 hours away.

A team's journey is never a straight line and for England a toxic combination of a schedule which appeared to have been drawn up by the Marquis de Sade, injuries and their own failings have thrown results off course and stopped the momentum they had built in its tracks.

Entering their third year together as a group, they had blazed a trail through the 2014 Six Nations. Had it not been for a slow start in Paris in the opening match, they would have taken the Grand Slam. The French game was the only one England lost in a promising championship in which they scored 14 tries.

Owen Farrell flourished as a distributor, showing an evolving attacking side to his game, and Mike Brown was a revelation from full-back. He was man of the match in three of the five games. Even the centre combination, a headache for a succession of England coaches ever since Will Greenwood stepped aside in 2004, looked good.

After scouring the horizons of English rugby to fill the considerable hole left by the absence of the half-man, half-monster Manu Tuilagi, Lancaster had gone back to his Leeds roots and called up his one-time academy boy Luther Burrell to partner Billy Twelvetrees.

It was a bold call – Burrell was an inside centre at his club Northampton – but he was asked by Lancaster to use his power down the outside-centre channel filled ineffectively by Joel Tomkins in the preceding autumn series. The switch asked a lot of Burrell, particularly defensively in the clearer waters occupied by a No. 13, but Lancaster's faith was vindicated. Burrell scored on his debut at the Stade de France and continued to impress through the rest of the championship in a balanced midfield.

After whitewashing Scotland 20-0 on a Murrayfield pitch infested with parasitic worms, England took down eventual champions Ireland 13-10 at Twickenham in an altogether higher-quality encounter on an altogether higher-quality surface. Brown's broken-field running across the pristine green grass of Twickenham was, in the estimation of the Ireland coach Joe Schmidt, the difference between the teams.

The frustration for England was that they created more chances than they finished so Mike Catt came up with a novel idea to try to improve the strike rate – introducing disco lights in training. Different coloured lights despatched decision-makers to different areas of the training centre at Pennyhill Park to improve their visual awareness and teach them to rely less on vocal instructions which could be drowned out in the bedlam of 82,000 people on match day.

The in-house nightclubbing worked. Champions Wales were made to look stale and stodgy by comparison and beaten more convincingly than the 29-18 scoreline suggested at Twickenham.

Wales prop Adam Jones said he had never encountered an England side with such pace. 'England,' reflected Jones, 'were like no other England side I've played against.'

The limited England who took their first baby steps under

Lancaster had grown to resemble white lightning and their first Triple Crown since 2003 was secured in some style.

As Chris Robshaw stood outside Twickenham's Good Health Bar giving his verdict on the side's development, the location was spot on. England looked in rude health. 'We were a side that was very defence-orientated and we prided ourselves on that defence – we probably won a lot of games because of it. But our attack has now caught up with it and I think we have come a long way. We can threaten with our attack and have that dominant defence as well,' said a justifiably excited Robshaw.

England suddenly had attacking options coming out of their ears and they put 50 points on Italy in Rome to conclude the campaign.

The final table, after Ireland won in France on the final day to give the peerless Brian O'Driscoll the perfect send-off into retirement, indicated there had been no improvement for England. They had finished second again for the third season running. But the threat level was completely different.

The comparison with 2012, Lancaster's first championship in charge, was illustrative. England scored twice as many tries, offloaded three times as often and beat almost four times as many defenders – 133 to 37.

They could hardly have been in better shape to take on the ultimate challenge of a tour to New Zealand that summer. Unfortunately, any continuity England might have enjoyed from a settled Six Nations was destroyed by a ludicrous tour schedule which had been agreed by the RFU without due care and attention in the height of the 2011 World Cup fall-out.

The proximity of the first Test in Auckland to the Premiership final on the other side of the world meant Lancaster was duty bound not to select any of the players involved. That meant 14 players from Northampton or Saracens could not be considered for Eden Park.

An example of the disruption this provided came in the pivotal stand-off position. With no Owen Farrell or Stephen Myler – and with the promising George Ford out of the tour injured – Lancaster had to switch to Gloucester's Leicester-bound No. 10 Freddie Burns, the fourth choice.

With a makeshift team at a ground where New Zealand had not lost for 20 years, England were up against it, so, ahead of tackling this huge hurdle, Lancaster played the team a video from Henry Fraser. He was the twenty-two-year-old brother of Saracens flanker Will Fraser and had been paralysed from the neck down five years earlier after diving into a hidden sandbank. He knew all about challenges. His life was one big challenge.

His recorded message was both poignant and inspiring. These were his words: 'Being challenged in life is inevitable: being defeated is optional,' said Fraser.

'We cannot change the cards we are dealt, it's all about how you and I play the hand. You have to accept what is and adapt.

'I was told I would need a head-controlled electric chair for the rest of my life. Bullshit. As soon as I saw someone else pushing themselves around, I knew it was for me. Personally, being in a completely electric chair would have been like giving up. It is unheard of for someone with my severity of injury to be in the chair I am in now.

'This was the fight I needed. It's an ongoing fight I live with daily. It is the striving which makes life meaningful. It's the challenge, the quest, the undone which really is the meaning life offers me. I now have the belief that the greater the challenge life offers you, the more alive you feel.

'The greater the challenge, the greater the opportunity. The greater the challenge, the greater your memory. The greater the challenge, the greater you can become.'

England – despite being deprived of the talents of Courtney Lawes, Billy Vunipola, Dylan Hartley and many others – embraced the challenge of Eden Park.

They were the better side in the first half and still level at 15-15 with three minutes to play. It was a heroic shot at history but then the All Blacks, as they so often do, came up with the killer play near the end with Conrad Smith crossing for the match-winning try.

It was a heartbreaking conclusion. Nevertheless the performance promised much for the two Tests to come when the cavalry would be available. This was take-off time.

Lancaster changed horses for the second Test in Dunedin and called up some of the Premiership finalists to strengthen the side, but the upheaval proved counter-productive. A potent third quarter from the All Blacks ripped the game away from England and while a 28-27 defeat sounded breathless, in reality the late tries from Mike Brown and Chris Ashton sugar-coated the scoreline.

England had attempted to carry on with the exciting rugby which had lit up Twickenham in the Six Nations but outplaying the All Blacks at their own high-skill, high-speed game proved beyond them. New Zealand remained the brand leaders when it came to integrated rugby and the series was lost.

'The difference between the All Blacks and ourselves is when they have periods of ascendency they convert that into points,' observed Lancaster at the time. 'When we're in the same position, we perhaps don't.'

There was still something to be taken from the tour. A Test

victory in New Zealand, even in a lost series, is something to cherish and England had, with the exception of the injured Farrell, most of their front-line side available for the third Test.

It was a chance to land a punch but instead they were knocked out. England were blown to pieces, shipping 29 points in the first 34 minutes. It was New Zealand at their breathtaking best in the first half but England all at sea.

Half-time in Lancaster's world is usually an ocean of calm. Half-time in Hamilton was different. It was, in Lancaster's words, 'an old-school rev-up'. The coach was livid at the slump in standards and exploded. The second half – a 7-7 draw – was more like it but of no consequence in terms of the result.

A tour which had offered the chance to achieve so much had ended in disappointment. Because they had to fly straight home next day, the players received their feedback from the third Test on their iPads, complete with text and audio bollockings from their coach.

They left behind an improved reputation in New Zealand. There were no headlines for misbehaviour off the pitch at the scene of their World Cup crimes. The bloated 46-man party included several who had encountered trouble there on England visits before – and Danny Cipriani, who had also blotted his copybook off the field in the past – but in Lancaster's more austere environment they proved excellent ambassadors. They took part in community activities in Auckland, Dunedin and Hamilton as well as helping raise funds for Canterbury Rugby Earthquake Relief. Ahead of the third Test, the players paid a visit to a traditional Maori meeting ground and surprised their hosts by singing a version of the Bill Withers classic 'Lean on Me'. But on the field New Zealand, rugby union's peerless standard bearers, had once again been the ones hitting all the right notes – and in the right order.

Against the best, England had come up short and it left them with some deep thinking to do. Playing the sort of ambitious rugby they had in the Six Nations was all very well but they needed to up-skill considerably if they wanted to make it stick against sides like the All Blacks.

Despite the whitewash in New Zealand, RFU chief executive Ian Ritchie handed Lancaster and his assistants unprecedented contract extensions stretching beyond the 2019 World Cup. As a demonstration of faith, it was resounding and underlined Twickenham's belief that England were on the right track.

However, an uncomfortable autumn lay in store. Three successive defeats became four with a narrow home loss to New Zealand. Jonny May's brilliant individual try, delivered perversely after listening to the soundtrack of the Disney film *Frozen* on the team bus, left scorch marks across Twickenham early on but he hardly touched the ball after that. The masters of rugby's universe again proved themselves tactically and technically superior, backing England into corners from which they could not escape. Their third try from Charlie Faumuina, which came after 22 phases in the pouring rain, was a masterpiece.

When four became five with another three-point loss to South Africa a week later, as England fought their way back from conceding a first-half interception try only to cede the momentum in the last half hour, the air was escaping from the balloon at a rapid rate.

A run of defeats has consequences. The players knew a storm was coming and in the huddle on the pitch after the Springboks defeat the message to each other was to batten down the hatches and look after one another.

As for Lancaster, his England revamp came in for the most concerted external fire of his three years in charge.

Being on the wrong end of the media's ire was a new experience for the coach. The extent of his media responsibilities had been an eye-opener from the start. Having served his apprenticeship in Yorkshire, where rugby union was not front-page news, and with the Saxons, who tended to attract a paragraph in the paper on the morning of Six Nations' games, the massed ranks of camera crews and journalists represented a quantum leap. He did not mind it when the side was going well – in fact he quite enjoyed it – but being on the back foot was something new.

The string of losses, with a home World Cup looming in ten months' time, had allowed the headline writers to run away with themselves and changed the tone of the questioning. Why couldn't he pick a settled midfield? Why couldn't England deliver a wet-weather game plan? Was he over-loyal to Owen Farrell who had played very little rugby all season because of injury?

There was a legitimate answer to the first one. A high injury toll had depleted England particularly badly in the midfield and deprived Lancaster of both Manu Tuilagi and Luther Burrell. And with Billy Twelvetrees all fingers and thumbs for Gloucester, he had no choice but to look elsewhere.

When it came to question two, the England management had twigged that running at onrushing brick walls in greasy conditions was not a smart tactic and had devised a more conservative game plan for the Springboks but, with the adrenaline flowing and the Twickenham crowd roaring, the half-backs had departed from the script. Lancaster made a mental note to be more direct with them in future.

As for the third question, well, there the coach appeared bang to rights. While Farrell had been on the treatment table, George Ford had been outstanding running a bubbling Bath side from stand-off over the first two months of the season. Farrell had been a long way short of his best in the first two games of the autumn series. Hindsight, always the wisest selector, suggested Lancaster had gone for the wrong man.

Sitting in front of the fireplace in the Carolean Room at Pennyhill Park, the faithful Collins A4 diary on the table in front of him, Lancaster came out fighting to his inquisitors. He could hardly be accused of being a conservative selector when it came to young talent. It was one of the calling cards of his tenure. From Farrell himself, who he had picked for his first side as a twenty-year-old, to second row Joe Launchbury, who he threw into the furnace of Test forward play in 2012 at twenty-one; from the Vunipola brothers to Jack Nowell, who had been refused entry to *The Wolf of Wall Street* on the week of his debut in 2013 because he didn't look eighteen, Lancaster had consistently pinned his faith in youth. He had just handed the Bath wing Anthony Watson his first Test start at twenty against South Africa, the same age as Ford had been when he made his debut off the bench in the 2014 Six Nations. But having missed the New Zealand tour, he did not feel Ford had been familiar enough with the England system to take control of the team against the top two sides in the world.

Lancaster's defence was robust but inwardly he accepted that the team was not playing well enough and changes would have to be made. He had stuck by his men after the All Blacks reverse but decided enough was enough after South Africa. He jettisoned Billy Vunipola and Danny Care from the squad, shifted Farrell to No. 12 and brought in Ford for his first start against Samoa as the side's quarterback. Dylan Hartley, who had been warned over his discipline after he had been sent off and suspended for swearing at referee Wayne Barnes in the 2013 Premiership final, was also dropped after being sin-binned for trampling on Duane Vermeulen.

The captain Chris Robshaw was under fire too. He had been one of the linchpins of Lancaster's England and a relentless workhorse in the back row but he was not delivering the turnovers that were the prime currency of attacking rugby at Test level. The name of Toulon's Steffon Armitage, arch-breakdown poacher and the European player of the year, kept cropping up. Was it time to play the 'exceptional circumstances' card and bring in a French-based player against RFU policy?

In an attempt to stop top English players moving across the Channel, where they could earn more money with a top French club, Twickenham had brought in a directive binding England into picking only those based at home. Lancaster had circumnavigated the geography before in naming Tom Palmer, from Stade Français, in his first squad, using the fact that he had signed his contract in Paris before the directive came out by way of justification.

The Armitage case was different because he had knowingly extended his contract with Toulon after the directive had been brought in, but if Lancaster wanted him badly enough the craftily phrased 'exceptional circumstances' caveat was there to assist him. Lancaster remained reluctant, partly because of the precedent it would set and partly because he would be unavailable for the majority of England's training sessions and camps.

The truth was he did not, at the time, see Armitage as the final piece of the jigsaw in the way that others did. Lancaster accepted the theory of the poacher at No. 7 but he still had reservations about Armitage's fitness and how he might blend into the England formula. The defensive patterns of the England back row required the No. 7 to stand in the tackling front line and compete hard for the ball once a tackle was made. Armitage at Toulon was much more of a freelance, lurking deep before choosing the right time to turn over the ball at a ruck.

Would parachuting him in add more to the side than excluding Robshaw would take away? Lancaster thought not. So Robshaw was retained to face Samoa, the game which stood at the edge of the abyss.

England had, as usual under Lancaster, prepared meticulously. If the outcome could have been pre-ordained by hours of analysis and intensity of training there would have been no need to worry. The Samoans, by dint of circumstance, were a rabble in comparison. But a highly unpredictable and proud rabble.

What if the Samoans played the game of their lives? What if the ball and the officials sided against England? What if? What if? What if?

Under the Twickenham lights, in what was a dry run for the evening kick-offs to come at the World Cup, the rot was stopped with a 28-9 victory. The England players joined the Samoan prayer circle on the pitch at the final whistle; their relieved coach felt like joining in too, to offer up a word of thanks.

The coach's loyalty, misplaced in Farrell's case, had been well placed in that of Robshaw. His captain was named man of a very important match.

The overall performance, though, was no great shakes. The forwards were again England's strength but the running game fragmented in the rain against the eager Samoan tacklers. Sometimes the passes stuck; sometimes they did not and against better opposition they would have been made to pay. The heat had not gone yet.

So the approach changed along with the personnel the following week. Lancaster stripped things back to basics against Australia. England's attacking game was mothballed and the pack was given licence to grind the Wallabies into submission. Farrell was dropped to the bench and twenty-one-year-old Ford was ordered to orchestrate a kick-chase game whatever the weather. It was old-school English rugby reborn.

Think of England as a rugby team and the historical image is of a well-tuned forward steamroller, a pair of kicking half-backs and five other blokes who stand around chatting and have no need to wash their kit after matches.

The stereotype is an exaggeration, obviously, but it is based loosely around the truth. England have traditionally built their rugby on collective pack power with what comes when the ball is occasionally let out as something of an afterthought.

Even England's World Cup-winning team, after a carefree start when Clive Woodward breezed in and told the side to play without a game plan, won the Webb Ellis Cup with a brand based on gnarled old forward nasties and a world-beating goal-kicker. So if rumbling rugby can win a World Cup why depart from the template?

As an ex-flanker himself, Stuart Lancaster knew the importance of forward dominance but he had seen the array of skills which the national junior sides deployed to great effect during his time lower down the RFU food chain and he thought the senior team would be selling themselves short as simply a route-one side. He wanted a multi-faceted England, one which would play a ball-in-hand game. That was what his Leeds side had attempted – they just never had the ammunition to do so successfully at Premiership level. Under Lancaster, the Saxons too were an expressive team given licence to move the ball. They had better players but very little time together and so the framework was necessarily simple. With England, he had both the players and the time to develop it and he had done so.

An enlightened philosophy is all very well but in times of strife it is best to forgo the fancy stuff and lower the portcullis. Minimising the mistakes was the priority against the Wallabies. The game plan for Australia was: kick, chase, scrum, squeeze. End of. Lancaster spelled out bluntly there would be no deviation from it. George Ford and Ben Youngs kicked the leather off the ball, the pack mauled and mauled and the defence held Australia's lethal backline out. Just.

The plan had worked, England had won and a stressful series had ended on an upturn. The sense of release at the end was palpable. Lancaster's team had stuck together when the attack dogs had been snarling and come through the other side.

Robshaw, who had again been outstanding against the Wallabies and had played all 320 minutes during the series, approached Lancaster on behalf of the squad and asked if they could head out into Richmond to unwind with a few beers. 'I understood what he was saying but with 82,000 people pouring out of Twickenham, us going to the Sun Inn probably wasn't a good idea,' said Lancaster. The last thing he needed was a load more negative headlines.

In the cold light of day, taking into account the absence of players such as Tuilagi, Alex Corbisiero, Dan Cole and Launchbury and the knock-on effect this had on the bench strength, two victories and two three-point defeats against the top two sides in the world was no disaster.

But while Lancaster insisted publicly afterwards that his team had continued to make progress, the impression from the outside was of a team in a holding phase. The surge had been replaced by stagnation.

What that testing autumn had proved to him was that the changes he had made to England beneath the surface had worked.

In the bowels of Twickenham, an hour-and-a-half after the end of the Australia game, he explained to a small huddle of journalists how he felt all the time he had invested in the cultural makeover had been vindicated. It had, along with the trust built in all the one-to-one sessions with his players, provided the anchor in the storm.

'What was apparent to me is that because we've got a strong belief in what we're doing, there was no sense of panic,' said Lancaster. 'When you lose a couple of games your culture and everything else you stand for can be challenged. People start questioning what you're doing internally. But there was none of that.

'That's when you really get tested – when the pressure's on. Can you hold it together under pressure? I think internally, within the camp, throughout the course of the week, I always had a strong sense of belief that we were going to perform against Australia. It reminded me a bit of the week we played New Zealand in 2012 after we'd lost to Australia and South Africa. There was a calmness in the squad. We were rock-solid.'

14

The Miracle Shot

I see you stand like greyhounds in the slips,
Straining upon the start. The game's afoot:
Follow your spirit, and upon this charge
Cry 'God for Harry, England and Saint George!'

Henry V, Act 3, Scene 1

The start of England's World Cup year – Tuesday 27 January 2015.

On a bright winter's day, the England squad gather at Pennyhill Park for the first time in 2015. The pine trees in the grounds are sharply defined against the blue sky and bird calls carry clearly across the still, crisp air. It is an afternoon on which to feel energised. The training pitch, though, is deserted.

Instead, England's players are inside their private training complex, screened from nosy passers-by. The shutters on the windows of the hangar are pulled down. Unblinking security guards flank the door. This is work time and they do not wish to be disturbed.

Mike Catt is putting the squad through a series of drills with the opening match of the Six Nations' Championship against Wales ten days away. Wales's defence is formidable and England are busy assembling the building blocks of their strategy to unlock it.

This is an enormous game in itself – Friday night at the Millennium Stadium, Cardiff, is quite a prospect – but in the context of Wales and England residing in the same World Cup group later this year, it is even more important. This season's Six Nations is anticipated as keenly as usual but there are additional psychological blows to be landed with the tournament looming large.

Catt played in four World Cups for England. He experienced everything from being steamrollered by Jonah Lomu in the 1995 semi-final to having the last touch in the 2003 final, a languid clearance kick off the pitch which meant England were world champions. He knows what is coming in eight months' time. A home World Cup makes this the most important year of these players' professional lives.

On the wall of England's hotel hangs a photo montage of the 2003 triumph. A few paces further along the corridor is a curving staircase down which lies the team room. In there that morning, with the area sealed off by a strategically placed easel warning 'This area is closed for a private function', the players had been reminded by Stuart Lancaster and Bill Beswick of the significance of 2015. It would not be a year for short cuts, it would be a year when the squad's mantras of self-sacrifice and hard graft had to be lived. In a tournament of tight margins, the small things would make the big difference.

Inside the training building, underneath the roof lights, the atmosphere is intense – studious almost. You can sense the concentration. The players are zoned in, hanging on Catt's every word. In his black T-shirt, the slight figure of the skills coach is dwarfed by the giants in red surrounding him in the centre of the green artificial pitch. He relays his instructions in his clipped South African accent.

'Remember, the defence is coming to get us, so stay nice and square and run at the space. OK, off we go.'

The players, silent and still to this point, are suddenly animated, filling the room with deadened sound as they organise their small, diamond-shaped attack units, trying to hold the defenders in their yellow bibs with dummy runners and make holes to flood through.

Catt, a whistle round his neck, prowls constantly, checking on the delivery of the passes. The action is fast and precise, replicating as closely as possible the speed of a Test match. On his haunches, watching the angles of running, like a golfer studying the line of a putt, is Lancaster.

Behind him on the wall is a sign which reads 'Kill Zone'. Underneath it is the explanation – 'The intensity at which we physically and emotionally break the opposition'. They had talked about the kill zone, and what they needed to do to visit it, at their squad meeting that morning.

There is a quote, too, on the wall from Ulysses S. Grant, the American Civil War general and later president. 'In every battle there comes a time when both sides consider themselves at their limit, then he who continues the attack wins.'

England are training to attack.

'Silver, silver,' bawls James Haskell above the din to Ben Youngs as he bursts through on to a short ball.

Wales defence coach Shaun Edwards observed before the opening game of the championship that when he watched England's style he was reminded of Wigan, his old rugby league side. He was partly right. With Andy Farrell as Lancaster's key lieutenant, there was always going to be a Wigan flavour but there was some Leeds Rhinos and Warrington Wolves thrown in there, too.

In fact, watch any top Super League game closely and there is a resemblance to the way England attempt to pull apart defences. The first session Lancaster took with the squad back in 2012 at West Park Leeds revolved around just this style of attack.

When Lancaster was quizzing Tony Smith in his formative Leeds days, the pair weren't talking rolling mauls. He was very interested in what rugby league could bring to rugby union and after they went their separate ways they kept in touch.

'We don't meet up that often but when we get together he'll often bring a video clip of my team and ask what we are doing in a certain situation tactically. I'd show him a clip of his team of how some things cross over into both codes,' said Smith. 'We've learned a lot from each other over the years. I can see some rugby league influence in some of the plays England use now. I remember talking to him about why some of those plays work in rugby league and I can see he's adapted those to rugby union and they have been successful in that code as well. I now do watch England play rugby union and that's all because of him. It's the only reason I would!'

In the training facility, watching by a punchbag, stands Graham Rowntree. On an unused tackle shield, Andy Farrell is talking to Geoff Parling and Tom Wood. Both players are injured. Parling has a blue wire attached to his leg, Wood is in a protective boot, two of the casualties of a punishing weekend of European club action.

The treadmill of the domestic game has again taken its toll ahead of an England campaign. Farrell's son Owen has been ruled out of the entire championship by a knee injury. He is nowhere to be seen; nor is Courtney Lawes, who will miss the start of it too. In all a dozen front-line players are injured including Manu Tuilagi who, through a set of glass doors, can be seen exercising with a rope in a gym housing weights like Formula One tyres. Every one bears the logo of the England rose.

None of the players involved in the European ties 48 hours beforehand are training either, which means there are almost as many people around the indoor pitch as on it. Beswick is there, alone by the one unshielded window from which sunlight streams in, interpreting the body language. Matt Parker is watching, too, with his 2015 World Cup plan in its penultimate refinement stage. The conditioners and physios are there as well. Dylan Hartley calls one over for a stretching session in a brief break between drills and then the next one begins as Ben Youngs charges off to trigger the play while the runners align themselves rapidly.

'If it's not on, boys, just set it up. Don't force it,' says Catt, preaching patience to his attackers as they urgently go through their phases.

For most, it is a case of slotting back into the England way after two months with their clubs; for one – Nick Easter – it is his first day at a new school after almost four years away from England.

The broken leg sustained by Ben Morgan, the player of the autumn series, has left a hole which Lancaster, after some deliberation, has filled with Easter. The thirty-six-year-old had been tainted by association with the 2011 World Cup squad and had not been part of the England scene since Lancaster's makeover.

Yet, despite his self-confessed 'old-school' rugby outlook, Easter had been defying Old Father Time by performing consistently well for Harlequins and in pure playing terms more than justified his selection. Conor O'Shea, Quins' director of rugby, had been trying hard to persuade Lancaster of his merits for a long time.

It was a call-up which made sense on rugby grounds. England had been exposed by the powerful Welsh when they deployed a fill-in No. 8 in Cardiff two years earlier and they needed a specialist back-up No. 8 to Billy Vunipola but, in terms of personality, it appeared to go against the grain for Lancaster.

Before he recalled Easter, he had arranged to meet him on his territory. In a pub. Easter, who had been so convinced he would again be overlooked by England that he had booked a Caribbean holiday for the training week, made sure he arrived early and had just bought himself a drink when Lancaster turned up at the Stag in Ascot. 'It was a pint with a triple whisky chaser,' joked Easter.

The pair talked for an hour.

'We went back through time and went back to the World Cup. To me, he expressed his desire at not finishing his England career on the 2011 World Cup and to come back and finish the story. He convinced me he would buy into us as a group and add real value,' Lancaster explained when he announced Easter's inclusion in a boardroom of sponsors QBE in the City of London.

The coach was confident that the England environment he had created was now so robust it could not be bent out of shape by mavericks. Instead it would make loyalists out of the rebels.

So Easter was in, as was Danny Cipriani who had been rewarded for his form at Sale. He was another who had been in trouble at various stages of his career off the field but Lancaster had seen a reformed character on the tour to New Zealand the previous summer and was sure he would swim in the right direction.

Both were training with the national side again as eagerly as puppy dogs for a game which England would start as clear outsiders.

With England's injury list the odds were logical but from the way they were shaping it did not look as if Lancaster's men were planning to give Wales a free ride at the Millennium Stadium. There was no tackling or contest for the ball but the execution was impressive. In their first 40-minute session of the year – and first together for two months – only one pass was dropped.

England's private training complex is gleamingly modern. An electronic board, bearing the name of every player, lists the extra physical activities each will be required to do that day. It is also meticulously organised. Each player has a cubby hole which houses his personal weight-training schedule.

The set up is state of the art yet the connection with England's rugby ancestry is also highly visible. The first thing the players see as they enter the building, to the stirring accompaniment of the voiceover to their team DVD, is an England shirt worn by Wavell Wakefield, the great forward and captain of the 1920s. At the head of the stairs, on their way to the indoor training pitch, is a picture of Arthur Harrison VC. Next to it is a quote from him – 'It takes a certain kind of man to wear the shirt' – and a list of the winners of England's defensive awards since they were instigated. It is a working environment designed to fuse the inspiration of the past with the perspiration of the present.

Quite what Wakefield and Harrison would have made of the racket emanating from the indoor training centre eight days later is anyone's guess. Blasting out 'Hymns and Arias', the Welsh rugby anthem, at full volume as England trained 48 hours before the game was an interesting – and deafening – call by Lancaster.

England had been taken aback by the atmosphere on their last visit to the Millennium Stadium and the coach wanted no surprises on what promised to be a raucous Friday-night opening to the championship.

He had taken the recording from the referee's microphone in the closing stages of the 2013 game, had Steve Walsh's voice removed and fed the remix through a powerful speaker hired from a stockist in nearby Camberley to give the England players a taste of what lay ahead. Eight of them had never played there before.

'One of the bits of feedback we gave the players before the game two years ago was that the acoustics of the stadium are so loud that sometimes you can't hear the communication on the field,' Lancaster explained after announcing his side for the game at Pennyhill Park.

'Mike Catt kept repeatedly saying this and all the players nodded their heads and said: "yeah, yeah, yeah". Until they had actually experienced that they didn't really know, but afterwards they all came round and said: "You were right".

'I didn't want to leave it to chance this time around. It was only for ten minutes but I wanted them to get the sense of what it feels like to play there. We did some phase-play attack inside without the players being able to hear themselves think.'

Tom Croft, one of the survivors of 2013, thought the technicians might have gone over the top. 'It was probably louder in the training indoor facility than it is actually in the Millennium Stadium,' he said.

Despite the goading of Wales coach Warren Gatland, England had chosen to leave the roof open for the match which in theory served to diffuse the noise but there was still an intimidating edge to the atmosphere on game night. Actually, it was worse than that. It was downright lairy. This was no setting for the faint-hearted.

Wales's plan was to send England out into the lion's den as early as possible – and keep them waiting before their own grand entrance. The ploy might have worked had the attention of England's management not been drawn to the pre-match running order they received before the game.

According to the timings they had been given, there would be a six-minute gap between England taking the field and the match starting. Not even Ireland or South Africa's anthems took that long. Lancaster smelled a rat.

After a discussion between the management team, Chris Robshaw was told that under no circumstances was he to lead England on to the field and into the nightclub-style sound and light show which was scheduled to take place until Wales appeared in the tunnel.

When they were asked to do so on the night, Robshaw stood firm. When they were asked again to go out by Welsh officials his Harlequins henchman Mike Brown added his two penn'orth and asked the Wales substitutes, who had appeared, if they wanted to go out first. England were going nowhere.

The stand-off lasted five minutes. In the end referee Jérôme Garcès had to give Robshaw his assurance that if Wales had not appeared within a minute of England heading out on to the field they could come back in.

He had made his point and out they went to be roundly booed by sections of the Cardiff crowd.

'You just have to listen to the captain and trust what he says is the right thing,' said England second row George Kruis, one of the Millennium Stadium new boys. 'We cut our time down on the field standing there getting shouted at by the Welsh so I think it was a good call.'

Wales did keep England waiting for a couple of minutes before they came out but the message was clear. England were in no mood to be pushed around. When they subsequently went on to shock Wales and deliver an outstanding 21-16 victory to open the championship the two events were immediately linked.

Actually, England's show of defiance did nothing for their start – they were 10-0 down inside eight minutes – but the resilience and belief they showed to claw their way back into the game before half-time spoke of a side on a mission.

The second-half performance was so dominant that Wales were hardly in the game and had the rampaging James Haskell not spun out of a tackle and into a post, rather than over the line, the margin of victory would have been more comfortable.

'My neck is broken but apparently the post's had to retire,' winced Haskell afterwards.

England had made a significant statement against their upcoming World Cup opponents. As with Australia, the other piranhas in a crowded pool, the result made it successive wins over their main group rivals for England.

For Lancaster, the immediate reaction was elation. The 30-3 defeat in Cardiff two years beforehand had been the nadir of his time with England; this was an exhilarating flip side.

England's big runners had battered their way through Wales's inside defence as he had planned and Anthony Watson and Jonathan Joseph had taken advantage to score the tries on the outside. Joseph's second-half score was particularly pleasing, coming after Wales's defence had been manipulated through 20 phases of patient attack. Just what England had been practising away from prying eyes ten days earlier.

It was a monumentally satisfying win for the England coach. There was even a show of emotion from Lancaster as he appeared to leap for joy on his way down the tunnel. Pictures can be misleading – he was actually trying to reach an England fan up above to respond to an offer of a high five – but even so the grin told its own story. It was after midnight when he met Andy Farrell at the bar of the St David's Hotel. The one beer he stretched to probably tasted unusually good.

Elation does not last long for a coach. After a few hours' sleep, Lancaster was up and running around Cardiff Bay clearing his head to plan the following week.

When the squad reassembled, the injured Wood addressed the team to tell them how proud he was of them. Like Tuilagi, Wood had sent Lancaster a good-luck message for the team the night before the Wales game. Their words reinforced the sense in the coach that this was an England side who had long since passed the point of playing for themselves.

The next challenge was Italy at Twickenham. They had never beaten England and, despite the concession of an early try to Sergio Parisse, there never looked the remotest chance that they would do so. The game turned into a showcase for England's flowering attack – and in particular the Bath axis of George Ford and Jonathan Joseph.

Handed his debut three years earlier by Lancaster in South Africa, Joseph had drifted so far from the England picture that he had not even made the 46-man squad for the tour to New Zealand in 2014. His omission had been a kick up the backside which had sparked a big change in his approach at Bath.

Despite being relocated to the wing early on when Watson took the concussed Brown's place at the back, Joseph carried on where he left off in Cardiff, scoring two of England's six tries with his graceful running. It helped enormously that he had his clubmate Ford, on the other side of the battering ram Burrell, pulling the strings. Still only twenty-one, Ford was bringing defenders on to him like bulls to a matador before, with a swirl of his cape, sending his team-mates through gaps with his skilfully delayed passes.

Owen Farrell, at Twickenham on crutches, must have had mixed feelings. Here was one of his closest friends, who had done his homework for him as a kid on occasions so they could escape the academic grind to kick a rugby ball around, making the England No. 10 shirt his own.

Round three, though, a dogfight in Dublin, would serve as a reminder that Ford – and England – were not yet the finished article.

Ireland stand-off Johnny Sexton, one game back from a long concussion lay-off, was outstanding as Ireland, the Six Nations' champions, took charge of the championship with a 19-9 win.

The rugby, frankly, was pig-ugly but forensically precise. The straitjacket Sexton and Conor Murray imposed on England with their pinpoint kicking proved almost impossible to escape from. They finally did so in the last quarter when Sexton went off but by then it was too late.

For Ireland, the ends more than justified the means. They had attempted to outrun England at Twickenham 12 months earlier and lost out narrowly in a high-calibre rugby match. Joe Schmidt, their savvy Kiwi coach, had moved Ireland into a much more pragmatic phase and it was paying rich dividends. This was their tenth win in a row.

England were unable to counteract the aerial barrage that came their way and they compounded their problems with the penalties and turnovers they conceded at the breakdown. Throw in a brain-freeze moment when Chris Robshaw chose to kick for the corner in the first half in search of a try, only for line-out caller Dave Attwood to order a long throw to the tail where 6 foot 11 inches Devin Toner was waiting, and England were becalmed.

Ireland captain Paul O'Connell admitted afterwards he never, for a moment, expected a 19-3 scoreline with half-an-hour left but that was how the scoreboard read after Robbie Henshaw outjumped Brown's stand-in Alex Goode to score the game's only try.

England belatedly rallied with a couple of penalties and, had Easter's try not been ruled out for obstruction with ten minutes left, there could have been a frenetic finish but as it was the last play saw even a consolation try from Jack Nowell disallowed by referee Craig Joubert for a forward pass by Billy Twelvetrees.

'This championship might come down to points difference. I hope that doesn't come back to bite us,' said Andy Farrell afterwards in what turned out to be a prophetic observation.

Ireland were deserved winners, fair and square, but there was a huge amount of frustration for England. They had anticipated and trained for an Ireland kick-a-thon; they had just failed to cope with its accuracy.

'We knew how difficult it was going to be. It was right up there alongside the Wales game, if not tougher, because of the quality of the opposition and the run they were on. But some of the problems were of our own making,' reflected Lancaster, a few days later back at Pennyhill Park.

'The indiscipline and penalty count had a bearing on the score, as did not taking a chance when we did go to the corner. You have to be able to control the big moments and we didn't get enough of those right to win the game. When you are away against a team that has won nine on the bounce, you have got to get accuracy and decision-making to the highest level and we didn't achieve that.'

Had Lancaster picked the right team? In theory he had the experience of Courtney Lawes, Tom Wood and Brad Barritt available – they were all playing Premiership rugby that weekend – but to throw any of them straight into a Test match after a lengthy injury lay-off would have gone against the coach's usual *modus operandi*.

'Selection-wise, the hand was pretty much dealt given the lack of game time of the more experienced players I had available. That is, they had not played at all so there was not a huge amount that could have been done there,' concluded Lancaster.

Had he dealt the cards he held correctly? The decision to leave Danny Cipriani, who had scored within a minute of coming on against Italy, unused on the bench in the usual flurry of second-half substitutions attracted some criticism.

'There are two hard positions to change as a coach – captain and fly-half,' said Lancaster. 'I do trust Cipriani to come on and make a difference and I could have done so after seventy-two minutes but I had made that many changes in a relatively short space of time and momentum was clearly going our way.'

Had Joe Schmidt out-thought him tactically? Schmidt and Lancaster are different sorts of coaches. Both pride themselves on their attention to detail but they tend to prioritise different areas.

Where Schmidt will spend hours choreographing set moves for his team to follow to the letter, Lancaster is not an overly prescriptive coach. He has his favoured starter sequences but he prefers to spend time working on what players might do once play has opened up. In Ireland the game remained firmly clamped shut.

If he'd had that preparation time again, Lancaster would have placed more emphasis on the breakdown. The fast, attacking possession the likes of Ford and Joseph thrived on was slowed to a trickle by Ireland's domination in this area.

But the bald fact was that Ireland had simply outplayed England in the type of game which materialised at the Aviva Stadium. 'We knew exactly what type of game Ireland were going to bring but they executed their game better than we did,' said Lancaster.

'They're a high-quality team across the board. They have a simple game plan that they execute well, primarily when Johnny Sexton is on the field. We needed to be nine or ten out of ten in our execution. We were six in the first fifty minutes, eight by the end.'

Lancaster's message to the team in their review session the following week was not to give up hope on the championship because Ireland had been put in exactly the same position by England the previous season and had come through to win the title. They still had to go to Wales.

When the Welsh duly re-enacted Rorke's Drift with a heroic defensive stand in round four to end Ireland's winning streak, the door suddenly reopened for England. But the convincing win they needed over wooden-spoon-bound Scotland to assume control of the title race never materialised.

They ripped Scotland's defence apart almost at will but 12 line breaks were converted into only three tries. Scotland's scramble defence was wholehearted but the wastefulness was criminal. The atmosphere afterwards among the England players was almost as if they had lost, rather than won 25-13.

If all the hours they had spent training together during the Six Nations had been added up, breaking down defences and finishing would have topped the time-distribution chart. While Part A had been spot on, Part B had been miles off.

'It was frustrating. We just tried to do too much, tried to force the offloads and the passes a little bit. We have to take our time and realise they are the ones under pressure,' said Joseph, who was on the scoresheet again. 'It's not always going to be the same picture every time – we have to see what's in front of us and react accordingly.'

The upshot was that the final Six Nations before the World Cup would come down to a three-way shoot-out on the last day. England led the table by a points differential of four from Ireland with Wales 25 adrift but they had to face France at Twickenham while their rivals had the tournament makeweights, Italy and Scotland, to play, albeit away from home.

It was a unique situation with such a labyrinth of imponderables as to be mentally exhausting. Lancaster distracted his players in the build-up with key messages on defence and breakdown speed and himself with his customary walk around Virginia Water. On the way there and back he would play his Bill Walsh CD for guidance.

And so to the day itself. The staggered kick-off times were manifestly unfair on the teams, distracting for the players and coaches but magnificent for the viewer. What transpired was one of the greatest days in the tournament's history.

The Welsh, first up in Rome, looked to be going nowhere at half-time when they led by a single point. The second half, though, was a turkey shoot with the Italians picked off at will. The England squad, watching at the team hotel, saw the margin of victory they needed against France expanding with each try by George North. When Wales breached the 60-point barrier, England were heading into mission-impossible territory.

Lancaster, who had avoided most of the action, saw three tries in the space of five minutes and elected to avoid the rest.

A late converted breakaway try from Leonardo Sarto brought some respite but the victory target a remarkable Welsh performance had set was still an imposing 16 points.

By the time the England team bus had pulled into the West Car Park, Ireland were well on their way to extending it. The supporters watching there on a giant screen cheered the sporadic Scottish attacks but they were few and far between as the holders pushed their way past Wales, showing they too could play handling rugby when the mood took them.

Lancaster, watching in the coaches' annexe next to the players' changing room, saw the total rise inexorably. When the final whistle blew, Ireland's 40-10 win left England needing to beat France by 26 points to take the championship. France may have been their annual disappointment but they had not lost a game by more than ten in the Six Nations since 2009.

Lancaster took a deep breath and broke the news to the players 35 minutes before kick-off, just before they headed out for their final warm-up. He told them it would take 80 minutes but that if they did not panic and did not go for broke too early they could do it. He believed in them.

'There was no panic whatsoever when he told us,' said Luther Burrell. 'As a group of players we are very confident and we know we're a very fit squad and in the last twenty minutes of any game we are going to put the hammer down. It was about putting in an eighty-minute performance. It was very quiet in the changing room but you could feel the energy from the players.'

England had been training all week with the intention of moving the French giants around. Castigated domestically for their dreary rugby, France had decided to take a day off from drudgery and go the same way. The result – with the title on the line – was one of the all-time classic Six Nations' games.

From the moment Ben Youngs went over for England's first try inside two minutes, it was a riotous blur of movement. It was less a rugby match than frantic, fantastic, urgent lunacy.

There was a length-of-the-field try finished by a prop, Vincent Debaty, a murderous tackle from Lawes which temporarily turned Jules Plisson into a rag doll, a yellow card for a trip by Haskell . . . it was the game that had everything.

When England trailed 15-7 after a try by Noa Nakaitaci, their championship race looked run but they refused to accept their fate and fought back with score after score. It was the attacking rugby they had trained for made real. The trouble was the French had come to play as well and they were also reeling off the tries. Just as soon as the target moved tantalisingly into range, *Les Bleus* moved it out again.

With five minutes left to play, England still needed two converted tries but they simply would not give up the chase. When Jack Nowell went over for his second try from Ford's pass, Twickenham was in tumult.

With one minute left, England won a scrum penalty and Ford kicked to the corner. The line-out drive, with full-back Mike Brown and replacement centre Billy Twelvetrees adding their weight, rumbled mesmerisingly to within two metres before buckling. Penalty try? No. Not even a penalty. England came again but, short on numbers, referee Nigel Owens, an outstanding contributor to a magnificent game, penalised Easter for sealing the ball off. The French, in one last blast of insanity, attempted to run from their own line in overtime but England could not force the turnover and Rory Kockott put the ball out of play to end the game. France had denied England the title and the scrum-half clenched his fists in celebration.

England had won 55-35 but the silence which followed in that moment was as deafening as the noise during the game. Lancaster put his head in his hands. The presentation podium under the North Stand would remain unused. The trophy belonged to Ireland once again.

On the pitch afterwards in a huddle, Lancaster parked his own crushing disappointment to try to help his players process the pain of heroic failure. He told them it was the most courageous performance he had ever seen and that he was proud of them all. 'I tried to move them, immediately afterwards, to a point where they understood the game they'd just played in,' explained Lancaster. 'But it is very hard when you're Chris Robshaw or Mike Brown who's played in four championships and come second four times.'

The crestfallen players broke up to take a walk around Twickenham and thank their supporters. They received a standing ovation. None of the fans there that day would ever forget what they had just witnessed. It was a phenomenal game and a scintillating England display. Even Joe Schmidt thought so. 'I spare a thought for England,' he said. 'They were superb and probably deserved a share of the spoils.'

Despite scoring more than twice as many tries as Ireland in the championship and making more than twice as many breaks, England had lost out to Schmidt's side in the photo finish. While they had hit more highs, they had also suffered more lows than the consistent Irish so, once again, they had to make do with runners-up spot.

It seemed like there could be no short cuts for England rugby sides. They simply had to suffer their battle scars.

England had lost one game per season in four successive Six Nations' campaigns under Lancaster; Sir Clive Woodward's World Cup winners lost one championship game for five successive seasons before their epiphanous 2003.

The transition from base metal to gold is never instantaneous. England, by now up to 440 caps as a starting 15, had evolved from spirited stoppers to a side capable of tearing apart major Test nations. That they could still find a way to lose to the best sides indicated the alchemy process was not yet complete.

The journey from a rabble to a good team was complete; now they had to take the next step. To become a great team.

'From good to great is the toughest job of all,' reflected Bill Beswick. 'The last 10 per cent is the hardest. A lot of coaches can get a team to good but to get to great is very difficult. It's not one thing that does it but a lot of little one per centers. A lot of it is holding your nerve while a team builds the experience to become great. You can't shortcut to greatness – that's the mistake football makes all the time.

'In many great teams there would be initial excitement and progression, a period of levelling-off and then a kick-start as the team find themselves and then a plateau when they reach 90 per cent. Then it is a case of searching for those one per cents – finding the right selection balance, changing the training load . . . trying to find the formula – and, all of a sudden, they catch fire.'

What England had proved beyond all doubt in the 2015 Six Nations was that they could incinerate teams with their attack when they got it right. Their total of 18 tries was the most in the championship for nine years.

The bookmakers rubber-stamped them as second favourites for the World Cup behind holders New Zealand. Post-France, no one in their right mind would look forward to playing them at Twickenham. Not even the All Blacks.

It was going to be some event, the biggest in the history of rugby union. For the England head coach, though, it could wait. The following weekend he was back on the touchline at Pocklington with West Park Leeds under-14s.

15

Leadership

How sweet a thing it is to wear a crown;
Within whose circuit is Elysium
And all that poets feign of bliss and joy.
                Henry VI Part 3, Act 1, Scene 2

A game of rugby union is like a giant jigsaw. With 30 players on the pitch, it is all a bit of a muddle but occasionally, gloriously, order breaks out. For this to happen, and for a coherent picture to emerge, 15 individuals need to do the right thing at the right time. For rugby union's devotees, this inter-reliance makes it the ultimate team sport.

Jonny Wilkinson may have dropped the goal which won England a World Cup in Sydney in 2003 but 'zig-zag' – the call which won them the Webb Ellis Cup – was a team move. In the 32 seconds from the ball leaving Steve Thompson's hands at the line-out to Wilkinson becoming a national hero many players were involved.

Wilkinson could not have performed his party trick if Thompson had not thrown in straight at the line-out and Lewis

Moody caught the throw. If Mike Catt had not made the initial inroads into the Australian midfield, England would not have enjoyed forward momentum; if Matt Dawson had not garnered a few more precious metres and Martin Johnson had not taken the ball up again they would not have been in such good position. And if Dawson's pass had been wide, Wilkinson would not have been given the split second he needed to send the ball over the onrushing Wallabies and between the posts.

Everyone needed everyone else.

The inter-connectedness can be extended further – beyond the team itself. The skills of those great players had been honed over countless hours by fine coaches in Andy Robinson, Phil Larder and Dave Alred. Without their input, something might have gone awry in the sequence.

The ultimate team game ultimately relies on one man – the visionary who pulls it all together, the head coach. In 2003 that was Clive Woodward.

If there is no shepherd to lead the flock, no one pointing the side in the right direction on and off the field it all falls apart. The buck stops with the head coach. Win and he is a man of letters; lose and he is a fool. Woodward was knighted for his remarkable achievement of winning the World Cup; two years later he was pilloried for his stewardship of the Lions in New Zealand.

Being head coach of a national rugby union team can bring with it tremendous elation and satisfaction but it can also be a lonely role, as Stuart Lancaster has found out since taking charge of England. There are, inevitably, dark times involved as the leader.

'It was tough when we lost in the Millennium Stadium when we were on for the Grand Slam . . . it was tough losing in New Zealand. I had a pretty rough ride in the autumn of 2014 and it was difficult, if I'm being honest,' admitted Lancaster.

'When you're going through those tough times you have to think to yourself: "I'm in a leadership position, I've got to stand up in front of these people and tell them why we are going to win the next game and why everything is on track". In a leadership position you've got to find a way to absorb the pressure and to deal with it. You have to work out in your own mind why you have put yourself in that situation.'

The answer is not always immediately obvious. At times it is a painful existence. In *The Score Takes Care of Itself*, Bill Walsh runs through the side effects of coaching a top team.

'How do you know if you're doing the job?' asks Walsh. 'If you're up at 3 a.m. every night talking into a tape recorder and writing notes on scraps of paper, have a knot in your stomach and rash on your skin, are losing sleep and losing touch with your wife and kids, have no appetite or sense of humour and feel that everything might turn out wrong... then you're probably doing the job. There is a significant price to pay to be the best.'

Lancaster recognises the symptoms but he knows the cure too. 'In the tough times, sometimes I have questioned my sanity and why I have put myself in this position. I've got my wife and two kids in Leeds and I'm in London all the time. I have put my neck on the block,' he said.

'But actually when you arrive at Twickenham with 82,000 people in England shirts shouting and screaming, it makes it all worthwhile. I never have days when I don't want to get out of bed, I never feel like that. I still bound out of bed at six in the morning on game day and wonder what the hell I'm going to do until kick-off.'

The business of leadership is often misunderstood. To those of a certain vintage, when leadership is mentioned, an image of Windsor Davies bawling – eyes popping – into his troops' faces in the TV sitcom *It Ain't Half Hot Mum* springs to mind. That is not leading. It is shouting.

A leader may shout but more often he considers, he plans and he acts. A leader sets the tone for the whole organisation and delivers a vision for his players to buy into. He is the compass for the side, the figurehead who sets the co-ordinates for where the team is heading and tells them how they will find their way there. He directs. While he may invite the thoughts of others, he makes the calls.

'The difference between offering an opinion and making a decision is the difference between working for the leader and being the leader,' Lancaster said. 'If you take selection, there are plenty of opinions in rugby that I have thrown at me from the coaching team downwards. Faz has a view, Wig has a view and Catty has a view. So does Stuart Barnes, Clive Woodward ... everyone has a view. But ultimately you are in a position as the leader where you have to make a decision. And sometimes people just want to know what the decision is and then back it.'

Selection is where Lancaster earns his bucks and he is meticulous in his approach. He collates two lots of data – objective and subjective – to help him make a decision for each position. The objective data is collected by OPTA from all games involving Premiership clubs and will cover areas such as tackles, offloads, defenders beaten and breakdown effectiveness. The subjective data comes from Lancaster and his assistant coaches.

Lancaster will watch DVDs of all six Premiership games on a club weekend and sometimes attend one in person. All three of his coaching staff will do likewise. Then England's management will mark each squad member out of ten across a variety of categories. These will vary depending on position. These scores will be pooled and the numbers crunched. Jonathan Joseph was picked for the 2015 Six Nations on the back of the fact that he was the highest-scoring centre in this ranking system.

The marks do not dictate selection entirely – Lancaster will add in any pertinent information on form or attitude from club directors of rugby and any injury updates and, like any coach, he retains the right to follow a hunch. His tenure has been marked by a willingness to go out on a limb. He selected Tom Youngs, a converted centre, as hooker for the 2012 tour to South Africa before he had started a Premiership game in the position. As the leader, calls like this have to be his. He stands or falls by them.

In Becker and Hill's book *Secrets of Winning Coaches Revealed*, Lancaster outlined his thoughts on leadership.

'I think people are born with it. Through whatever your life-style has been, through the genes, through your own personality and the way you've been shaped during your formative years, you will have some leadership quality about you. The best will have 50 per cent but that's at least 50 per cent which you can learn to grow,' he wrote.

To release the other 50 per cent requires constant study of other coaches and leaders in other fields.

Becoming England coach might have stopped the process of harvesting knowledge for others – if he had made it to the top he must be good – mustn't he? – but in Lancaster it accelerated his drive to accumulate it. He met with leading football managers such as Arsène Wenger, chief executives of multi-national companies and in his spare moments continued to read widely.

There were no trashy whodunits on his holiday reading list. Apart from absorbing the thoughts of World Cup-winning coaches like Woodward and Graham Henry, he also read books by military men like General Colin Powell and management gurus like Jim Collins. He even dipped into Abraham Lincoln and the American Civil War.

Top-level rugby coaching has moved on a long way since a moustache, tracksuit and whistle were all that were required. A coach is no longer just a coach, according to the man who trains them at the RFU, Kevin Bowring.

'Coaching on the field is fine but leadership and management are also part of the coaching process,' said Bowring. 'I think Stuart sees his role as a combination of all three. What keeps him sane is his on-field coaching which is really important to him, but he really bought into the concept of a coach as a leader and manager.'

Lancaster loves coaching – he is England's head coach and he enthusiastically does what it says on the tin – but ask him which he views as the most important element of the trinity and he will say, without hesitation, leadership. If he is not providing the lead for England, they will go nowhere.

So what sort of leader is he? From a management point of view, he provides clarity, says Matt Parker. 'Winning teams absolutely have to have a clear direction and strong leadership which Stuart gives us in abundance. He knows what he wants,' said Parker. 'He is not too dissimilar to Dave Brailsford in many ways – both are visionary, both inspirational and both incredibly hard working.'

From a player's point of view, he provides direction. No one inside the England squad is in any doubt where the line is drawn when it comes to behaviour. When Manu Tuilagi was found guilty of three counts of assault in May 2015 after an altercation with a taxi driver and two female police officers, he knew what was coming. Potential World Cup-winner for England when fit or not, he was out on his ear. When Dylan Hartley head-butted Jamie George and picked up a suspension which stretched beyond the opening game of the World Cup, he was gone too. 'Stuart has no tolerance – which is exactly what you need if you are controlling

English rugby. You certainly know your place as a player with England,' said Courtney Lawes.

The Northampton second row likes to wear his hood up; Lancaster prefers it down. So it stays down. The demarcation lines are clear.

Lancaster is strict but he is not a dictator. Bowring often calls in on England training camps and sees a leader who balances discipline with a human side in his dealings with his players. 'He has an immense knowledge of them as people and players. He cares about their feelings. Even though he has to give them tough messages at times, he does it in a humanistic way but still a totally honest way,' said Bowring. 'His processes are based on communication, people management, trust and delegation. And he uses a lot of positive psychology.'

There is a pastoral element to his stewardship despite the crew cut and ramrod posture.

When he was running the Leeds Academy, Lancaster under-went a personality profiling test to see how he rated as a leader. It concluded he had a:

> '...calm unruffled manner, consistent and steady under pressure.'
> '...positive overall approach, diplomatic and sensitive to the needs of others.'
> '...personality capable of influencing others to his point of view.'

But it also pointed out that he:

> '...may allow others to take advantage of him.'
> '...may be over-tolerant of non-producers.'

i.e. he could be too nice.

Whenever any of his players has been faced with a choice of putting family or England first he has always advised family. Joe Marler missed the concluding game of the 2013 Six Nations to be at his partner Daisy's bedside for the birth of their child, Jasper; Tom Youngs missed the 2014 tour to New Zealand because of his wife Tiffany's serious illness.

He may deliver the odd dressing room hair-dryer – the changing rooms in Hamilton in 2014 had the paint peeled off – but the Sergeant Major approach is rare.

'Stuart is pretty controlled. He's not generally a shouter and bawler,' said Tom Palmer, who has been in club and country dressing rooms with him. Lancaster relies on a more rounded approach. His communications skills are excellent.

When Jack Rowell summoned wide-eyed schoolboy Paul Sampson to train with his England squad in 1996, the acerbic coach greeted him with the words: 'They told me you were bigger.'

It is hard to imagine Lancaster delivering such a deflating opening line. He has a natural ability to connect on a personal level with players. 'What is the key quality of a high-performance coach? I always come back to emotional intelligence. That involves an awareness of yourself and your own emotions and an awareness of others in order to get the best out of them. He's got it,' said Bowring.

After he has finalised the selection of the England side, Lancaster will always make a point of meeting individually with every player in his squad to outline his involvement. He will tell each player face-to-face whether he is in the side and, if not, why.

'I've worked with some coaches who will turn over a flipchart and say: "There you are, lads, that's the team, away you go and get on with it," but my belief is that I should explain to the players why I have made the decision I have,' said Lancaster.

'I genuinely believe that if you don't do it that way with England it would fall apart very quickly because the stakes are so high and the margins so small. I spend a lot of time with the non-twenty-three players making sure they have feedback as to why they're not getting picked and tell them how to get picked.'

As someone who was not always an automatic selection during his own modest career, he has an understanding about these matters which a superstar player-turned-coach may not.

Lancaster also likes to sit down one-on-one with each assistant coach to run through his thinking before finalising his team for a match. Graham Rowntree will have specific input on the forwards and Andy Farrell and Mike Catt the backs. If the discussion surrounds Owen Farrell – Andy's son – Lancaster trusts his backs' coach to give a professional, rather than personal, opinion, when consulted.

He notes their thoughts but it is Lancaster, as leader, who draws up the 15 names to start the game. 'There might be a fifty-fifty call but ultimately I will make the final call and they will back it,' said Lancaster. 'It's the toughest part of the job – of that there is no doubt. It is easy with hindsight but the margins are so small. Deciding on the team and then communicating that decision to the players is difficult because they are all passionate about playing for England.'

Once players are in for the start of a tournament or series, there is rarely change for change's sake. Lancaster tends to remain loyal to those who have served England well in the past. One of his favourite phrases is 'credit in the bank' and once this has been accumulated by a player it takes a while to use it up. Despite the radical overhaul he undertook at the start of his tenure, Lancaster had picked just 67 players by the end of the 2015 Six Nations, which made England one of the most stable international set-ups. Of the major Test-playing nations, only New Zealand, with 57, had selected fewer players over the same period. 'It's an environment where they know they can do things without fear of failure or getting dropped without any reason. There has to be a security in the team' is Lancaster's view.

The players have to trust and believe in the leader otherwise it is a relationship built on quicksand. Lancaster believes every coach has an internal credibility scale with his players which rises or falls depending on his performance each day.

This is how he sees it. Let us say he headed into his first squad camp as England's interim coach with a score of 20 out of 100 – many players were unfamiliar with him and needed first-hand proof he was up to the job.

If he had messed up his first presentation, exposed himself as a novice on the training field and called Chris Ashton 'Brian' or Tom Wood 'Dudley' by mistake he could have lost the squad completely and gone down to zero. From that point, there would have been no way back.

But, having started off on the right foot with his one-to-one sessions with players, he would have edged up towards the 40 mark with his players. The kudos he gained through the rest of that formative week may well have sent him into the Six Nations on the 50 mark. A couple of wins to start the championship and he was probably up to 70 with the players beginning to trust that he had them on the right track.

But if his standards had happened to slip – perhaps if he had lost his cool after a bad training session or criticised the team in public – his score would quickly have plunged.

In *Secrets of Winning Coaches Revealed*, Lancaster also outlined what he believed were the ten points that marked out a top coach in his dealings with his players.

He must:

- Command respect – if the players do not respect their coach they will not play for him.

- Be a great leader – one who gives clear direction for his players to follow willingly.

- Be a great communicator – an inspiring, persuasive coach can motivate the team and bring more out of them.

- Be able to create a winning environment – one full of integrity where the players and coach share the same set of values.

- Show emotional stability – a coach who goes up and down like a raisin in a glass of champagne according to results is no use to anyone.

- Set the tone for the team – he has to balance approachability and affability with maintaining the distance required of a figurehead.

- Care for the players – if a player has a problem in his domestic life a coach must be prepared to prioritise that over rugby.

- Be trustworthy – do not let players down. If they are told they are being rested one week and will be back the following week make sure they are.

- Be honest – players want to hear the truth even if hurts. Sometimes it has to be 99 per cent of the truth because 100 per cent would be detrimental to their morale but misleading players only stores up trouble.

- Be fair – treat the new cap just the same as the captain. No special favours.

Spot Lancaster at England training sessions and it would not be immediately obvious that he was the leader. Aside from his Monday afternoon session, it is his assistants – Farrell, Catt and Rowntree – who attend to most of the nuts and bolts of England training.

The presence of Farrell is felt in particular. The former Wigan and Great Britain rugby league great is much more than simply a backs' coach in the England set-up. He is the energy pulse of the team.

As for Lancaster, he might occasionally provide input but for the main part he will act as an impassive overseer. He will stand there in his tracksuit, arms folded, whistle around his neck, quietly observing his deputies. 'I trust them implicitly,' he said.

It may look odd for the man in charge to choose to be hands-off – and it is certainly a change from his Leeds days – but this is leadership through delegation. While there is a risk of eroding his own position in devolving responsibility downwards, they are the ones who have played international rugby and Lancaster is happy to give them their space.

Bill Beswick cites this willingness to assign coaching time as vital.

'The great Italian football coach Arrigo Sacchi said the greatest quality of the greatest coaches and the greatest athletes was humility and one of Stuart's strengths is leaving his assistant coaches room to breathe,' said Beswick.

'A lot of head coaches with lower self-esteem than Stuart feel they have to be the boss and they dominate the session. The best coaches can be left stood on the side-line watching him trying to coach. It's not about Stuart, it's about the team.'

Detached from the action, Lancaster will use the space to assess how the players are training and how they are feeling. 'I'm always looking out for body language,' said Lancaster. 'I also use the physios, the conditioners and the masseur – all the people on the ground who see the players on a regular basis – to assess the mood and the mental state of players. They will naturally manage their image a bit more towards me because I am the coach who makes the decisions.'

The watcher is also being watched. When Beswick makes one of his regular visits to England's training camp he will scrutinise the body language of the head coach.

'I think we're all on stage as members of staff; we are all responsible surrounding these challenged young men. But Stuart is the leader and he should be aware of how he presents himself. He is the head of corporate energy and corporate confidence. How he looks and how he talks affects how players deal with a situation,' said Beswick.

'It is very important that the head coach, regardless of the weight on his shoulders, walks out of the office door positively. Stuart has some big advantages. He is fairly unflappable. He has great body posture as a trained teacher. He looks people in the eye. And generally he is able to surmount the many difficulties facing the team. I think it was Arsène Wenger who said the mood of the team is reflected in the face of the coach and I'm a great believer in that.'

When England win, Lancaster's phone goes into meltdown with congratulatory messages. Everyone wants to be on the bus. When they lose, as in sport they must, it all goes quiet – except for the criticism. That is when the leader needs the backing of his corner men, Beswick and Bowring.

'Those guys provide the silent support that people are unaware of which is absolutely critical because it's a lonely job. It's a tough job,' said Lancaster.

Beswick will make a point of contacting him when England are beaten. 'I was head coach of England basketball for five years and I know how vulnerable I felt pre-game and how alone; I know how devastated I felt post-game when we lost,' said Beswick. 'You swing to anxiety when you lose and the team need him to recover quickly for the next week so I will try to inject some confidence.

'I know how grateful I was for a message after a game. I don't know if it helps him or not but I send him very simple texts – "hold your nerve", "something to work on" – just something to tell him he has a friend. Or I might get one of my other coaches to get in touch and tell him "now you're facing it, son – welcome to the club!"'

When a team loses, the prism through which everything is viewed suddenly changes and the media agenda changes for the man in charge. 'It comes with the territory. If you don't win consistently, you are going to get asked difficult questions,' shrugged Lancaster. 'You've got to make sure you are considered with your responses. From my point of view, I always try to be honest and fair.

'Your patience does get tested, if I'm honest, but I don't think it serves any purpose to lose it. You have to keep working at it because people's understanding of the England team is going to be governed about what they hear about it through the media. I have to find ways to get the message through to the England rugby fan.'

Beswick, who had seen Steve McClaren endure the 'Wally With The Brolly' headlines as England football manager, tells Lancaster to lump it.

'I expect him to deal with the criticism. It's natural. I have no issue with it. That's part of what you take on when you take on the job of head coach,' said Beswick. 'It's a game within a game and the main thing is not to lose focus on the team winning. He has good people around him and he's not easily distracted.

'I expect him to be tough and he is. He's a tough man. He can deal with it. Sometimes the best advice is just to get on with it.'

With one or two strident exceptions, the England coach had enjoyed a pretty favourable ride from his inquisitors. It helps that they tend to think him a good bloke who is straight with them. When, in 2014, he felt he had not been honest enough over the impending arrival of Sam Burgess in rugby union – because the deal might have collapsed if he had admitted it was on – Lancaster took time out in a Test week to ring leading journalists to apologise in person.

The media relationship is one of eight parts to Lancaster's role as England head coach, as he sees it. There are three other relationships to manage – with his England management team, his bosses at the RFU and the Premiership clubs and four other strands comprising selection, coaching, team culture and his own thinking space.

At any given moment one will vault above the other in terms of its importance but the one he has to fight hardest to preserve room for is his own head space. Halting the carousel for long enough to pause and consider is something he constantly has to remind himself to do. Switching off is not his strong suit but living in Leeds helps in this respect. He has no choice but to stop and think in the long hours spent travelling there and back.

On the Tuesday evening of a home Test week Lancaster will often drive the 220 miles north from Pennyhill Park to his family home, sometimes arriving in Leeds after 10 p.m., so as to be able to do the school run on Wednesday morning with his two teenage children. He says goodbye to his wife then sets off back south again at 10 a.m. It sounds mad but the schedule allows Lancaster to live the family-first values he espouses among his squad and affords him precious thinking space. No one can tap him on the shoulder in his BMW X5.

The real mark of a leader is to create other leaders, not followers. It remains an ongoing process for Lancaster with England. The search for authentic leaders has probably been the most exacting part of Lancaster's tenure.

For someone who sets such great store by leadership, the issue of on-field direction for England is one which has occupied a lot of Lancaster's thoughts. He comes from an interesting angle on the subject. He believes that in general there is a leadership void in English sports teams because the current generation have been given too much on a plate.

'I think today we've got – certainly in England – leadership problems,' he once wrote. 'And I think there are a lot of reasons for that. I think young people have to be less dependent. We give them too much. In the sport I'm involved in, we give them the training schedules, we give them drinks to drink, we give them the diets to follow, we give them the weights programme to do. So, all that independent learning and thinking that you do as a child, the decisions you make, and as a teenager when you go to university, for the elite player they're taken away. They've been done for you.

'That said, though, you can still spot the leaders. And I think the trick is we've got to invest more time in developing the leaders. Previously . . . the leaders grew and emerged just through the environment that we're in, or the strength of their character or personality. But now, I think we actually almost have to artificially accelerate that process because the environment is not the same . . . If we can grow them then we will have more effective elite athletes in the end.'

This may be his boarding-school background speaking. Sent away for term time as a ten-year-old, he had to fend for himself and grow up quickly. He does not see the same attributes in many of the players who have come up through rugby's professional academies.

When he took over as England coach, potential candidates to captain the side and flank the leader were not exactly forming a queue around the street corner.

Down the years, English rugby has embraced many different styles of captain – of which the three most successful of recent times were Martin Johnson, Bill Beaumont and Will Carling.

Handed the England captaincy by coach Geoff Cooke as a twenty-two-year-old just out of Durham University, Carling appeared to the manor born with his dimpled chin and suave, officer-material manner. He held the position for eight years during which time his cool authority inspired and aggravated in equal measure.

'I have been criticised by players and journalists for appearing aloof, for not being one of the boys. Whatever people say, you can't. You can be, should be, very relaxed with the team but there has to be a distance, a gap which sets you apart,' advised Carling in his autobiography. 'A captain has to be setting standards and pushing people to meet those standards. That is part of the job. Sure, great captaincy involves persuading others to take on responsibility but you are the ultimate role model.'

Carling could be perceived as cold and arrogant but behind the scenes he was more tactile with his team than his detractors would imagine. He would make a point of finding out the birthdays of their partners and send them flowers on the appropriate day. He would reach out to his players in other surprising ways, too.

'I pushed individual notes under the doors of the players' hotel rooms on the night before the match against France when England clinched the 1991 Grand Slam, the first Grand Slam since Bill Beaumont's side in 1980. I'm sure it didn't work for every player but if it worked for one or two it was worth doing.'

Beaumont had little truck with these more theatrical elements of captaincy. The Lancastrian second row was a head-down grafter whose only thought of impressing people was by sweat and toil alone. He was a 'do as I do' rather than a 'do as I say' captain.

'People have to believe you are worth your place in the side. A leader shouldn't be there just because he can make speeches, be nice to people, open village fetes and speak at the local Rotary Club meeting. He has to perform in the arena,' said Beaumont, who went on to make plenty of decent speeches as RFU chairman.

England's greatest captain of all, Martin Johnson, the only man to lead the Lions twice, had a similarly clear approach. 'I have to be myself. I don't set out to make rousing speeches, stick notes under doors or engage in too much management speak. I am a fairly straightforward bloke and that's how I captain,' said Johnson in his autobiography. 'Much of what I do involves trying to gauge the mood of the team and either calm them down or rev them up accordingly.' Johnson's win ratio as England captain was 87 per cent.

Lancaster had gone into his first week with the squad in Leeds with an open mind about who would captain his England side.

The anaesthetic-free surgery he performed on the squad when he took over cut out the dead wood but it also removed experienced figures who could guide the side, on the field at least, in the right direction.

Looking around his first squad he found two possibilities – Chris Robshaw, who had been omitted from the 2011 World Cup squad, and Tom Wood, who went to New Zealand but largely to hold the tackle bags. As relentless back-row work-horses, they were cut from similar cloth. Both were selfless individuals respected by their team-mates.

Wood, the more compelling speaker, was chosen to accompany Lancaster as England's playing representative at his first Six Nations' media launch. The conspiracy theorists interpreted this as a clue that he was the chosen one. In fact, he was the injured one.

The toe problem which ruled Wood out for the first couple of games of the championship meant he had free time on his hands and with England up against the clock in trying to bring a brand-new team up to speed he was the most expendable.

The job was Robshaw's. Lancaster saw in him a character he could build a side around, someone who would cherish the England jersey rather than take it for granted, whatever the commercial spin-offs it brought with it.

Lancaster respected him as a man not least because he had been forced to fight for everything that had come his way. Lancaster is drawn to people who have paid their dues.

He once showed the England squad an ESPN documentary on the New England Patriots quarterback Tom Brady. He had been rejected early in his career because he was deemed not strong enough for the demands of the NFL, not mobile enough to avoid the defensive rush and not mentally sharp enough to think on his feet. Brady was draft pick No. 199 which basically meant he was the afterthought after the afterthoughts.

Six quarterbacks were chosen ahead of Brady in the draft including Giovanni Carmazzi. He is now a goat farmer. Brady was not rated by anyone. But through his sheer force of will and desire to be the best he became one of the most decorated NFL quarterbacks of all time, with 2015 seeing his fourth Super Bowl victory.

In the documentary, former San Francisco 49ers coach Steve Mariucci explained how it could have been that his local team overlooked the Californian in 2000. 'We didn't open up his chest and look at his heart. We didn't look at what kind of spine he has and resilience – all the things that have made him really great,' said Mariucci.

Brady's explanation of his subsequent success is that those early hardships made him the player he became. 'It's not really a chip on your shoulder. It's just that feeling that maybe nobody wants you,' he said. 'That's what gets me up and motivates me. I always want to feel like I am the best quarterback for this team. I want to earn it every single day.'

Bottle that attitude, multiply it by 15 and you have the outline of a decent rugby team.

Robshaw, who had lost his father to a heart attack at five, had never been an automatic choice for England at any age-group level and his early career at Harlequins had been blighted by foot and knee injuries. Nothing had come easily to him. But he would not take no for an answer.

He was carved from the same unyielding oak as others whom Lancaster had chosen to lead his sides down the years like Stuart Hooper at Leeds, who went on to become Bath's long-time leader, and Northampton's Phil Dowson, who he had chosen to lead the Saxons.

Robshaw, too, had captained the second string under

Lancaster, against Ireland A and Italy A in 2011, and came highly recommended by Conor O'Shea at Harlequins where he led the side in a low-maintenance fashion.

He was not the finished article at first – hardly surprising with so little Test experience – but Lancaster was prepared to wait for him to grow into the role. 'Experience matures players and captains,' he said. 'When you are captaining England there is a bigger role to play than just on the field.'

England under Lancaster became England under Robshaw. He led the side in 36 of Lancaster's first 39 Tests with Dylan Hartley leading the side when he missed the third Test in South Africa in 2012 through injury and Tom Wood filling in when he was rested for the tour to Argentina in 2013.

In the Hampton Room at England's Pennyhill Park base, the Monday after their 2015 Six Nations' victory over Wales, Lancaster outlined to a semi-circle of national newspaper journalists why he had stuck by Robshaw as captain. It boiled down to two factors. Robshaw, with his relentless work ethic, was one of the first names on the team sheet and he led by example.

'You've got to be secure of your place in the team. He's earned that and he earns it on a weekly basis with the number of tackles he makes, the turnovers he makes and his contribution to the game. We look at people's involvement and in their work rate off the ball. He's continually at the top of that as well. He's earned the respect of all the players and as a consequence he's leading them effectively,' said Lancaster.

With Robshaw, it was never about him it was about the team, which fitted the identikit of the leadership model Lancaster desired. The side which had beaten Wales contained four serving Premiership captains – Ben Youngs, Dylan Hartley, James

Haskell and Joe Marler. Another, Billy Twelvetrees, had come off the bench.

'I've never done the job on my own, there's always been this core group around me,' said Robshaw. 'We've increased the numbers in the leadership group as we've gone along so that when we're out there on the pitch we're a bit more experienced and know exactly what's going on. It really is a core group of leaders of ten or eleven players that continues to drive this squad and push it. A lot has been made over the captaincy but everyone in the squad is out there to achieve the same goal.'

The likes of Hartley had provided important back-up to Robshaw from the start, which was part of the reason Lancaster had turned a blind eye to his disciplinary excesses, but the process of turning foot soldiers into generals had not been straightforward. That was why Sam Burgess's arrival from rugby league was so interesting. Here was a ready-made leader, teleported into English rugby union. All he had to do was learn to play the game.

Slowly, a greater depth of leaders had begun to emerge in the squad.

'The captain as the iconic leader is not how it works in rugby,' continued Lancaster. 'You have leaders across the field and our strength is in the collective. Chris represents the collective which is great and he does it brilliantly,' said Lancaster. 'But he's backed up by some pretty strong foot soldiers which is what we want. If you go back to the 2003 team you had Johnno as captain but there was also Dallaglio, Back, Hill and those guys in the same category. I'd like to think we have that type of group growing together.

'I'm trying to develop leadership in the team and trying to get that player ownership so they take more of a lead. It is their team. You get players who are all first choice for their clubs who aren't necessarily for England, so in that environment they wait until selection is made before they step in and lead.

'What I'm trying to say to the senior players who have been around from the start is that this is their team now. Irrespective of whether they are in the starting team or on the bench it is up to them to drive it. You have to give them self-belief and then hopefully they can take it and run with it.

'I spend time with the senior players to help direct them and motivate them and give them some leadership. They're a good group. We get on well. I enjoy their company and I enjoy trying to develop them and I enjoy watching them succeed.'

There remains some way to go on the path to player power. The England team who won the 2003 World Cup was so packed with leaders that when Sir Clive Woodward came on to the field before extra time in the final he was entirely superfluous. The players had it covered.

Look at the 2015 New Zealand team and it is a similar story. 'If I look at the All Blacks I would say they are led 60 per cent by the players and 40 per cent by the coaches. I'd say we are probably the other way round,' admitted Lancaster.

'The stage we are in as a team is in developing the players to take more ownership. The players now prepare the preview and while we provide suggestions for the game plan they give their input into it, too.

'Hopefully, as the players mature and get more experience they will gather more and more ownership of this England team and ultimately drive the team, which is what I want. We're not at that stage yet because a lot of them are around the ten-cap mark as opposed to forty or fifty caps – or one-hundred-and-thirty caps in Richie McCaw's case.'

Letting go can be one of the hardest parts of the job for a coach but it is a necessity if a team wants to fly. Lancaster's England may have been centrally controlled at the start by necessity but it has never been a dictatorship; it has always involved the players. The review of the previous week's game on Monday, which will double as the scene-setter for the week ahead, is less of a lecture than a discussion. While Lancaster may lead it, his squad feel able to join in.

'The environment that's been created here allows for anyone to pipe up and say their piece. And also for people to take responsibility for the mistakes they made,' explained Harlequins prop Joe Marler.

But while the players will also have an input into the game plan as it takes shape early in the week there is no doubt as to who is directing it. As game day approaches, the emphasis shifts. 'From Thursday I pretty much let the players run it. They have to take ownership. I let them drive the meetings and stand in front of each other and talk,' said Lancaster.

'As a coach you can select and make substitutions but it isn't American football. You don't stop the game to tell them which play to make. You have to set the team up to make the decisions themselves. You hope they make the right ones.'

A generals group comprising the captain, the half-backs and the defensive leader meets to talk through match tactics and preview the game on Thursday. While the coaches attend, it is led by the players.

In the evening, while the management head for one restaurant, the players head for another. There is no alcohol ban for the team – a player is allowed a glass of wine if he wants one – but there are few, if any, takers. The captain's run at Twickenham the following morning is led by the players, too.

On match morning itself the backs and forwards will separately walk through a few drills at the hotel before their pre-match meal. There is one last squad meeting in the team room two-and a-half hours before kick-off. Lancaster will address the squad for the final time, in the team room downstairs at Pennyhill Park, reminding them of the key messages of the week, sometimes reinforcing his words with a motivational video.

The team bus collects the squad and deposits them at Twickenham 90 minutes before kick-off for the walk through the tunnel of supporters and into the stadium.

Aside from a last huddle on the pitch with Andy Farrell in the warm-up, where he gives a final briefing on defence, it is the players' voices which are heard from now on. Lancaster can do nothing more. He has ceded control. He will watch the warm-up on the pitch before leaving and finding a quiet room of his own to collect his thoughts. Sometimes in those tense few minutes he will write down, left-handed, on a piece of paper two or three key prompts for himself to use during the game.

Test match rugby is a high-emotion atmosphere with the noise of 80,000 people swirling around and these words act as his anchor. They are often very simple – 'composure', 'focus', 'help the team win' – words which strip away the distractions of the occasion. Sometimes he will just stew.

He knows that aside from getting messages on to the pitch via Catt, one of England's water carriers, he is out of the game until half-time. Even then he has to be careful not to do too much. The half-time talk will consist of two or three key points and no more. Players are unable to take any more than this in under the stress of a match.

Lancaster will often use a visual image to help illustrate his point through a clip on the giant screen in the dressing room.

He will underline what he wants to see more of in attack and defence before the team split into forwards and backs for a conference with the specialist coaches and finally a word from the captain.

Once they retake the field for the second half, Lancaster will be thinking when to deploy his eight substitutes. There is no pre-set change time and injuries can alter everything but Lancaster's pattern is to have swapped his props and scrum-half by the hour mark and to have emptied his bench by the final whistle. That is the extent of his input.

For the rest, it is watch, wait and worry – which is ultimately a leader's lot.

Conclusion

Let the end try the man

Henry IV Part 2, Act 2, Scene 2

Stuart Lancaster is sitting inside a spotless England dressing room at Twickenham. Surrounding him are some of the pillars of his England revolution – the history board, the honours wall, the pristine plaques that link the present jersey-holder with those who have worn the shirt before. Above him, like a hovering spaceship bringing a message from on high, is the giant oval disc displaying rugby's core values – teamwork, respect, enjoyment, discipline, sportsmanship.

If Twickenham is the cathedral of English rugby, this is the altar and its high priest is delivering a stirring sermon. Lancaster is talking about game day, the witching hour when the chosen few pull on the white shirt and give themselves to England.

'The feeling inside the changing room is incredibly powerful,' he said. 'Look at the history and the heritage that is on the walls here. You know who has sat here and you know it is a very special, unique place to be. Very few people have had the privilege of being in here before an international.

'When you are preparing to go out there and sing the national anthem in front of so many people and for the people to care so much and be behind the team it's an unbelievable feeling. I'm sat here looking at the boys preparing to go out and play and I have got so much respect for them, for what they do and how they do it.

'They prepare in different ways, some go quiet, some are energetic, some are vocal but they are all preparing themselves individually to go into a battle against the opposition, put their body on the line and make decisions that will be judged by millions of people. You've got to respect any player who is prepared to put himself in that position.'

Lancaster never did it himself as a player. But if he sees out the full term of his contract extension, he will become the longest-serving coach in England history, eclipsing Sir Clive Woodward. He may not make it that far – the waters of international sport are stormy, the pressures intense and the bounce of a rugby ball capricious – but whatever happens, English rugby will owe him a profound debt of gratitude.

When he took charge of the England team it was a lost cause, deprived of meaning and honour. The pride is back in the jersey now. The players know who they are, what they stand for and what is expected of them.

'I think earning the respect of the sporting public, your opponents and referees in the way you conduct yourself is important. The players have got that now. They understand that it is about giving back,' said Lancaster. 'It is about getting the players to understand that they represent England. We have history, traditions and legacy. They need to leave the shirt in a better place.'

For those who experienced the previous England environment, it feels like another world. The change amounted to nothing less than a revolution.

'It was a whole new rebirth. Sometimes when regimes change, the wallpaper changes but not the structure. He came in and changed everything,' said Wasps captain James Haskell. 'When Stuart came in he did so with a completely new broom and swept everything clean. He set up his system and his way of doing things and made everyone believe in it. It was a re-education process which, for some people, needed to happen so we were clear why it was important to play for England and what was expected of us as England players.

'It was a case of making sure everything was connected so the fans came on a match day knowing the players were playing for the shirt and the players knew they were going to have a good atmosphere. I will say this. It was never as bad as it was painted in the England camp before. But people look forward to going into camp now.'

Bill Beswick sees the Lancaster transformation as a revisionist return to higher ideals that had been lost to professional rugby in England. 'Stuart reintroduced a concept which had gone to some extent in the game with the arrival of short-termism and commercialism. It was the concept of a value-based culture where good people worked hard to try to do good things,' he said.

Word has got out about how England have overhauled their beliefs and behaviours. Barely a week goes by now when the squad are in camp without a coach from another sport looking in.

'I've spent a lot of time going to other sports to see how they do things but what has been nice recently is that people are coming to us. They can see there has been a change and they want to know how we've made it,' said Lancaster.

The recipe has involved taking the performance standards of the San Francisco 49ers, adding British Cycling's marginal gains and stirring in some All Blacks-style heritage and culture. The magic ingredient has been a lot of down-to-earth Cumbrian good sense.

The foundations Lancaster has put down should serve England well into the future. Nearly all of the players schooled in what it means to play for England and what is expected of them will still be around at the 2019 World Cup in Japan.

'The thing that motivates me most is creating a long-term team,' said Lancaster. 'The plan has to extend beyond winning the World Cup in 2015 because it's no good for England Rugby to keep going through peaks and troughs of success and failure. We had a fantastic team in 2003 and we've never really reached those heights since.

'It's about continuous high performance. We don't want to arrive at the Six Nations in 2016 and fall off a cliff.

'The future is only going to get better. We don't have any players who we will have to transition out. We have a youngish group emerging that should go way beyond 2015. There will be real competition for places with a whole generation of players coming through together. Knowing some of the talent that is coming through the system now, we should be right at the top of the world game for a long time.'

Outstanding young players such as Maro Itoje, of Saracens, Captain of England's Junior World Championship-winning side in 2014, are next in line.

Even when the squad was under colossal pressure ahead of the Australia Test in November 2014, Lancaster still thought it right in the build-up to introduce six of the England under-18s players to training with the senior team at Pennyhill Park. The invitation provided them with a taste of what to expect when they make the step up. His background at the RFU, where he was in charge of the conveyor belt for four years, means he will always have an eye out for the next George Ford or Owen Farrell.

'He's developed into a superb strategic thinker and leader. He's someone who understands the big picture but also the necessity of succeeding short term. He's got that balance absolutely spot on,' said Phil Davies, the man who gave him his coaching break at Leeds.

The nature of the England head-coach post, from its long-term vision to the more immediate priority to deliver victories, is a challenging one. As Kevin Bowring knows from experience, coaching at Test level is a wonderful job but a demanding one.

'International coaching, with its media profile, is like waves coming crashing down on you. One lot hits you and then you come up for air and, crash, another one arrives and you have to fight again. It's coming at you at a hundred miles per hour,' said Bowring. 'Sometimes as a coach you can't see the wood for the trees and Stuart needs his time away – whether that is going for a walk or being on the running machine.'

Harlequins director of rugby Conor O'Shea, who helped choose Lancaster for the post in the first place, knows the pressures and sometimes worries that he gives too much of himself. 'Stuart's heart is on his sleeve. He cares ridiculously. Maybe at times too much. He'll give his last waking minute to the job,' said O'Shea.

The way Lancaster approaches the role, it is trebly demanding. Aside from his official titles as England head coach and head of the RFU's international performance department, he also views himself as a carrier of the flame he has lit. He feels he should spread the message of England Rugby and rugby in general to as wide an audience as possible. When he receives an invitation to speak at a rugby club or open a new artificial pitch at a school he ends up saying 'yes' more times than he should. Lancaster is discharging what he sees as his wider responsibility.

'Sometimes he gets involved in too many things but he sees himself not only as head coach of England but as someone who is a leader in developing rugby throughout the country,' said his other sounding board, Bill Beswick. 'He feels that very keenly. He feels he is doing something for the English rugby public. That is a very big agenda.

'His work ethic is unbelievable and that is a great quality but I wish he was less busy. The problem is prioritisation. Sport is about reality and illusion. A head coach will hover between the reality of selection, injuries, what the team is doing each day and the illusion of the external world with its dinner invitations and speaking events. Stuart's work ethic enables him to embrace both, but in a non-threatening way I will sometimes point out to him: "What's the most important?"'

Lancaster, though, is a man on a mission, leading England and English rugby with an almost messianic zeal. 'I have to connect the England team back to the community because that is the lifeblood of the game. I don't say that because it is the right thing to say, I say it because I believe it,' he said.

'I've coached at every level of the game from under-7s to England. Because I've come from the grass-roots game, I don't think anyone has anything to fear in the England team getting carried away with ourselves and losing the connection with real rugby.'

Nor is there much chance of Lancaster losing his own head in the clouds. He is as anchored as they come. 'Those who know me know I haven't changed at all,' he told the *Daily Express* in

2014. 'When I go home to Leeds and spend time with family and friends I like to think I am exactly the same person and that they would agree.'

The journey from comprehensive school PE teacher to England head coach has been an inspirational one. If he can do it maybe some other day-dreaming teacher on a windswept, wintry field somewhere can do it too.

If the route has been unconventional, it has been the stop-offs along the way that have shaped Lancaster. From farm life to boarding school to Bill Walsh, it has been one long learning journey, which continues every day, but one ultimately founded on iron principles.

Stuart Reid, who has known him since their schooldays at St Bees, says he has never met a man with such high moral standards. It has been England's good fortune to have those standards inflicted upon them.

'Fundamentally my belief is that the culture is set by the head coach,' said Lancaster. 'The high-performance environments which have won consistently have all been driven by the head coach rather than anyone else.'

If you are going to talk the talk to a team, you have to live by the ideals. Lancaster puts the cones out before every England training session and is the man who brings them back in at the end. Without fail.

A team is a complex matrix comprising many moving parts but ultimately it is a window into the soul of its leader. 'The England team is a reflection of Stuart,' said Bill Beswick. 'He models what he talks about.'

Lancaster would love to finish the job he has started and lead England in two World Cups but, however the story plays out, he pledges to remain true to his roots.

'The ultimate thing for me would be to go on to 2019, for the team to be successful in the long term and to leave the shirt in a better place,' said Lancaster.

'But once this journey is finished I don't think I will struggle to get motivated to go back into coaching. If someone said to me I had to go and coach at Harrogate or Yorkshire under-16s I would enjoy it just as much. I love coaching. I love being part of teams and helping people get better.'

The house of Lancaster has been built on granite foundations.

Postscript

In Bill Walsh's final game in charge of the 49ers, against the Cincinnati Bengals – Super Bowl XXIII in 1989 – his team trailed 16-13 with three minutes and eight seconds remaining. They were on their own eight-yard line.

The 49ers had the ball but they were one slip-up from defeat. Under the most intense pressure, in front of 75,000 fans at Miami's Joe Robbie Stadium and a TV audience of more than 80 million, they required a perfect sequence of plays.

As the offense huddled in the end zone to hear quarter-back Joe Montana call the first play, he suddenly noticed the actor John Candy in the crowd and pointed him out to the team. It was a surreal aside before the serious business of what followed. The 11 successive plays which the 49ers delivered were as near to perfection under pressure as sport produces. It came to be known as The Drive and culminated in an 18-yard pass from Montana to John Taylor to win the Super Bowl.

'There was just a sense of inevitability,' recalled Walsh in *The Score Takes Care of Itself*. 'All we had to do was adhere to the standard of performance that we had been sculpting for a decade.

'I was at peace knowing the score – one way or another – would take care of itself. And it did.'

England Tests Under Lancaster

(up to 1 June 2015)

Date	Opponents	Venue	Result	Score
04/02/2012	Scotland	Murrayfield	Won	13-6
11/02/2012	Italy	Stadio Olimpico	Won	19-15
25/02/2012	Wales	Twickenham	Lost	12-19
11/03/2012	France	Stade de France	Won	24-22
17/03/2012	Ireland	Twickenham	Won	30-9
09/06/2012	South Africa	Kings Park	Lost	17-22
16/06/2012	South Africa	Ellis Park	Lost	27-36
23/06/2012	South Africa	Port Elizabeth	Drew	14-14
10/11/2012	Fiji	Twickenham	Won	54-12
17/11/2012	Australia	Twickenham	Lost	14-20
24/11/2012	South Africa	Twickenham	Lost	15-16
01/12/2012	New Zealand	Twickenham	Won	38-21
02/02/2013	Scotland	Twickenham	Won	38-18
10/02/2013	Ireland	Aviva Stadium	Won	12-6
23/02/2013	France	Twickenham	Won	23-13
09/03/2013	Italy	Twickenham	Won	18-11
16/03/2013	Wales	Millennium Stadium	Lost	30-3
08/06/2013	Argentina	Salta	Won	32-3
15/06/2013	Argentina	Buenos Aires	Won	51-26
02/11/2013	Australia	Twickenham	Won	20-13
09/11/2013	Argentina	Twickenham	Won	31-12

Date	Opponents	Venue	Result	Score
16/11/2013	New Zealand	Twickenham	Lost	22-30
01/02/2014	France	Stade de France	Lost	24-26
08/02/2014	Scotland	Murrayfield	Won	20-0
22/02/2014	Ireland	Twickenham	Won	13-10
09/03/2014	Wales	Twickenham	Won	29-18
15/03/2014	Italy	Stadio Olimpico	Won	52-11
07/06/2014	New Zealand	Eden Park	Lost	15-20
14/06/2014	New Zealand	Forsyth Barr Stadium	Lost	27-28
21/06/2014	New Zealand	Waikato Stadium	Lost	13-36
08/11/2014	New Zealand	Twickenham	Lost	21-24
15/11/2014	South Africa	Twickenham	Lost	28-31
22/11/2014	Samoa	Twickenham	Won	28-9
29/11/2014	Australia	Twickenham	Won	26-17
06/02/2015	Wales	Millennium Stadium	Won	21-16
14/02/2015	Italy	Twickenham	Won	47-17
01/03/2015	Ireland	Aviva Stadium	Lost	9-19
14/03/2015	Scotland	Twickenham	Won	25-13
21/03/2015	France	Twickenham	Won	55-35

Tests played: 39

Won: 24

Lost: 14

Drawn: 1

Test Nations' Results During Lancaster's Tenure

(up to 1 June 2015)

Country	Played	Won	Drawn	Lost	Win ratio
New Zealand	42	38	2	2	92.8
South Africa	37	26	2	9	72.9
England	39	24	1	14	62.8
Ireland	35	20	2	13	60.0
Wales	40	22	0	18	55.0
Australia	44	22	2	20	52.2
France	37	15	2	20	43.2
Argentina	44	16	1	27	37.5
Scotland	39	13	0	26	33.3
Italy	39	9	0	29	23.6

Bibliography

Books

Beaumont, Bill, *The Autobiography* (HarperCollins, 2003)

Becker, David and Scott Hill, *Secrets of Winning Coaches Revealed* (Sports Wisdom, 2011)

Burns, Peter, *White Gold* (Arena Sport, 2013)

Carling, Will, *Will Carling: My Autobiography* (Hodder & Stoughton, 1998)

Catt, Mike, *Mike Catt: Landing On My Feet* (Hodder & Stoughton, 2007)

Easterby, Simon, *Easter's Rising* (Y Lolfa, 2011)

Jackson, Phil and Hugh Delehanty, *Sacred Hoops* (Hyperion, 1995)

Johnson, Martin, *Martin Johnson: The Autobiography* (Headline, 2004)

Jones, Stephen and Nick Cain, *Behind the Rose: Playing Rugby for England* (Arena Sport, 2014)

Kerr, James, *Legacy: What the All Blacks Can Teach Us About the Business of Life* (Constable, 2013)

Lombardi, Vince, *The Lombardi Rules* (McGraw-Hill, 2002)

McCaw, Richie, *The Real McCaw* (Aurum Press, 2013)

McConnell, Robin, *Inside the All Blacks* (HarperCollins, 1998)

Walsh, Bill, with Brian Billick and James Peterson, *Finding the Winning Edge* (Sports Publishing Inc., 1998)

Walsh, Bill, with Steve Jamison and Craig Walsh, *The Score Takes Care of Itself: My Philosophy of Leadership* (Penguin, 2009)

Whitaker, David, *The Spirit of Teams* (Crowood Press, 1999)

Wiggins, Bradley, *My Time* (Yellow Jersey Press, 2012)

Wilkinson, Jonny, *Jonny Wilkinson: Lions and Falcons* (Headline, 2001)

Woodward, Clive, *Winning! The Autobiography of Clive Woodward* (Hodder & Stoughton, 2004)

Multi-media

Sinek, Simon *How Great Leaders Inspire Actions* (Ted.com, 2009)

ERTV, *Stuart Lancaster: Country Behind The Team Is A Powerful Motivator* (Rfu.com, 2014)

ERTV, *RBS 6 Nations 2015 player diary II* (Rfu.com, 2015)

The Brady 6 (ESPN.com, 2011)

Papers

Hodge, Ken 'A Case Study of Excellence in Elite Sport: Motivational Climate in a World Champion Team' (*Sport Psychologist*, 2014)

Lancaster, Stuart 'An Analysis into the Effectiveness of Changing My Coaching Behaviour to Create Mentally Stronger Individuals and a More Cohesive Team' (RFU. com, 2009)

Articles

Paul, Gregor, 'Graham Henry's Revolution' (*New Zealand Herald*, 2007)
'Promoted Tykes Look To Finish On a High' (*Yorkshire Post*, 2007)

Wheeler, Sam, 'Leeds Begin Hunt For New Coach After Lancaster Quits' (*Yorkshire Post*, 2008)

Souster, Mark, 'England Rugby Players Cared More About Money Than Sport' (*The Times*, 2011)
Bale, Steve, 'Lancaster Plans England Crackdown' (*Daily Express*, 2011)

Lancaster, Stuart, 'My Upbringing In Cumbria Has Completely Shaped My Career' (*Cumberland Herald*, 2012)
Reid, Alasdair, 'Revealed: The Picture That Shows Stuart Lancaster's Scottish Roots' (*Daily Telegraph*, 2012)
White, Jim, 'Why Stuart Lancaster's Squad Need Yorkshire Roots' (*Daily Telegraph*, 2012)
Benedict, Luke, 'From St Bees U-12s to England: The Making of Coach Lancaster' (*Daily Mail*, 2012)
Kervin, Alison, 'The Pursuits Interview' (*Financial Times*, 2012)
Croft, Tom, 'Ben Was Screaming For the Ball But He Has Enough Tries' (*Daily Express*, 2012)
Bale, Steve, 'Stuart Lancaster's Vision Validated As England Destroy All Blacks' (*Daily Express*, 2012)
Brown, Oliver, 'England Head Coach Stuart Lancaster Believes The Next Step For His Team Is To Make Them Genuinely Feared' (*Daily Telegraph*, 2012)

BIBLIOGRAPHY

Bale, Steve, 'World Is Turned Upside Down' (*Daily Express*, 2012)

Brown, Oliver, 'All Blacks Told: 'We Are The Most Dominant Team In History'' (*Daily Telegraph*, 2013)

Lothian, Bill, 'Why Scotland Cannot Underestimate Lancaster's England' (*Edinburgh Evening News*, 2014)

Bale, Steve, 'Lancaster's Labours of Love! Boss Seeks Extraordinary Achievements With England' (*Daily Express*, 2014)

Jones, Adam, 'Ready to make it 100 caps' (bbc.co.uk, 2014)

Acknowledgements

This is not the sort of book Stuart Lancaster would ever write – or want written. When I told him I was writing it he was not best pleased, so this is not an authorised biography, but rugby union, blessedly, remains generous in its ways, and in writing it I have been fortunate to enjoy excellent access to the England head coach through briefings and business talks, interviews and press conferences, and to those who have shaped his thinking.

It is a long journey for an idea to become a book and there are many people who make the transition possible.

To John Burton, late of the *Daily Express*, my gratitude goes out for allowing me to undertake this project. I know you'd have preferred it to have been on West Ham. To my *Express* writing colleagues past and present, Steve Bale and Andy Elliott, thanks for your assistance with the words – particularly the long ones.

To Will Chignell and Dave Barton at the RFU, thanks for opening locked doors and to Bill Beswick and Kevin Bowring for generously sparing me time on the other side of them.

ACKNOWLEDGEMENTS

To those England players, past and present, whose insight since 2012 has shed a light on a unique environment, I am very grateful; likewise to Phil Davies, Gary Hetherington, Stuart Hooper, Hendre Fourie and Joe Bedford for the Leeds memories and, in Phil Daly and Mike Bidgood's case, photos too. To Yorkshire's fine scribes, Nick Westby, Dave Craven and Sam Wheeler, my thanks, and likewise to Tony Rolt for the St Bees recollections and visual confirmation that Stuart Lancaster once had hair.

Also, to the Bard of Burley, Graham Greensit, thank you for reintroducing me to Shakespeare.

Special thanks to Matt Phillips at Yellow Jersey, who believed in this project, and Fran Jessop, who steered it skilfully in the right direction, and to super-agent John Pawsey who made sure I was paid for it.

Finally, to Louis and Issy, sorry for being locked in the office for so long, and to Andrea – thanks for being a rock while everything came together. This definitely could not have happened without you.

List of Illustrations

1. Wakefield's Caldy Sevens-winning squad in 1991 (Richard Lowther); St Bees on tour in Split to play Yugoslavia under-21s (Tony Rolt)

2. Stuart Lancaster playing for Leeds (Yorkshire Carnegie); coaching Leeds (Yorkshire Carnegie); Lancaster talking to Leeds squad (Yorkshire Carnegie); winning promotion at Leeds (Yorkshire Carnegie)

3. Training at Pennyhill Park (Getty/David Rogers); Lancaster's first Six Nations match as England coach against Scotland (Offside); preparing at Twickenham (Offside)

4. Lancaster, Mike Catt, Graham Rowntree and Andy Farrell at Pennyhill Park (Getty/David Rogers); the England dressing room at Twickenham (Getty/David Rogers); Chris Robshaw and Lancaster (Getty/David Rogers); Lancaster at a training session (Getty/Clive Mason)

5. Joe Launchbury in a line-out again New Zealand in 2012 (Offside); victory against New Zealand for the Hillary Shield (Offside)

LIST OF ILLUSTRATIONS

6. Merchandise available outside the Millennium Stadium prior to the game against England in the 2013 Six Nations (Offside); Wales fans at the Millennium Stadium (Getty/Stu Forster); despair following the 30-3 defeat (Getty/David Rogers)

7. Elation after beating Wales in the opening 2015 Six Nations match against Wales (Corbis); Jack Nowell scores a try against France in the 2015 Six Nations Championship (Getty/David Rogers); disappointment after coming so close to winning the title (Getty/David Rogers)

8. Training during the 2015 Six Nations Championship (Getty/David Rogers); Lancaster walking down the Twickenham tunnel (Getty/David Rogers)